REFORMATION TO F

D0087804

'. . . an excellent teaching tool.'
Sears McGee, *University of California, Santa Barbara*

'Margo Todd as an experienced scholar with a fine reputation in this field is well placed to write an outstanding introductory survey.
Anthony Fletcher, *University of Durham*

Few periods of English history have been so subject to 'revisionism' as the Tudor and Stuart era. This volume offers a quick introduction to the complex historiographical debates currently raging about politics and religion in early modern England. *Reformation to Revolution*:

- draws together 13 articles from familiar and less accessible sources
- embraces revisionist and counter-revisionist viewpoints
- combines controversial works on both politics and religion
- covers Tudor as well as Stuart England
- includes a glossary, explanatory notes and suggestions for further reading.

These carefully edited and introduced essays draw on the new evidence of newsletters and ballads and ritual, as well as the more traditional sources, to offer a new and broader understanding of this transformative era of English history.

Margo Todd is Associate Professor of History at Vanderbilt University.

Rewriting Histories focus on historical themes where formerly standard conclusions are facing a major challenge. Each book will present 10–15 papers (edited and annotated where necessary) at the forefront of current research and interpretation, offering students an accessible way to engage with contemporary debates.
Series editor **Jack R. Censer** is Professor of History at George Mason University.

REWRITING HISTORIES
Series editor: Jack R. Censer

REFORMATION TO REVOLUTION

Politics and Religion in Early Modern England

Edited by Margo Todd

London and New York

First published 1995
by Routledge
11 New Fetter Lane, London EC4P 4EE

Simultaneously published in the USA and Canada
by Routledge
29 West 35th Street, New York NY 10001

Phototypeset in Palatino by
Intype, London
Printed and bound in Great Britain by
T.J. Press Ltd, Padstow, Cornwall

British Library Cataloguing in Publication Data
A catalogue record for this book is available from the British Library.

Library of Congress Cataloging in Publication Data
Reformation to revolution : politics and religion in early modern
England / edited by Margo Todd.
p. cm. — (Rewriting histories)
Includes bibliographical references and index.
1. Reformation—England. 2. England—Church history—16th
century. 3. England—Church history—17th century. 4. Great
Britain—History—Tudors, 1485–1603. 5. Great Britain—History—
Early Stuarts, 1603–1649. I. Todd, Margo. II Series: Re-writing
histories.
BR756.R44 1995
942.05—dc20 94–11831

ISBN 0–415–09691–X (hbk)
0–415–09692–8 (pbk)

CONTENTS

v

EDITOR'S PREFACE

Rewriting history, or revisionism, has always followed closely in the tow of history writing. In their efforts to re-evaluate the past, professional as well as amateur scholars have followed many approaches, most commonly as empiricists, uncovering new information to challenge earlier accounts. Historians have also revised previous versions by adopting new perspectives, usually fortified by new research, which overturn received views.

Even though rewriting is constantly taking place, historians' attitudes towards using new interpretations have been anything but settled. For most, the validity of revisionism lies in providing a stronger, more convincing account that better captures the objective truth of the matter. Although such historians might agree that we never finally arrive at the 'truth', they believe it exists and over time may be better and better approximated. At the other extreme stand scholars who believe that each generation or even each cultural group or subgroup necessarily regards the past differently, each creating for itself a more usable history. Although these latter scholars do not reject the possibility of demonstrating empirically that some contentions are better than others, they focus upon generating new views based upon different life experiences. Different truths exist for different groups. Surely such an understanding, by emphasizing subjectivity, further encourages rewriting history. Between these two groups are those historians who wish to borrow from both sides. This third group, while accepting that every congeries of individuals sees matters differently, still wishes somewhat contradictorily to fashion a broader history that incorporates both of these particular visions. Revisionists who stress empiricism fall into the first of the three camps, while others spread out across the board.

Today the rewriting of history seems to have accelerated to a blinding speed as a consequence of the evolution of revisionism. A variety of approaches has emerged. A major factor in this process has been the enormous increase in the number of researchers. This explosion has reinforced and enabled the re-testing of many assertions. Significant ideological shifts have also played a major part in the growth of revisionism. First, the crisis of Marxism, culminating in the events in Eastern Europe in 1989, has given rise to doubts about explicitly Marxist accounts. Such doubts have spilled over into the entire field of social history, which has been a dominant subfield of the discipline for several decades. Focusing on society and its class divisions implied that these are the most important elements in historical analysis. Because Marxism was built on the same claim, the whole basis of social history has been questioned, despite the very many studies that had little directly to do with Marxism. Disillusionment with social history simultaneously opened the door to cultural and linguistic approaches largely developed in anthropology and literature. Multiculturalism and feminism further generated revisionism. By claiming that scholars had, wittingly or not, operated from a white European/ American male point of view, newer researchers argued other approaches had been neglected or misunderstood. Not surprisingly, these last historians are the most likely to envisage each subgroup rewriting its own usable history, while other scholars incline towards revisionism as part of the search for some stable truth.

Rewriting Histories will make these new approaches available to the student population. Often new scholarly debates take place in the scattered issues of journals which are sometimes difficult to find. Furthermore, in these first interactions, historians tend to address one another, leaving out the evidence that would make their arguments more accessible to the uninitiated. This series of books will collect in one place a strong group of the major articles in selected fields, adding notes and introductions conducive to improved understanding. Editors will select articles containing substantial historical data, so that students – at least those who approach the subject as an objective phenomenon – can advance not only their comprehension of debated points but also their grasp of substantive aspects of the subject.

Empiricists have been mainly responsible for the most recent shifts in understanding the English Revolution and its precedents. These newcomers enter a situation with a venerable historiography. Traditionally scholars had seen this period in terms of a struggle both over religion among Catholics, Puritans and Anglicans and over politics between the king and the Parliament. Although Marxists and other social historians endeavoured to inscribe class conflict into these battles, this kind of interpretation gave way once again to the pre-eminence of politics and religion as the most potent forces for historical change. But now even these factors are questioned. In this work, Margo Todd presents a conflict between those who deprecate religious and political principle and those who still see the conflict turning on major disagreements about fundamental ideas. Essentially, such a debate pits those willing to focus more on a narrative of events against those searching for a cause equivalent in dimensions to the event itself.

Jack R. Censer

ABBREVIATIONS

BIHR	*Bulletin of the Institute of Historical Research*
BL	British Library
Bodl.	Bodleian Library, Oxford
CJ	*Commons' Journal*
CSPD	*Calendar of State Papers, Domestic*
EHR	*English Historical Review*
HJ	*Historical Journal*
HMC	Historical Manuscripts Commission
KAO	Kent Archive Office
JBS	*Journal of British Studies*
JEH	*Journal of Ecclesiastical History*
JMH	*Journal of Modern History*
LJ	*Lords' Journals*
PRO	Public Record Office
RO	County Record Office
ST	*State Trials*, ed. W. Cobbett and T. B. Howell, 33 vols (1809–26)
TBGAS	*Transactions of the Bristol and Gloucestershire Archaeological Society*
TRHS	*Transactions of the Royal Historical Society*
VCH	*Victoria County History*

Place of publication is London unless otherwise indicated.

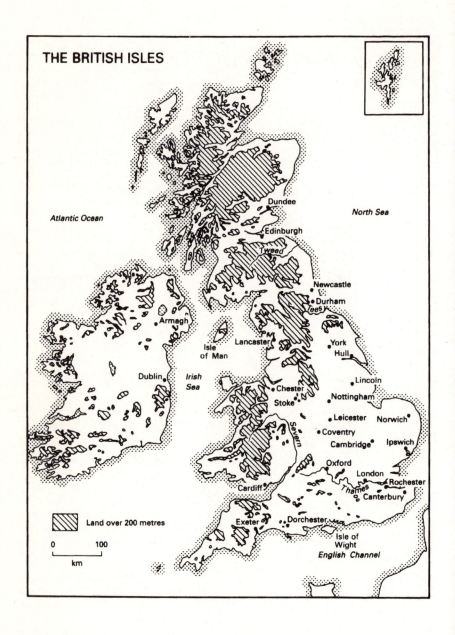

THE BRITISH ISLES

Atlantic Ocean

North Sea

Dundee

Edinburgh

Tweed

Newcastle

Durham

Armagh

Isle
of Man

Lancaster

York

Hull

Dublin

Irish
Sea

Lincoln

Chester

Nottingham

Stoke

Leicester

Norwich

Coventry

Cambridge

Ipswich

Oxford

London

Severn

Cardiff

Thames

Rochester

Canterbury

Exeter

Dorchester

Isle of
Wight

English Channel

Land over 200 metres

0   100

km

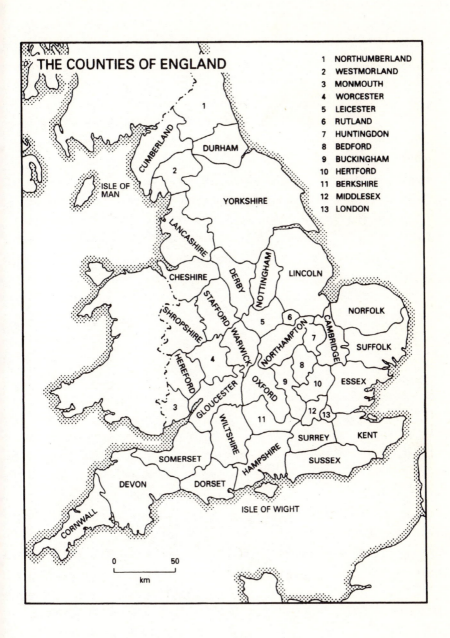

THE COUNTIES OF ENGLAND

1 NORTHUMBERLAND
2 WESTMORLAND
3 MONMOUTH
4 WORCESTER
5 LEICESTER
6 RUTLAND
7 HUNTINGDON
8 BEDFORD
9 BUCKINGHAM
10 HERTFORD
11 BERKSHIRE
12 MIDDLESEX
13 LONDON

CUMBERLAND
DURHAM
ISLE OF MAN
YORKSHIRE
LANCASHIRE
CHESHIRE
DERBY
NOTTINGHAM
LINCOLN
SHROPSHIRE
STAFFORD
WARWICK
NORFOLK
CAMBRIDGE
SUFFOLK
HEREFORD
NORTHAMPTON
OXFORD
ESSEX
GLOUCESTER
WILTSHIRE
SURREY
KENT
SOMERSET
HAMPSHIRE
SUSSEX
DEVON
DORSET
ISLE OF WIGHT
CORNWALL

0   50
km

INTRODUCTION

Margo Todd

Generations of students have learned that the foundations of modern England were laid in the century between the Henrician Reformation of the 1530s and the Civil War of the 1640s. During that century, England underwent the religious revolution that made it a protestant nation – divided within itself between puritans and conformists, but much more clearly divided from Rome, the presumed seat of Antichrist. And during that century of demographic growth and inflation, England's 'political nation' – the men who by right of birth or wealth participated in the political process and the administration of the realm – expanded dramatically and became self-conscious and active defenders of what they construed as constitutional liberty. Marxist historians have traced these changes to socio-economic factors – the decline of feudalism and the emergence of a new mercantile capitalist class.[1] One need not accept their now largely discredited notions of causation and their anachronistic theme of a rising middle class, however, in order to acknowledge that what happened under the Tudors and early Stuarts was revolutionary: it was, after all, the traditional Whig historians who in the last century gave us 'Puritan Revolution' as the interpretive name for the Civil War of the 1640s.[2] As they traced what they saw as England's inevitable progress towards liberal enlightenment, the Whigs depicted the war as the culmination of a century of religious and political maturation and accelerating conflict with the forces of conservatism, and from this broad perspective they made it comprehensible to students. However they disagreed on whether the causes of change were socio-economic or political and religious, Marxists and Whigs

1

both accepted this 'high road' to civil war, and both presumed the revolutionary nature of the conflict.

In the last decade or so, the most basic assumptions underlying this received version have been seriously questioned by both religious and political historians. On the basis of impressive work with archival sources, these 'revisionists' have proposed a very different picture of England during the century of revolution: while the traditional view of the Reformation had protestantism triumphant in the first generation and an oppositionist puritan movement emerging soon after Elizabeth's accession to demand a more thorough reform of the Church, revisionists like Christopher Haigh and J. J. Scarisbrick now argue that the Reformation was unpopular and slow in coming. They stress instead the health and perceived social usefulness of the Catholic Church on the eve of the Reformation and the continuity of English Catholicism through the sixteenth century.[3] The revisionists have in turn stimulated further revision. A recent variation on the theme of unpopular Reformation finds that people in the south-west of England were willing to forego their Catholicism under government pressure, but they did not find Protestantism sufficiently compelling to convert them; rather they tended to revert to irreligion.[4] Others have acknowledged a slow Reformation, but not quite as gradual and reluctant as Haigh has suggested: Patrick Collinson finds that, by the middle of Elizabeth's reign, England had been culturally as well as formally converted into a Protestant nation. Collinson's more serious departure from the received version of Elizabethan religion is to depict the Church of Elizabeth and James as more consensually protestant than the old version of 'puritan versus Anglican' had it. He finds the Church at this stage characterized by an evangelical consensus uniting bishops and Puritans, magistrates and ministers, on the importance of preaching, sabbath observance, Calvinist orthodoxy, and opposition to 'popery'. Historians of his camp now use the term 'puritan' very sparingly in order to convey concord rather than conflict as the hallmark of the Church of England in this era.[5]

Obviously, the historians grouped together here and elsewhere as 'revisionists' do not form a single school of interpretation; in fact, they disagree heartily with each other on many points. What they have in common is rejection of an older view on the basis of research that has shifted focus from the exceptions to the rule. While earlier scholars looked at the minority on the radical fringes (early protestant preachers and martyrs, and later nonconformist, presbyterian puritans), the focus now is on the vast majority of the religious population occupying the middle of the road, struggling to cope both with changes imposed from above and with the demands of radical reformers on the one hand and reactionaries on the other. These moderates, in Collinson's version, adopted and disseminated a thoroughly protestant *via media* within which limited toleration was at least tacitly allowed to a wide spectrum of reformed belief and practice, so long as order and episcopal authority were upheld.

What, then, upset this consensus and gave rise to a war of religion in the 1640s? Of those who now see consensus as the rule in the Elizabethan and Jacobean Church, some identify as the stimulus to violent confrontation the theological innovation of Arminianism (denying the traditional Calvinist understanding of grace and predestination) and the revival of 'popish' ceremonies by associates of Archbishop Laud, especially during the decade of Personal Rule (1629–40). This is the argument of Nicholas Tyacke, who reverses the older Marxist and Whig versions of radical puritans fighting a conservative Anglican establishment, into a view of Calvinist traditionalists (now labelled puritans by their enemies) as conservative counter-revolutionaries struggling against radical Arminians. Other 'consensus historians', however, react against both the received version and this revision with a more extreme alternative, rejecting the notion of fundamental theological conflict altogether, even in the 1620s and 1630s. Peter White, for instance, posits instead a broad theological consensus *not* based on Calvinist predestinarianism, and a wide spectrum of tolerated views of grace throughout the first century of English Protestant history. Laud, in the view of this revisionist cohort, represents the religion of protestants, rather than a radical departure from it; thus Kevin Sharpe argues that Laud's desire was to maintain order, obedience and unity in the Church, and to quiet, not exacerbate, theological disagreement.[6] Again, the revisionists do not necessarily agree with each other, except in dismissing absolutely the old 'Puritan Revolution' as a struggle of the godly reformed against resurgent popery in Laudian guise.

On the political front, too, the focus of historians has shifted away from radicals and fomenters of conflict, and towards the much more numerous parliamentary moderatés and local administrators who were quite willing to co-operate with instructions from the centre and anxious to ameliorate tensions and avoid conflict. In Parliament, as in the Church, the agenda may be set on high, and the loudest voices at the meeting may come from the fringes, but when in the end a vote is taken, it is the great middle that determines the outcome. It is the great middle, therefore, that has of late drawn the attention of historians like Geoffrey Elton, and that has produced a more consensual view of Tudor politics than we have seen before. Thus, while the Whigs showed us Elizabethan and early Stuart parliaments as battlegrounds between monarch and political nation, with members especially of the House of Commons waging an unremitting campaign to increase parliamentary privilege, the revised version instead finds fundamental agreement between parliaments and monarchs, and co-operation between provincial magistrates and the centre.[7] Just as there was a religious consensus, so there was a political consensus – on the divine right of the queen or king to rule, on the subordinate though important advisory role of Council and Parliament, and on the absolute need to avoid conflict in the political process. The political revisionists tell us that when conflict is visible in early modern parliaments, its sources can generally be traced to personal animosities and rivalries within the aristocracy at Court and in the Council, not to parliamentary partisanship or ideology. Some Tudor revisionists have even chosen to shift focus completely away from Parliament to the Court as the crucial political arena.[8] As for the old Whig assessment of the increasing strength of parliaments and the Commons' drive to confirm and expand their privileges, revisionists now find that early modern parliaments were relatively weak and declining in power relative to King and Court.[9]

Revisionist historians of the seventeenth century have continued this theme, producing a dilemma for those who seek causes of the Civil War: if Parliament and the early Stuart kings were able to work out their differences on the basis of a commonly held understanding of the structure and function of government, what drove them to take up arms in 1642? In his monumental work of revision, Conrad Russell has answered that the Civil War, far from being a principled conflict between divergent views of law and liberty, was the result of short-term causes, rooted in fundamental structural weaknesses of the monarchy, especially bureaucratic and financial. These contingencies, including inflation, the increased costs of early modern warfare, and the difficulties of ruling the multiple and religiously diverse kingdoms of Scotland, Ireland and England, led to a functional breakdown of the centre, and thence to war – or, more properly, wars: of Charles I's three realms, Scotland rose violently in 1639, Ireland in 1641, and England in 1642. Russell warns against viewing the outbreak of the English Civil War as a single event, rather than 'a somewhat unpredictable sequence of events' in all three kingdoms. Eliminating even one of many contingent events from the five years preceding the outbreak of the English war would have prevented it.[10] The conflict was thus at its outset not particularly revolutionary, and as John Morrill has found, allegiance during the war owed more to family loyalty, local quarrels, or the proximity of either army than to political ideology.[11] In their most recent work, both Morrill and Russell have come back to religious commitment as the greatest source of the conflict that broke out in the 1640s, though they have divergent views of the nature of the religious problem.[12] Even religion, though, forms but one element in a constellation of contingencies in which political ideology finds no place, and in which the collapse of the centre preceded the revolt of the provinces. The furthest edge of the revisionist view is Kevin Sharpe's recent book, *The Personal Rule of Charles I*, which denies any role for either religious division (whether doctrinal or liturgical) or political ideology.[13] Far from being a struggle for law and the liberties of subjects against attempted absolutism, or for reformed religion against Laudian tyranny, the Civil War now appears something of a fluke, 'an accidental war'.[14]

Not all scholars, however, are satisfied with the new version. Many find it incomprehensible that the idea of law and liberty articulated early in the Long Parliament sprang from a vacuum; that the violence that erupted in the summer of 1642 found no cause deeper than 1637; and that the fears of religious innovation expressed by Calvinist Members of Parliament in 1641 were themselves departures from traditional English Protestantism. These scholars are sometimes called 'counter-revisionists', though most would eschew the term and prefer to avoid categorization. Working just as closely with archival sources and producing just as detailed political narratives and theological analyses as their opponents, they find that evidence of long-standing conflict within church and state is not after all wanting, and that the Civil War is more comprehensible when placed in this context. The old 'high road' may have oversimplified the issues, and crude notions of class conflict in this pre-industrial society are not about to be reinstated; however, the new picture of broad-based consensus until the end of the 1630s appears just as flawed. Accordingly, A. G. Dickens, who in the 1960s wrote the classic work on the English Reformation as early and popular, has continued to defend his version. He responds to the revisionists by amassing more evidence of vigorous and widely successful protestant evangelism from the first generation of reformers, setting the stage for the sort of earnest anti-popery and evangelical zeal that would almost inevitably spell trouble for an inclusive and consensual national church. Peter Lake, who accepts many elements of Collinson's and Tyacke's revisions, nevertheless finds that even among moderate Elizabethan puritans, the divide between the self-perceived godly and the world was pronounced, and that for those who understood themselves to be the elect, the comprehensive national church was a precarious enterprise despite the unifying factors of Calvinist theology and anti-popery. In his view, contrasting understanding of the visible and invisible church – the institution over against the truly elect, or 'saints' – in the context of Laudian ceremonial and theological innovation in the seventeenth century, would prove the bane of church unity and peace in the realm.[15]

Lake examines the broad middle ground of an intellectual élite – the clergy; other historians have looked instead at ordinary people in the provinces to challenge the revisionist denial of ideological conflict building for decades before the war. David Underdown's study of regional patterns of allegiance, and more recently of the puritan conversion of Dorchester, has identified deep cultural divisions at all social levels that underpinned and now help to explain conflict over political and religious principle. Far from being a 'fortuitous accident', as the revisionists would have it, the Civil War (or 'English Revolution' as he prefers) resulted in his view from political and social processes at work in the half-century before the conflict to create fundamental instability at the popular level. The result in the 1640s was a struggle 'between adherents of two different conceptions of society and culture'.[16] Underdown's analysis has been vigorously criticized by those who question his correlation of political affiliation with geographic and socio-cultural categories, and his retention of the old Marxist connection of Puritans with the 'middling sort' of society, but they acknowledge that he has 'changed the agenda of Civil War studies'.[17] He has certainly challenged the tendency of revisionists to examine high politics in isolation from the concerns of the larger society, and their dismissal of the possibility that popular allegiance might be based on ideological commitment. Other historians with more specifically political concerns have in fact demonstrated that provincial society was not politically uncommitted and merely reactive to events at the centre. Rather, as Richard Cust shows, people in the localities were remarkably well-informed about events and ideas at Court and in Parliament, and they responded with principled action.[18] Close local studies like that of Warwickshire by Ann Hughes, and comparative surveys of regional diversity and complexity, likewise show provincial allegiance determined not merely by contingency, but by ideology expressed in terms both political and religious.[19] Seventeenth-century people apparently did see the political process in terms of conflict and division, even if some modern historians do not.

The 'counter-revisionists' accept many elements of the new revisions. No one would deny the enormous contribution of the revisionists in challenging old orthodoxies, reformulating in very basic ways the questions we ask about politics and religion, offering highly detailed and meticulously researched narratives of events, and guiding us further into the archives to seek answers from neglected manuscript sources. It would be foolish indeed not to build on what is firm in their new foundations. But it would be just as foolish to assume that if the foundation of the older view is cracked and crumbling in places, it must be entirely abandoned. The 'high road' theorists built on the perceptions of many contemporaries that there was division in the Church, and counter-revisionists have begun to identify the subtleties of this division in ways never clearly articulated before. Those who saw the high road gave us a great deal of useful knowledge about the concerns of some members of Stuart parliaments with liberty and law, and counter-revisionists now find these concerns among provincials as well. They knew that English culture was not monolithic, but a patchwork of conflicting beliefs, rituals, festivities, allegiances and commitments; the counter-revisionists now struggle to identify and categorize these with more precision and sophistication based on new archival research.

The historiographical quarrels presented here are thus not of the sort that generates more heat than light. The revisionists have stimulated new questions, a closer look at the evidence, examination of new kinds of sources (ballads, for instance, and accounts of popular riot and protest), and a much more detailed narrative of events. Even those inclined towards a Whiggish view have had to modify their stance and admit that lines of conflict were less clearly drawn than we would perhaps like, and that there was remarkable willingness to agree or compromise in order to co-operate in the administration of church and state in the Elizabethan and Jacobean era. On the other hand, the revisionists are perhaps justly criticized for 'explaining why no civil war broke out in England in 1642'.[20] And disagreement among revisionists muddies the waters even more: for instance, those whose work is focused on politics have been turning back to religious division as central to the ultimate outbreak of violence – hence the concern of so much of this volume with religion – even while religious revisionists downplay the division. The debate is ongoing; the articles in this volume simply represent the main arguments and allow students to see first hand how historians use their sources to interpret the past. At this stage, both revisionists and counter-revisionists must be granted some partial victories. The spoils go to their students, who now have much more highly nuanced understanding of the complexities that bring on war. If the picture is no longer as simple as it was, it is certainly more accurate and more credible.

NOTES

1 Christopher Hill, 'A Bourgeois Revolution?', *The Collected Essays of Christopher Hill*, III (Brighton, 1986).
2 S. R. Gardiner, *The First Two Stuarts and the Puritan Revolution* (1876), and *The History of England . . . 1603–1642*, 10 vols (London, 1884–6).
3 J. J. Scarisbrick, *The Reformation and the English People* (Oxford, 1984); Christopher Haigh, ed., *The English Reformation Revised* (first chapter reprinted here), and now *English Reformations: Religion, Politics and*

Society under the Tudors (Oxford, 1993); John Bossy, *The English Catholic Community* (Oxford, 1976); Eamon Duffy, *The Stripping of the Altars: Traditional Religion in England c.1400-c.1580* (New Haven, 1992).

4 Robert Whiting, *The Blind Devotion of the People: Popular Religion and the English Reformation* (Cambridge, 1989).

5 Patrick Collinson, *The Religion of Protestants* (Oxford, 1983); Ken Parker, *The English Sabbath* (Cambridge, 1988); C. M. Dent, *Protestant Reformers in Elizabethan Oxford* (Oxford, 1983). Collinson has departed in this from his own earlier work, which in the 1960s traced the history of a 'Puritan movement' in the later sixteenth century: *The Elizabethan Puritan Movement* (Berkeley, 1967).

6 Julian Davies, *The Caroline Captivity of the Church* (Oxford, 1993) follows Sharpe's line on Laud and White's on Arminianism, both represented in Part I of this volume. See also George Bernard, 'The Church of England, *c.* 1579-c.1642', *History*, 75 (1990), pp. 183–206; Kevin Sharpe, *The Personal Rule of Charles I* (New Haven, 1993).

7 Geoffrey Elton, *The Parliament of England, 1559–1581* (Cambridge, 1986); cf. J. E. Neale, *Elizabeth I and Her Parliaments, 1559–1581* (1953). For a similar view of early Stuart parliaments, see C. S. R. Russell, 'The Nature of a Parliament in early Stuart England', in H. Tomlinson, ed., *Before the English Civil War* (New York, 1984), pp. 123–50.

8 e.g., David Starkey, *The English Court: From the Wars of the Roses to the Civil War* (London 1987).

9 This is the conclusion of Conrad Russell, 'Parliamentary History in Perspective, 1604–29', *History*, 61(1976), pp. 1–27; and *Parliaments and English Politics, 1621–29* (Oxford, 1979), and Kevin Sharpe, 'The Political Rule of Charles I', in Tomlinson, pp. 53–78.

10 Russell, *The Causes of the English Civil War* and *The Fall of the British Monarchies, 1637–1642*, excerpted below, Part II. The quotation is from *Causes*, p. 10. See also *Unrevolutionary England, 1603–1642* (Oxford, 1990). The events leading immediately to war (from November 1640 to August 1642) have been recounted in minute detail by Anthony Fletcher, *The Outbreak of the English Civil War* (London, 1981), who stresses the mutual misunderstanding and distrust of king and Parliament.

11 Morrill *Revolt of the Provinces*, excerpted below. See also J. C. D. Clark, *Revolution and Rebellion* (Cambridge, 1986). R. C. Richardson, *The Debate on the English Revolution* (London, 1988) surveys some of these historiographical shifts.

12 John Morrill, 'The Religious Context of the English Civil War', *TRHS*, 5th series, 34 (1984), pp. 155–78. For Morrill, 'Puritan dynamism' is a more persuasive phenomenon than Russell's (and Tyacke's) radical Laudianism and static puritanism: Morrill, 'The Causes of the British Civil Wars', *JEH*, 43 (1992), pp. 624–33. A political revisionist, Morrill's most recent work aligns him more closely with the counter-revisionists on religious issues.

13 cf. J. P. Sommerville, *Politics and Ideology in England 1603–1640* (Harlow, Essex, 1986). Sharpe (1993) resorts to the Scots' invasion

as the *'diabolus ex machina'* of the war, but Russell has pointed out the weakness of this explanation by wondering why so many Englishmen aided a foreign invader against their own government. See his review of Sharpe in the *London Review of Books*, 15 no. 11 (10 June 1993), pp. 23–4.

14 'Accidental war' occurs in Conrad Russell's Introduction to *The Origins of the English Civil War* (London, 1973), p. 1; his more recent arguments for this thesis are represented in Part II of this volume. Among historians influenced by Russell's interpretation are John Morrill, also represented in Part II; Mark Kishlansky 'The Emergence of Adversary Politics in the Long Parliament', *Journal of Modern History*, 49 (1977), pp. 617–46, and *Parliamentary Selection* (Cambridge, 1986); and Kevin Sharpe, Introduction, *Faction and Parliament* (Oxford, 1973), and *Personal Rule*.

15 Lake, *Moderate Puritans and the Elizabethan Church* (Cambridge, 1982); *Anglicans and Puritans?* (London, 1988); ed. with Maria Dowling, *Protestantism and the National Church* (London, 1987). Students who wish to pursue the problem of religion in the early seventeenth century in more detail may now consult a collection of new essays edited by Ken Fincham, *The Early Stuart Church 1603–1640* (London, 1993); his introduction surveys at length the current contours of the debate.

16 David Underdown, 'A Reply to John Morrill', *JBS*, 26 (1987), p. 479. Underdown is replying here to Morrill's 'The Ecology of Allegiance in the English Revolution' in the same issue, pp. 451–67, criticizing Underdown's *Revel, Riot and Rebellion* (Oxford, 1987), excerpted in this volume. The 'fortuitous accident' reference is on p. x of the book, and the preface tells us that the book is in part a response to questions posed by Morrill. On Dorchester, see *Fire From Heaven* (New Haven, 1992).

17 *JBS* debate, p. 468. The Marxist view is best represented by Christopher Hill, *The Century of Revolution* (rev. edn, New York, 1968). More recent work building on many of Hill's assumptions about puritanism and the middling sort include B. Manning, *The English People and the English Revolution* (London, 1976); William Hunt, *The Puritan Moment* (Cambridge, Mass., 1983); and Keith Wrightson, *English Society* (New Brunswick, N. J., 1982).

18 In addition to the excerpt below, see Cust, *The Forced Loan and English Politics, 1626–1628* (Oxford, 1987); Thomas Cogswell, 'The Politics of Propaganda: Charles I and the People in the 1620s', *JBS*, 29 (1990), pp. 187–215; and Derek Hirst, *The Representative of the People?* (Cambridge, 1975).

19 Anne Hughes, *Politics, Society and Civil War in Warwickshire, 1620–1660* (Cambridge, 1987); see also Jacqueline Eales, *Puritans and Roundheads* (Cambridge, 1990).

20 John Morrill, *The Revolt of the Provinces*, 2nd edn (London, 1980), p. x.

Part I

REVISING RELIGION

1

THE RECENT HISTORIOGRAPHY OF THE ENGLISH REFORMATION

Christopher Haigh

In the 1950s, church historians following the lead of A. G. Dickens began to shift the focus of their research away from the classic documents of the Reformation and the central government's implementation of the break from Rome. They began looking instead at local records, especially diocesan court registers, to ask how protestantism was received by people in the provinces. Did the new supremacy of the king over the English Church mean that ordinary people also rejected the authority of the pope? Did the new English Bible and the very protestant Articles of Religion of Edward VI's reign mean that the people of England willingly accepted salvation by faith alone and willingly gave up their former regard for transubstantiation, purgatory, veneration of relics and icons, and masses for the dead? Dickens's early work on Lollards and protestants in the northern diocese of York led him to conclude that indeed the message of the first generation of protestant reformers was received with open arms in the countryside. People disgruntled with the abuses of the Catholic Church and prepared by the anticlericalist and Bible-centred Lollard heresy readily accepted the gospel of salvation by faith alone, the English Bible and service, and the freedom from clerical domination inherent in the Catholic view of priesthood rather than ministry. Other local historians echoed Dickens's conclusions; however, as more and more local investigations were done, it became evident that all counties and towns did not have the same experience of early and popular Reformation.

Christopher Haigh's work on Lancashire pointed in a very different direction from Dickens's. Haigh found that reception of the Reformation was rather slow and reluctant, that in fact a persistent Catholic traditionalism was more characteristic of Lancashire than eager protestantism, even in the Elizabethan period when Catholic recusancy was actively prosecuted. Since his study of Lancashire, historians like J. J. Scarisbrick in The Reformation and the English People *(1984) have joined him in arguing that the pre-Reformation Church was in fact broadly popular, that people gave up the old faith reluctantly and frequently only under duress. In an interesting departure, Robert Whiting's study of the south-western counties has found that for many people at the point of obediently renouncing Catholicism, irreligion was the preferred option. Protestantism, with its requirements of Bible-reading and sermon attendance, and its 'culture of discipline' – a move to replace disorderly traditional festivities with a more austere, 'godly' community – was simply not a very attractive alternative. The revisionists do agree, however, that at some point in Elizabeth's reign the old faith was reduced to a small and actively repressed minority. The debate continues as to precisely when and how this happened.*

In the following essay, Haigh summarizes the revisionist position, now fully expanded in his English Reformations *(1993). In the last section of this volume, A. G. Dickens will pick up the gauntlet and respond to the challenge of the new view.*

* * *

The English Reformation was not a specific event which may be given a precise date; it was a long and complex process. 'The Reformation' is a colligatory concept, a historians' label which relates several lesser changes into an overall movement: it embraces a break from the Roman obedience; an assertion of secular control over the Church; a suppression of Catholic institutions such as monasteries and chantries; a prohibition of Catholic worship; and a protestantization of services, clergy and laity. Though the political decision to introduce each phase of change and the legislative alteration of statutes and canons may be dated easily enough, it is much harder to ascribe responsibility and motive for such measures. Moreover, as the interest of historians has in recent years moved on from such political issues towards the administrative enforcement of new rules and popular acceptance of new ideas, so the identification and explanation of change have become even more difficult: the pace is likely to have varied from area to area, and the criteria by which progress should be measured are far from clear. It is therefore not surprising that there has been much dispute over the causes and chronology of developments in religion, and recent interpretations of the Reformation in England can, with some simplification, be grouped in relation to two matrices. One matrix relates to the motive force behind the progress of Protestantism: at one extreme, it could be suggested that Protestant advance was entirely the result of official coercion, while at the other it could be said that the new religion spread horizontally by conversions among the people. The second matrix relates to the pace of religious change: on the one hand, it could be suggested that Protestantism made real progress at an early date and had become a powerful force by the death of Edward VI, while on the other it could be said that little had been achieved in the first half of the century and the main task of protestantizing the people had to be undertaken in the reign of Elizabeth. These two matrices provide us with four main clusters of interpretations.

First, there are those historians, usually political historians and biographers, who have seen the English Reformation as taking place rapidly as a result of imposition from above. The doyen of this school is, without doubt, G. R. Elton, who has presented the Reformation as one aspect of the great reform programme which was initiated and carried far by Thomas Cromwell[a] in the 1530s. The political Reformation saw the 'nationalization' of the Church, and a religious Reformation sought to purge the parishes of superstition. These changes were enforced from the centre by deliberate governmental action: the people were persuaded to accept new policies by a carefully orchestrated campaign of preaching and printed propaganda, encouragement to conform was provided by a sharpening of the treason laws, and local dignitaries were instructed to report deviants to Cromwell for investigation. The reformist thrust was, according to Professor Elton, carried very much further under Edward VI, with the imposition of a Protestant liturgy, the destruction of Catholic church furniture, and a preaching campaign to carry the Gospel into the villages: 'The fact is that by 1553 England was almost certainly nearer to being a Protestant country than to anything else.'[1] This picture of a 'rapid Reformation from above' has received powerful support from Peter Clark's study of Kent: it is clear that Cromwell paid close attention to this strategically important county and built up, by the exercise of patronage, a reformist group among the governing gentry and in the urban oligarchies. Within the Church in

Kent, Archbishop Cranmer and the preachers he brought in were crucial to the progress of Protestantism, and reformers took control of the administrative machine. Clark claims that changes in the formulae of wills and the political complexion of town governments show that, under pressure from the archbishop, there was a Protestant breakthrough in the mid–1540s: indeed, by this point the 'Reformation from above' had been so successful that 'Reformation from below' may have taken over, and Clark has suggested that a swing to Protestantism in the Home Counties forced Henry VIII 'to commit himself to the Protestant cause' in 1546–7.[2]

Elton and Clark are in a well-established tradition of English Reformation historiography, and a picture of officially inspired and imposed reform is presented by several of the older and briefer textbooks. They have, however, added to earlier descriptions of statutes and injunctions studies of the enforcement machinery in action and of the changing political structure of a well-governed area. But one may have doubts on the wider applicability of such an interpretation of the Reformation. Elton has shown how Cromwell's reform programme came to be accepted at the political centre, and how Cromwell attempted to impose his policies on the localities: he has not, however, shown that reform was, to any significant degree, accepted in the provinces, and a growing number of local studies suggest that there was little progress. 'Reformation from above' depended for its effectiveness upon the co-operation of the justices of the peace and diocesan administrators, who seem to have been unsatisfactory proponents of reform. Even in the early part of the reign of Elizabeth there remained a strong conservative element on the commissions of the peace, and to avoid crippling county government the commissions could be remodelled only slowly,[3] while the social influence of bishops was weakened by expropriation and lesser diocesan officials were a distinctly conservative group.[4] It is true that in Peter Clark's Kent both secular justices and ecclesiastical administrators co-operated with the reforming regime, but the county was a far from typical area: Kent was close to London, so the gentry were embroiled in the web of Court politics; it was a maritime county, so the continental Protestant influence was strong; and at its head was an activist reforming archbishop who patronized Protestants and harassed conservatives. Elsewhere, in circumstances less favourable to the Reformation, local government proved a block rather than a spur to religious change.[5]

The most influential of the historians who have detected a 'rapid Reformation from below' in early Tudor England is A. G. Dickens, though his general view has been supported by, for example, Claire Cross.[6] Professor Dickens has stressed the religious rather than the political roots of the English Reformation, and has sought to demonstrate that links between an expanding late Lollardy and early Protestantism led to swift Protestant advance at the popular level. The seedbed of Protestantism had been prepared by Bible-reading Lollard conventicles and by itinerant Lollard evangelists, and the interaction between native Lollardy and new Protestantism was symbolized by the exchange of Wycliffe texts for Tyndale New Testaments arranged by Robert Barnes.[7] The higher clergy of the Catholic Church were too involved in politics and the lower clergy were too poor and uneducated to meet the rising lay demand for a more personal involvement in religion or to combat the dynamic force of a Bible-based evangelical Protestantism: Reformation was easy and it was fast. Although legislative changes created a climate in which reform could triumph, the Dickens Reformation is one of conversion rather than coercion, with Protestantism spreading in the localities by the uncoordinated efforts of radical clergy, itinerant clothworkers and Bible-reading anticlerical gentry. This analysis is, in part, based upon Dickens's own pioneering study of the progress of religious change at the popular level in Yorkshire, and his general conclusions have gained support from other local studies of areas where Lollardy had made progress and where early Protestant clergy were active: it seems that there was a 'rapid Reformation from below' in Essex, Bristol and the textile villages of Gloucestershire.[8] It could, however, be argued that, in concentrating their attentions upon the atypical heretics whose cases reached the pages of Foxe, Strype, episcopal registers and court act books, historians of this school are in danger of losing perspective on the pace of religious change. Of course there were Protestant heretics in the 1520s, and there were more in the 1530s, but they formed a very small minority whose real significance has been exaggerated because their own rejection of Catholicism was, much later and for accidental political reasons, to triumph nationally.

Acceptance of an overall interpretation of the English Reformation which presents it as rapid and essentially popular depends upon two assumptions which are being increasingly questioned by recent scholarships. First, we must assume that the institutions, personnel and beliefs of the English Catholic Church did not command the respect and commitment of the people, who were therefore open to the influence of new and heterodox ideas. But as Reformation historians have moved from the study of the Church through the printed propaganda of its anticlerical critics to the study of the Church through the records of its work, a picture of a moribund, dispirited and repressive institution which failed to meet the needs of its people becomes more and more difficult to sustain. We now know that the parish clergy were *not* negligent, immoral and inadequately educated clerics embroiled in regular conflicts with their parishioners over tithes and mortuaries: if their standards of spirituality and academic achievement would not satisfy the late-twentieth-century mind, they seem to have satisfied Tudor villagers, who complained remarkably infrequently about their priests.[9] Though the early Tudor bishops have been dismissed as lordly prelates rather than spiritual pastors, we know now that in the dioceses of Chichester, Ely, Lincoln, Norwich and Winchester, and probably elsewhere, colleagues of Thomas Wolsey were attempting to overhaul diocesan administration, improve clerical standards and exert pastoral discipline over the laity.[10] Our assessment of the ecclesiastical courts and response to them is no longer based upon the 1532 'Commons Supplication against the Ordinaries', an *ex parte* political statement which tells us little about real conditions: we now know that the courts were, by sixteenth-century standards, honest, speedy and cheap, that their discipline was accepted with little criticism, and that they met important social needs in the resolution of disputes and the regulation of relationships.[11] Those 'faults' of the late medieval Church which have been presented as symptoms of decline or causes of lay criticism are now shown to have been very much less significant than had been supposed, and it therefore seems unlikely that there was any serious alienation of the laity from the institutional Church. Indices such as will-benefactions to the Church and the demand for religious books show a stable or even increasing lay involvement in the conventional piety sanctioned by authority,[12] and the 'anticlericalism' seen by many historians as the springboard for religious change may not have been a widespread phenomenon. Much of the evidence cited for anticlericalism comes from literary sources (primarily the work of Protestant propagandists and not necessarily reflective of any wider opinion), or from the grievances of particular groups with their own specific interests (such as London merchants in conflict with Wolsey), or from assumptions that there must have been a revulsion against the Church's flaws – flaws we now know were not usually serious. London, which was jealous of its civic rights and where it was difficult to operate an effective parochial system, presented special problems, but there is surprisingly little solid evidence of conflict between clergy and laity elsewhere: the diocese of Lichfield, with over 600 parishes, produced only ten tithe suits in 1525 and four in 1530, while in the 252 parishes of Canterbury diocese there were only four cases in 1531. Tithe appears to have become a seriously divisive problem in the parishes only from the 1540s and it is difficult to see, in the early Tudor period, the breach in lay–clerical relations necessary to a 'rapid Reformation from below'.[13]

The second assumption which underpins an interpretation of the English Reformation as swift and popular relates to the attractiveness and the presentation of evangelical Protestantism. A 'rapid Reformation from below' means that the new religion soon seized the imaginations of artisans and peasants, but that this happened on any widespread scale seems improbable. Protestantism was above all the religion of the Word, the printed word and the preached word, and it stressed salvation through a God-given faith supported by a reading of the Scriptures and an attendance at sermons. It was therefore a religion which had a much stronger appeal in the towns than in the countryside. We know that in the late sixteenth century tradesmen were five times more likely to be literate than husbandmen, and that regular and popular preaching was a feature of the towns rather than the rural parishes.[14] This means that country people were less likely than townsmen to be introduced to the new religious ideas, and that such ideas were less attractive to them: a number of local studies have shown that Protestantism could spread quite easily among the merchants and artisans of English towns,[15] but the Reformation shift from a ritualistic to a bibliocentric presentation of religion was a disaster in the countryside. Richard Greenham preached six sermons a week to his parishioners at Dry Drayton in Cambridgeshire, but after twenty years of effort he left for London in 1591, partly because of 'the intractableness and unteachableness of that people amongst whom he had taken such exceeding great pains'. An experienced Lancashire evangelist recorded sadly in 1614:

> It doth not a little grieve the ministers of the Gospel to take great pains in teaching the truth, and that in good manner, and yet see most of their hearers to receive little or no profit at all, but still remain, after many years' teaching, as ignorant, as popish and profane as they were at the first. Yet let them not be dismayed, it was Christ's own case; the fault is in the hearers, not in the teachers.[16]

If Protestant proselytizing in the countryside often encountered hostility or sullen resentment, the reasons are not difficult to find. An earlier generation of English Protestant historians too often assumed that the new Gospel taught by Luther was so obviously *true* that sensible Englishmen would abandon without hesitation the superstitions of their forefathers. But more recent scholars have adopted a functionalist approach to popular religion, and have recognized that the magical and communal rituals of the late medieval Church met important parish needs. Rituals which were related to the harvest year and which offered protection from the hazards of agricultural life, and ceremonies which reconciled disputes in villages built upon willing co-operation, were not readily relinquished: it has, indeed, been suggested that when the enforcement of the Elizabethan settlement drove magic from the churches, the people sought from charms and 'cunning men' the protection from evil which had formerly been provided by the Church.[17] The Reformation abolished the symbolic rituals which had been at the centre of rural religion, and attempted to impose a brand of personalized religion more suited to the needs of the gentry and the literate townsmen: as a result, some members of the rural poor found the official Church had little to offer them. Late in the reign of Elizabeth the Kentish preacher Josias Nichols examined 400 communicants in one parish and found that only 10 per cent understood basic Christian doctrine and only 1 per cent expected to be saved through faith rather than works. In the 1640s John Shaw found the people of Furness 'exceedingly ignorant and blind as to religion', and he met an old man who, when told he would be saved through Christ, said 'I think I heard of that man you spake of once in a play at Kendal called Corpus Christi play, where there was a man on a tree and blood ran down'.[18]

It has been argued here, then, that a picture of a 'rapid Reformation', whether it is thought to have been imposed from above or to have spread among the people, cannot properly be derived from rural England as a whole. Though religious change proceeded more rapidly in some areas than elsewhere, this was usually as the result of special circumstances. Kent had trading contracts with Protestant centres abroad, and Bible translations and propaganda were smuggled in through Dover to be distributed among the Lollard groups of the clothing towns, while it is clear that the role of Archbishop Cranmer was crucial in the growth of Protestant opinion.[19] In Bristol and Gloucestershire the position appears to have been similar: there were already Lollards in the weaving villages, some of the county gentry were influenced by Tyndale through family contacts, members of the Bristol merchant oligarchy supported Latimer's evangelical preaching, and when he became bishop he organized a preaching campaign. Under Edward VI, Bishop Hooper was not only an active proselytizer, but he also exercised, through visitation and his consistory court, unusually careful pastoral supervision of the diocese of Gloucester. But despite the vigour of these efforts, the destruction of Catholic allegiance in Gloucestershire proved much easier than the creation of positive Protestantism, and though the county was later to become one of the most distinctively Protestant of the western counties it had not moved far in that direction by 1558.[20] In Kent and the Bristol area the twin influences of a port and episcopal pressure seem to have been significant, but in Hampshire the protestantizing influence of the port of Southampton was apparently neutralized by the long rule of a conservative bishop, and in the reign of Elizabeth Catholicism remained surprisingly strong in this Channel county. In Sussex, a little further east, continental influences established Protestant groups in the ports of Rye and Winchelsea under Henry VIII, but the conservative Bishop Sherburne and his officials at Chichester prevented radical inroads in the west of the county.[21] Even the diocese of London may help to show the need for both Protestant trade links and activist Protestant bishops if there was to be 'a rapid Reformation'. In the 1530s and 1540s Bishops Stokesley and Bonner tried hard to limit Protestant penetration, and there was a good deal of conservative resistance from clergy and laity in the city to the spread of the new religion. It may be significant that the main early Protestant centres in the diocese, outside the city itself, were in the north-east of Essex, close to the port of Harwich, while Elizabethan Catholic recusancy was to be concentrated closest to London itself, where episcopal influence had been strongest.[22] Of course, the forces which dictated the pace of religious change in a region were more numerous and complex than those discussed here, but it seems clear that Kent and Gloucestershire were far from typical counties, and the conjunction of pressures from a Protestant port and a Protestant bishop was an unusual one.

A third group of historians has presented a Reformation which was imposed from above by authority, but which had only a slow impact upon the localities. Penry Williams has suggested that the early Reformation infected the statute book more effectively than the parishes, and that popular Catholicism was broken only by official preaching, printing and prosecution in the reign of Elizabeth. A. L. Rowse has seen the Reformation in Cornwall as a struggle for power between two parties, the winner gaining an opportunity to dictate the religion of the 'mentally passive people'. There was a good deal of hostility in the 1530s and under Edward VI towards attempts to impose religious change upon the Cornish, though the repression which followed the Western Rebellion of 1549 may have weakened popular resistance. But major Protestant advance came only as a result of a political coup in the late 1570s: a coalition of aggressive, reformist coastal gentry with privateering interests broke the power of the conservative inland gentry, and thereafter there was no effective bar to the imposition of religious reform.[23] In Sussex the popular Reformation had barely begun by 1558 and Protestantism made real headway only from the 1570s, when the bishop brought in radical preachers from Cambridge and enforcement of the Elizabethan settlement was improved by the remodelling of the commission of the peace.[24] In northern counties, too, the early Reformation was ineffective, and there was substantial religious change in the reign of Elizabeth only as a result of the redistribution of political power.

The new religion had made minimal progress among the ruling order of Durham and Northumberland by 1564, but the crippling of the Percy and Neville interests after the Revolt of the Earls proved to be a turning point: in Durham the bishop became the main dispenser of patronage and focus of political aspirations, so that authority passed into the hands of supporters of the Reformation. In Lancashire, too, Protestantism had little impact until after a political reconstruction: in 1568 the Ecclesiastical Commission was purged, in 1572 the conservative third Earl of Derby was succeeded by a son more open to the influence of the Court, in 1579 the clearly Protestant Bishop Chadderton arrived at Chester and in 1587 the commission of the peace was remodelled. Thereafter the anti-Catholic laws were enforced in the well-governed parts of the county, and there radical preachers could work unmolested.[25]

A group of scholars who embrace a 'slow Reformation from below' might be sought among the most sophisticated of the recent historians of Puritanism, who are presenting what had been seen as a post-Reformation radical deviation as the mainstream of Protestant advance. Patrick Collinson has treated Elizabethan Puritanism as the evangelical phase of the English Reformation, following the first political phase, in which the new religion was carried to the parishes by the preachers, who created a godly community of committed Protestants. In Cambridgeshire, Margaret Spufford found that though there was little opposition to the official changes of the early Reformation and a few villages may have had handfuls of Protestants in the 1540s, in most parishes Protestantism had an impact only from the 1560s and not until the 1590s is there substantial evidence of Protestant enthusiasm. Similarly, Bill Sheils had found that, except for a very few parishes, there is little sign of shifts in religious allegiance in Northamptonshire and Rutland before the reign of Elizabeth, and that Protestant loyalties developed significantly among the laity only from the late 1560s, when the influence of new Protestant ministers was felt.[26] But interpretations of the English Reformation as a slow and tortuous process, whether it proceeds by official coercion or popular conversion, are, not surprisingly, as flawed as works of the 'rapid Reformation' school. If 'rapid Reformation' historians too easily assumed that an absence of serious recorded opposition to, let us say, the Edwardian reforms suggests acquiescence and even approval, then 'slow Reformation' writers are too willing to conclude that an absence of serious recorded heresy under Mary shows that the early Reformation had failed.[27] Again, if those who think change was swift exaggerate the importance of Henrician heresy cases, those who argue that Protestantism gained ground only slowly may exaggerate the significance of Elizabethan recusancy returns.[28] If the case for a 'rapid Reformation' is usually substantiated from areas where social and political conditions were favourable to change, the argument for a 'slow Reformation' tends to be supported with evidence from counties with poor communications and less effective government. Reformation historians have, in the main, concentrated their attentions upon the counties near to London, such as Essex and Kent, where both the official and popular Reformations are most likely to have been effective, and upon the outlying areas, Cornwall, Lancashire and York, where change was necessarily slower: it has been possible to argue that both groups represent special cases.

The publication of the second stage of Margaret Bowker's painstaking study of the diocese of Lincoln is therefore of great significance, for Lincoln cannot be dismissed as untypical. The diocese sprawled across nine counties of midland England and had within it a representative sample of geographical locations. If the early Reformation could be effective, it surely ought to have been in Lincoln: it was a well-administered diocese which included one university and came close to the other; it embraced, in the Chilterns, an area of strong Lollard influence; and there were, in Leicester, Northampton and Stamford, important towns. But if Lincoln clergy conformed to the Henrician changes it was only because there were powerful career inducements; the bishop combatted Protestantism, and Buckinghamshire Lollardy was contained; and there is little evidence of shifts in belief among the laity until the late 1540s. Lincoln emerges as a classic case of 'slow Reformation', and Mrs Bowker concludes that when Bishop Longland died in 1547 'he left a diocese with priests and laity as conservative as he was'.[29] In the county of Lincolnshire the Edwardian Reformation seems to have been entirely destructive in its impact, and though the Marian visitations discovered isolated critics of Catholic doctrine and practice there was no substantial sympathy for the new religion. The Protestant breakthrough came only in the reign of Elizabeth, through the evangelistic efforts of a new generation of university-trained ministers.[30] The case of Lincoln is likely to shift the consensus of historical generalization towards a recognition that the early phases of the Reformation were indecisive, and that major Protestant advance took place mainly in the Elizabethan period. It was only in the latter part of the sixteenth century, when a Protestant regime remodelled commissions of the peace and diocesan administrations to give power to supporters of reform, when the redistribution of clerical patronage weakened conservative interests and when the universities produced a supply of committed preachers of the new religion, that Protestantism had a real and widespread impact.

Such an interpretation is far from universal among historians of the English Reformation, and on a crude head-count it may not even be the majority opinion, but it seems to be the natural conclusion of trends in recent historiography. Much of the achievement of the last twenty years of English Reformation scholarship has been built upon the insights and example of A. G. Dickens and G. R. Elton. Professor Dickens led students of the Reformation from the pages of Foxe, Bale and Fish to the folios of visitation act books and sheaves of consistory cause papers. In these under-used sources was recorded not the Reformation of the politicians and preachers but the Reformation of the people, and it has proved possible to trace the impact of the official Reformation upon the parishes and the growth of reformed opinion. Perhaps Dickens did not follow through the implications of his own archival revolution, for in rightly attacking the myth of the thorough backwardness of the Tudor North he tried to show that even unpromising areas could be made to fit into the chronology and categories of established 'rapid Reformation' historiography.[31] Those who have followed Professor Dickens into the record offices of English counties and dioceses have more often challenged the Protestant orthodoxy and stressed the diversity of local responses to the Reformation pressure. If Dickens led a breakthrough in the provinces, G. R. Elton led one at the centre, taking historians from the pages of the statute book to the state papers and administrative records, from the enactments of Parliament to the processes of policy formation and enforcement. Scholars are now constructing an account of the political struggles within Court, administration and Parliament which produced the erratic official Reformation, and a historiography which stressed theologians and preachers is being replaced by a Reformation of factions, parties and coups.[32] But perhaps of even greater significance for Reformation historians was Professor Elton's stress on the problems of enforcement, a stress which resulted from his examination of the reports of disaffection in the counties as the Henrician changes were imposed. Elton thus became the first serious non-Catholic or non-Anglo-Catholic historian to present the English Reformation as a major struggle.[33] It is true that Elton's admiration for the achievements of Thomas Cromwell has led him to exaggerate the progress the Reformation had made by the time of that minister's fall, and to minimize the importance of the resistance which was to occur thereafter,[34] but others have carried his themes of coercion and conflict into the later stages of the Reformation.

Some of the historians who have followed through the insights of Dickens and Elton have now abandoned the conventional interpretation of the English Reformation, an interpretation which came to appear archetypally 'whiggish' in the sense exposed by Herbert Butterfield. The task of the historian is the explanation of events: he tries to show why things turned out as they did. Since the eventual outcome of the Reformation was a more or less Protestant England, too often 'the history of the English Reformation' has been written as 'the origins of English Protestantism': we have been given a history of the progressives and the victors in which those men, ideas and issues seen as leading towards the final Reformation result are linked together in a one-sided account of change. The Reformation in England thus appears, in the pages of a 'whig' historians, as an inexorable process, a necessary sequence unfolding easily to a predetermined conclusion: the medieval Church was in decline, the laity was anticlerical, Lutheran ideas were readily accepted, a centralizing state espoused reform, superstition was attacked and, after a brief Marian fiasco, a finally Protestant England was recognized in the legislation of 1559, the date at which many Reformation textbooks stop. But the Reformation in England was not an inevitable development, it was the contingent product of a series of conflicts and crises and of the interaction of social, geographical and political influences which varied from region to region.

So far, only one general account of the period has accepted the possibility of another outcome and presented the Reformation as a long and hard-fought contest.[35] But many more specific studies have supported a view of the Reformation as a struggle, a struggle to achieve political victory at the centre and a struggle to secure enforcement in the localities. It is clear from the work of, for example, Guy, Starkey, Ives, Elton, L. B. Smith, Slavin and Hoak[36] that the main period of the early Reformation, from 1527 to 1553, was one of swirling factional conflict at Court, in which religious policy was both a weapon and a prize. At a number of points, in 1529, 1532, 1536, 1538, 1539, 1540, 1543, 1546–7, 1549–50 and 1553, events could have developed in dramatically different ways if the balance of power had shifted only slightly. It may be that the settlement of 1559 was the result of a preconceived plan by Elizabeth and her advisers rather than, as Neale thought, of pressure from Protestants in Parliament, but the outcome was decisively influenced by the challenge of conservatives in the House of Lords and the government had to fight hard for even its qualified victory.[37] Thereafter, there were still times when a political decision to revert to Catholicism was not entirely beyond the bounds of possibility.[38] In the counties, too, the Reformation was a struggle between the reformers and both deliberate Catholic resistance and the strong force of inertia – there were, in the middle of the reign of Elizabeth, still places like Ripon in Yorkshire and Weaverham in Cheshire where religious change had had hardly any effect.[39] At the local level the Reformation was not a walkover for the Protestants, it was a real contest: at Bristol, Gloucester, Oxford and Rye in the 1530s, at Canterbury and London in the 1540s, at Poole, Bodmin and Exeter in the reign of Edward VI and at Hereford and York in the 1560s there was powerful opposition to the Reformation in the towns.[40] The 1570s in Cornwall and Norfolk and the 1580s in Suffolk and Lancashire saw fierce battles for supremacy between conservative and reformist gentry, and only the political victories of the latter allowed an easier growth of Protestantism.[41] Sullen hostility towards novelty was apparently widespread in the countryside, and it took the Elizabethan episcopate some fifteen years to impose reasonable observance of the Prayer Book upon clergy and parishioners; there was more militant opposition to aspects of the official Reformation from nine counties in 1536, at least six counties in 1549 and two counties in 1569. Such resistance was not the despairing reflex response of a defeated cause, and its influence on the development of the Reformation at the centre and in the localities suggests that there was nothing inevitable about the final Protestant victory. The plans and achievements of the reign of Mary show, too, that there was no inevitability in the final Catholic failure. Rex Pogson's work on Cardinal Pole and studies of specific dioceses indicate a far-sighted approach to the needs of English Catholicism,[42] and some officials were attempting to present the old religion in forms more palatable to the articulate laity,[43] Marian visitations, even of Bonner's London, demonstrated that the bishops faced not an intractable problem of crushing entrenched heresy but a rather more solvable difficulty in re-indoctrinating a partially indifferent people.[44] It has, indeed, been argued that until as late as the mid-1570s conservative priests were quite successful in sustaining Catholic allegiance at the popular level, and that collapse came only when the Marian generation was replaced by missionary priests with new priorities.[45]

These are some of the strands from which an 'anti-whig' interpretation of an overall 'slow Reformation' might be constructed, but the production of a revised synthesis will be difficult. The great advantage of a view of the English Reformation which stressed its speed and its one-sidedness was that it made the subject manageable; the narrative method lends itself easily to a 'whig' interpretation of events, as progressives implement their policies step by step. But the writing of studies which do justice to the Catholics as well as the Protestants, to the ignorant as well as the theologians, which demonstrate the interplay of factions and forces at the centre and in the localities, and which trace the shifts in popular opinion in different parts of the country, will be a much more arduous task. History, however, must not be made to fit the convenience of the historian, still less the demands of the publisher; we must show the past in all its variety and irreducible complexity, no matter how far art has to be sacrificed to accuracy.

EDITOR'S NOTES

Reprinted from *The Historical Journal* 25 (1982), pp. 995–1007, with the permission of Cambridge University Press and the author.

a Cromwell was the most important of Henry VIII's ministers from 1534 to 1540, acting as architect and administrator of much of the legislation of the Reformation Parliament (1529–36), including the dissolution of the monasteries. Elton credited him with the creation of a modern bureaucracy in *The Tudor Revolution in Government* (Cambridge, 1953).

NOTES

1 G. R. Elton, *Reform and Reformation: England 1509–1558* (London, 1977), especially pp. 157–200, 273–95, 353–71, with the passage quoted at p. 371; *Policy and Police: The Enforcement of the Reformation in the Age of Thomas Cromwell* (Cambridge, 1972).

2 P. Clark, *English Provincial Society from the Reformation to the Revolution: Religion, Politics and Society in Kent, 1500–1640* (Hassocks, 1977), pp. 34–68.

3 W. R. Trimble, *The Catholic Laity in Elizabethan England* (Cambridge, Mass., 1964), pp. 25–6, 52–3; R. B. Manning, 'Catholics and Local Office Holding in Elizabethan Sussex', *BIHR*, 35 (1962), pp. 47–61; J. H. Gleason, *The Justices of the Peace in England, 1558–1640* (Oxford, 1969), pp. 68–72; C. Haigh, *Reformation and Resistance in Tudor Lancashire* (Cambridge, 1975), pp. 213, 284–6; D. MacCulloch, 'Catholic and Puritan in Elizabethan Suffolk', *Archiv für Reformationsgeschichte*, 72 (1981), pp. 232–5.

4 F. Heal, *Of Prelates and Princes: A Study of the Economic and Social Position of the Tudor Episcopate* (Cambridge, 1980), pp. 101–327; R. Houlbrooke, *Church Courts and the People during the English Reformation, 1520–1570* (Oxford, 1979), pp. 24–5; Haigh, *Reformation and Resistance*, pp. 210, 212; F. D. Price, 'An Elizabethan Church Official: Thomas Powell, Chancellor of the Gloucester Diocese', Church Quarterly Review, 72 (1939), pp. 94–112.

5 Elton, *Policy and Police*, pp. 85–9; Haigh, *Reformation and Resistance*, pp. 102–7, 140–2, 213, 284–90; R. B. Manning, *Religion and Society in Elizabethan Sussex* (Leicester, 1969), pp. 61–125.

6 A. G. Dickens, *The English Reformation* (London, 1964); 'Heresy and the Origins of English Protestantism', in J. S. Bromley and E. H. Kossman, eds, *Britain and the Netherlands* (London, 1964), II, pp. 47–66; C. Cross, *Church and People, 1450–1660* (London, 1976).

7 Dickens, *English Reformation*, p. 34; M. Aston, 'Lollardy and the Reformation: Survival or Revival', *History*, 49 (1964), pp. 161–3.

8 A. G. Dickens, *Lollards and Protestants in the Diocese of York, 1509–1558* (Oxford, 1959); J. E. Oxley, *The Reformation in Essex to the Death of Mary* (Manchester, 1965); K. G. Powell, *The Marian Martyrs and Reformation in Bristol* (Bristol, 1972); 'The Beginnings of Protestantism in Gloucestershire', *TBGAS*, 90 (1971), pp. 145–8.

9 M. Bowker, *The Secular Clergy in the Diocese of Lincoln, 1495–1520* (Cambridge, 1968); P. Heath, *The English Parish Clergy on the Eve of*

the Reformation (London, 1969); Houlbrooke, *Church Courts and the People*, pp. 177–9.

10 Houlbrooke, *Church Courts and the People*, pp. 10–11; Steven Lander, 'Church Courts and the Reformation in the Diocese of Chichester, 1500–58', in C. Haigh, ed., *Reformation Revised* (Cambridge, 1987), pp. 37–46; F. Heal, 'The Parish Clergy and the Reformation in the Diocese of Ely', *Proceedings of the Cambridge Antiquarian Society*, 66 (1975), pp. 147–50; Bowker, *Secular Clergy*, pp. 18–20, 33, 36, 90.

11 M. Bowker, 'The "Commons Supplication against the Ordinaries" in the Light of Some Archidiaconal *Acta*', *TRHS*, 5th series, 21 (1971), pp. 61–77; *The Henrician Reformation: The Diocese of Lincoln under John Longland, 1521–1547* (Cambridge, 1981), pp. 51–7; Houlbrooke, *Church Courts and the People*, pp. 42, 50–1, 95–6, 114–15, 263, 271–2.

12 Bowker, *Henrician Reformation*, pp. 48, 93, 147–8, 176–9; A. Kreider, *English Chantries: The Road to Dissolution* (Cambridge, Mass., 1979), pp. 89–92; W. K. Jordan, *The Charities of Rural England, 1480–1660* (London, 1961), pp. 438–40; H. S. Bennett, *English Books and Readers, 1475–1557* (London, 1952), pp. 57–8, 65–70, 74–5; J. Rhodes, 'Private Devotion in England on the Eve of the Reformation' (University of Durham Ph.D. thesis, 1974), I, pp. 6–7, 181, 194; II, pp. 98–9.

13 S. Brigden, 'The Early Reformation in London, 1520–1547; The Conflict in the Parishes' (University of Cambridge Ph.D. thesis, 1979), pp. 23–86; Heath, *English Parish Clergy*, p. 152; Houlbrooke, *Church Courts and the People*, pp. 146–7, 273–4; Bowker, *Henrician Reformation*, pp. 135–6; *Secular Clergy*, pp. 3, 110–11, 114, 152; Haigh, *Reformation and Resistance*, pp. 14, 56–62.

14 D. Cressy, *Literacy and the Social Order: Reading and Writing in Tudor and Stuart England* (Cambridge, 1980), pp. 146, 152; P. Seaver, *The Puritan Lectureships* (Stanford, 1970), pp. 77–117, 121, 297–300.

15 W. J. Sheils, 'Religion in Provincial Towns: Innovation and Tradition', in Heal and O'Day, eds, *Church and Society*, pp. 156–76.

16 S. Clarke, *A General Martyrology* (London, 1677 edn), pp. 12–15; W. Harrison, *The Difference of Hearers* (London, 1625 edn), sig. A3. On the ineffectiveness of evangelism in some areas, see my 'Puritan Evangelism in the Reign of Elizabeth I', *EHR*, 92 (1977), pp. 30–58, and the chorus of complaints from Elizabethan preachers too numerous to note here.

17 K. Thomas, *Religion and the Decline of Magic* (London, 1971), pp. 27–188, 252–332; J. Bossy, 'Blood and Baptism: Kinship, Community and Christianity in Western Europe from the Fourteenth to the Seventeenth Centuries', *Studies in Church History*, 10 (1973), pp. 129–43.

18 J. Nichols, *The Plea of the Innocent* (n.p., 1602), pp. 212–13; *Yorkshire Diaries and Autobiographies* (Surtees Society, 65, 1877), p. 137. See also Clark, *English Provincial Society*, pp. 155–7.

19 Clark, *English Provincial Society*, pp. 36, 40, 47, 60, 74.

20 K. G. Powell, 'The Social Background to the Reformation in Gloucestershire', *TBGAS*, 92 (1973), pp. 96–120; F. D. Price,

'Gloucester Diocese under Bishop Hooper', *TBGAS*, 60 (1939), pp. 51–151.

21 Houlbrooke, *Church Courts and the People*, pp. 227, 237–8; J. E. Paul, 'The Hampshire Recusants in the Reign of Elizabeth I' (University of Southampton Ph.D. thesis, 1958), pp. 128–30, 391; S. J. Lander, 'The Diocese of Chichester, 1508–1558' (University of Cambridge Ph.D. thesis, 1974), *passim*; Manning, *Religion and Society in Elizabethan Sussex*, pp. 37–8.

22 Brigden, 'Early Reformation in London', pp. 127–34, 141–5, 227–61; Oxley, *Reformation in Essex*, pp. 210–37; M. O'Dwyer, 'Catholic Recusants in Essex, *c.*1580 to *c.*1600' (University of London M. A. thesis, 1960), pp. 27–40.

23 P. Williams, *The Tudor Regime* (Oxford, 1979), pp. 253–92; A. L. Rowse, *Tudor Cornwall* (London, 1941), pp. 184, 253–4, 257–8, 263–89, 320, 345–65.

24 R. B. Manning, 'The Spread of the Popular Reformation in England', in C. S. Meyer, ed., *Sixteenth Century Essays and Studies* (St Louis, Missouri, 1970), pp. 36–8; *Religion and Society in Elizabethan Sussex*, pp. 63–4, 154, 256–60.

25 'Letters from the Bishops to the Privy Council, 1564', ed. M. Bateson, *Camden Miscellany*, 9 (1895), pp. 65–7; M. E. James, *Family, Lineage and Civil Society* (Oxford, 1974), pp. 51, 67–70, 78–9, 147; Haigh, *Reformation and Resistance*, pp. 209–46; 295–315.

26 P. Collinson, *The Elizabethan Puritan Movement* (London, 1967), especially pp. 14–15; 'Towards a Broader Understanding of the Early Dissenting Tradition', in C. R. Cole and M. E. Moody, eds, *The Dissenting Tradition: Essays for Leland H. Carlson* (Athens, Ohio, 1975), pp. 10–13; M. Spufford, *Contrasting Communities* (Cambridge, 1974), pp. 239–65, 320–44; W. J. Sheils, *The Puritans in the Diocese of Peterborough, 1558–1610* (Northamptonshire Record Society, 30, 1979), pp. 14–24.

27 For example Elton, *Reform and Reformation*, pp. 367–71; Haigh, *Reformation and Resistance*, pp. 183–5, 190.

28 For example Dickens, *Lollards and Protestants*, pp. 240–6; Haigh, *Reformation and Resistance*, pp. 269–78.

29 Bowker, *Henrician Reformation*, especially pp. 181–5.

30 R. B. Walker, 'Reformation and Reaction in the County of Lincoln, 1547–58', *Lincolnshire Archaeological and Architectural Society*, 9 (1961), pp. 50, 58–9; 'The Growth of Puritanism in the County of Lincoln in the Reign of Queen Elizabeth I', *Journal of Religious History*, 1 (1961), pp. 148–9, 150.

31 Dickens, *Lollards and Protestants*, pp. 1–7 and *passim*.

32 Professor Elton has summarized much of this work in *Reform and Reformation*, pp. 250–310, 328–52, 376–81.

33 Elton, *Policy and Police*, pp. 1–170.

34 Ibid., 393–6; *Reform and Reformation*, pp. 198, 294–5. See the remarks by C. S. L. Davies in *EHR*, 93 (1978), pp. 873–5.

35 C. S. L. Davies, *Peace, Print and Protestantism, 1450–1558* (London,

1977). See also J. J. Scarisbrick, *The Reformation and the English People* (Oxford, 1984).

36 J. A. Guy, *The Public Career of Sir Thomas More* (Brighton, 1980); D. Starkey, *The Reign of Henry VIII: Personalities and Politics* (London, 1985); E. W. Ives, 'Faction at the Court of Henry VIII: The Fall of Anne Boleyn', *History* 47 (1972), pp. 169–88; G. R. Elton, 'Thomas Cromwell's Decline and Fall', in his *Studies in Tudor and Stuart Politics and Government* (Cambridge, 1974), I, pp. 189–230; 'Tudor Government: The Points of Contact. III. The Court', in *Studies* (Cambridge, 1983), III, pp. 38–57; L. B. Smith, 'Henry VIII and the Protestant Triumph', *American Historical Review,* 71 (1966), pp. 1237–64; A. J. Slavin, 'The Fall of Lord Chancellor Wriothesley', *Albion* 7 (1975), pp. 265–86; D. E. Hoak, *The King's Council in the Reign of Edward VI* (Cambridge, 1976).

37 N. L. Jones, *Faith by Statute: Parliament and the Settlement of Religion* (London, 1982).

38 W. MacCaffrey, *The Shaping of the Elizabethan Regime* (London, 1969), pp. 77–8, 108, 211–12, 276.

39 K. R. Wark, *Elizabethan Recusancy in Cheshire* (Chetham Society, 1971), p. 16.

40 Elton, *Policy and Police*, pp. 85–90, 93–100, 112–23; Clark, *English Provincial Society,* pp. 63–4, 84; Brigden, 'Early Reformation in London', pp. 235–61, 322–7; *Narratives of the Days of the Reformation,* ed. J. G. Nichols (Camden Society, 1859), pp. 71–84; Rowse, *Tudor Cornwall,* pp. 262, 264, 276; J. Cornwall, *Revolt of the Peasantry, 1549* (London, 1977), pp. 57–8, 100–1, 110–11; 'Letters from the Bishops', ed. Bateson, pp. 14–15, 19–23; J. C. H. Aveling, *Catholic Recusancy in the City of York* (Catholic Record Society, 1970), pp. 25, 26, 27–8, 31–2, 33–4, 39.

41 Rowse, *Tudor Cornwall,* pp. 345–65; A. Hassell Smith, *County and Court: Government and Politics in Norfolk, 1558–1603* (Oxford, 1974), pp. 181, 201–3, 211–28; MacCulloch, 'Catholic and Puritan in Elizabethan Suffolk', pp. 236–47; Haigh, *Reformation and Resistance,* pp. 285–90, 313–15.

42 R. H. Pogson, 'Reginald Pole and the Priorities of Government in Mary Tudor's Church', *HJ,* 18 (1975), pp. 3–20; Haigh, *Reformation and Resistance,* pp. 195–207; Heal, *Of Prelates and Princes,* pp. 156–61.

43 A. Bartholomew, 'Lay Piety in the Reign of Mary Tudor' (University of Manchester M.A. thesis, 1979), especially pp. 1–42.

44 Gina Alexander, 'Bonner and the Marian Persecutions', in *The English Reformation Revised,* ed. C. Haigh (Cambridge, 1987), pp. 168–9; Houlbrooke, *Church Courts and the People,* p. 238; Walker, 'Reformation and Reaction in the County of Lincoln', pp. 58–9.

45 C. Haigh, 'From Monopoly to Minority: Catholicism in Early Modern England', *TRHS,* 5th series, 31 (1981), pp. 129–47.

2

PROTESTANT CULTURE AND THE CULTURAL REVOLUTION

Patrick Collinson

In The Elizabethan Puritan Movement *(1967), Patrick Collinson taught a generation of historians about divisions within the protestant movement between those satisfied with the Elizabethan Settlement of religion and those who thought that it had not gone far enough in a protestant direction. Under Elizabeth, the Church of England took a* via media, *or middle way, between Catholicism and radical protestantism. It retained the episcopal polity and liturgical worship of the medieval Church, but adopted a thoroughly Protestant doctrine of grace, an evangelical emphasis on preaching that doctrine, and encouragement of English Bible-reading by the laity. Those dissatisfied with the extent of these changes, called by their enemies 'puritans', wanted elimination of all 'popish superstitions', from worship (the sign of the cross and the wearing of clerical vestments, for example), greater stress on the sermon, and in some cases, replacement of bishops with a presbyterian form of church government.*

But as Collinson's research continued, he began to see the church of Elizabeth and James characterized more by consensus than by conflict. As he argued in The Religion of Protestants *(1982), most protestants, puritans and bishops alike, were bound together by a common theology and evangelical commitment and determined to work together within the national Church to bring about reform at the popular level, to impose a new, disciplined, protestant culture centred on the Word of God. Collinson's recent works have examined many aspects of that protestant consensus, from theology and preaching to political and social thought. The following essay is concerned with another aspect of the consensus – the development of a distinctively protestant culture over the last half of the sixteenth century. Notice that the author makes no fundamental distinction in this essay between puritans and other English protestants in his study of how protestants*

33

used, rejected, and then restructured the literary and visual arts as a means of expressing their beliefs. Collinson is discussing here the shared culture of all English protestants and the struggle in which they all engaged to communicate their message in a medium appropriate to the religion of the Word.

Collinson's sources – popular ballads and broadsides, poetry and drama, woodcuts and wall-paintings – are as great a departure from traditional ways of looking at church history as are his conclusions. As will be seen later in this volume, the focus of historians is increasingly on popular as well as élite belief and behaviour, and the nature of their research is increasingly informed by other disciplines.

* * *

If 'culture' be understood, not as anthropologists understand the word (or social historians when they speak of 'popular culture'), but as meant by Goering when he is supposed to have said that whenever he heard the word he reached for his revolver,[1] then according to a certain widespread prejudice there is no need to draw a gun on English Protestantism, since it produced no culture of its own but made an iconoclastic holocaust of the culture which already existed. The efflorescence of high culture in the age of Shakespeare is conventionally packaged and labelled as the English (or Elizabethan) Renaissance, a secular achievement which involved a degree of emancipation from the dominance of religion and was consequently facilitated by the Protestant Reformation, but only in a negative sense. No one turns Shakespeare himself into a chapter of the English Reformation.

Spenser may be another matter. *The Faerie Queene* is unmistakably a Protestant epic. And later there is Milton. With these poets the total incompatibility of Protestantism and high culture becomes more doubtful. C. S. Lewis discovered a paradox, in that the flinty rocks of Calvinism were to be seen pushing through the soft turf of Sidney's *Arcadia*.[2] But if Protestantism had a cultural history, surely Puritanism (in spite of Milton) was another matter. A long-running dispute about Spenser, whether he should be classified as a Protestant or a Puritan, is sterile,[3] since it rests on a distinction which cannot in fact be made. But in this discussion there is a sense of promising paradox. If one were to demonstrate that Spenser was indeed a Puritan one would have succeeded in proving something almost unprovable: the compatibility of Puritanism and great art. And yet Puritanism was neither alien to Protestantism nor even distinct from it but was its logical extension, equivalent to its full internalization: as R. H. Tawney suggested, the real rather than merely the official Reformation in England. So this is almost as much as to say that Protestant culture is a nonentity.

'The Bible, the Bible only I say is the religion of Protestants.' So wrote Henry Chillingworth in 1638. And since for Protestants religion was not one compartment of a segmented life but all-enveloping, this must also mean that the Bible only is the *culture* of Protestants. This will do as a starting point and I think that it has to do, uncompromising and unpromising though such a statement may at first sight appear. The Bible was no narrow straitjacket but a rich and infinitely varied source of imaginative and formal inspiration. Nevertheless, just as the God of the Bible advertised himself as a jealous God, so his book in the age of the Reformation made exclusive and intolerant claims. When Erasmus (and Tyndale following his lead) expressed the hope that wayfaring men and women would have the Scripture in their heads as they went about their business – 'that the ploughman holding the plough did sing somewhat of the mystical psalms in his own mother tongue' – they seem to have meant that *only* these lyrics should be on their lips. So it was in an authentically protestant tradition, but one of far greater antiquity than the Reformation, that Milton stood when in *Paradise Regained* he envisaged a choice and even a conflict between 'divine' and 'humane' literature. Christ tempted in the wilderness was confronted with the rival claims of both, with Satan cast, literally, as devil's advocate for secular, pagan literature: Christ is made to say to him that the classics are unworthy to compare with Zion's songs, to all true tastes excelling. If he would delight his private hours with song, 'where so soon/As in our native Language can I find that solace?'

Truth was all and truth for Protestants was plain truth, sufficiently contained in the Bible. All non-scriptural doctrine and practice, all non-scriptural art, amounted to lies, false religion. There was no gainsaying Scripture, no substitute for it: there was scope only for some debate as to the all-sufficiency of Scripture, as to whether or not there were areas of indifference where it could be supplemented by human reason and imagin-

35

ation.[4] For hardline Protestants 'imaginings' was one of those words always qualified by the same adjective, in this case 'vain', often in the formula 'vain imaginings and humane policy'. It was primarily Tyndale who had put the Bible into plain speech. If the wayfaring man and the spinning woman were to fill their mouths with Scripture, the Scripture must itself speak the language of the spinning woman and the wayfaring man. It has been said that Tyndale 'hated literature. Next to a papist he hated a poet.'[5]

But George Herbert's question still stands: 'Is there in truth no beauty?' Could it be said that the Bible was not only literally and dogmatically true but also aesthetically true? Moreover this rhetorical question (for of course the answer was yes) can be extended in the direction of a more popular culture. 'Is there in truth no pastime? no mirth? no enjoyment?' The protestant play *The life and repentaunce of Marie Magdalene* sold itself as 'not only godly, learned and fruitful, but also well furnished with pleasant mirth and pastime, very delectable'. Another biblical play, the *Historie of Jacob and Esau*, was described as 'merry and wittie', an interlude on the story of King Darius as 'pithie and pleasaunt'.[6]

Looking ahead, in the first century of English Protestantism the story of truth and beauty, religion and culture falls into three stages which work almost dialectically: positive, negative, positive nevertheless. First Protestantism embraced the cultural forms which already existed and employed them for its own purposes, both instructively and as polemical weapons against its opponents. Then, in the secondary phase of the English Reformation, roughly equivalent to the first ascendancy of Puritanism and dated quite precisely to 1580 in respect of its cultural impact, many protestant publicists turned their backs on these same cultural media, which now became the enemy no less than popery itself. The consequence of this rejection, seen most starkly in the case of the drama, was an advanced state of separation of the secular from the sacred, something without precedent in English cultural history. But in the third phase protestant biblicism delivered its positive answer in ever fuller measure to Herbert's question, heard most clearly in some of the greatest of the English poets. And it was at this point that an authentically protestant literary culture emerged.

Culturally speaking, the Reformation was beyond all question a watershed of truly mountainous proportions. On the far, late medieval side of the range, the landscape consists of images, concrete symbols, mime, the ritualized acting out of religious stories and lessons, a certain artlessness. Religion was 'intensely visual'. Seeing was believing, more than hearing and much more than the privatized mental discipline of absorbing information from a written text.[7] On this side of the divide we confront the invisible, abstract and didactic word: primarily the word of the printed page, on which depended the spoken words of sermon and catechism. In crossing this range we are making a journey from a culture of orality and image to one of print: from one mental and imaginative 'set' to another.

The mimetic presentation of religion which came to an exuberant climax in the last generation or two of pre-Reformation England lacked absolutely, in protestant perception, any sense of what might be thought to constitute blasphemy and was almost totally neglectful of the Second Commandment: 'Thou shalt not make unto thee any graven image.' As anyone knows who has shared as actor or audience in the modern revival of the mystery and miracle plays, the religious drama and pageantry treated divine things with a homely familiarity which was shocking and obnoxious to Protestants who had recovered their sense of God's awe-inspiring otherness. Thus it was thought in no way indecorous for King Richard II to be welcomed into the city of London in 1392 with ceremonies which explicitly identified this mortal monarch with Christ in his entry into Jerusalem on Palm Sunday, or as making his Second Coming to inaugurate a new Jerusalem. The Chester accountant who noted expenditure 'for gilding of little God's face' presumably felt no embarrassment.[8]

But this last reference dates not from 1392 but from 1566, at least thirty years into the official Reformation and six years after the definitively Protestant Elizabethan Settlement. At York for another six years still, until it was suppressed in 1572, the annual naivety (or indecent blasphemy) of the Christmas ride of Yule and Yule's Wife continued, with Yule distributing nuts 'to put us in remembrance of that noble Nut our Saviour's blessed body'. 'For the Nut hath in it[s] body a triple union, that is to wit, *Testam*, the shell, signifying the bones; and *Corium et nucteum*, the skin and kernel, signifying the flesh and inward Soul of our Saviour.'[9] Those who scrambled for the free nuts and cracked them in their teeth were supposed to bear this symbolism in mind. Our mountain range will have to accommodate some complex and overlapping geographical features, since elements of this mimetic religious culture survived long after the Reformation is supposed to have happened: long enough for the young Shakespeare to have witnessed the Corpus Christi plays in Coventry and to have included in *Hamlet* a likely reference to them in the player who 'out-Heroded' the blustering and comically villainous character of Herod.

By this time the plays were controversial. When the queen came to Coventry in 1575 'certain good-hearted men' petitioned to revive for her benefit the play called the Hock Tuesday Play, a piece which dealt with local history in the time of the Saxons and Danes, 'without ill example of manners, papistry or superstition'. They knew no reason why the play should have been abandoned 'unless it were by the zeal of certain their preachers: men very commendable for their behaviour and learning, and sweet in their sermons, but somewhat too sour in preaching away their pastimes'.[10] In 1580, the year of the earthquake as its direct consequence, the Coventry pageant was finally 'laid down', to be replaced four years later by a new and protestant play 'of the Destruction of Jerusalem' which had a brief run before, towards the end of the reign, the indigenous homegrown drama of Coventry was finally extinguished and the principal promoter jailed for his truculent behaviour towards both preachers and magistrates.[11] At York, Wakefield and Chester the plays had been put down in the mid–1570s, victims of the vigorous new broom of the Protestant regime in the north headed by Archbishop Grindal and the President of the Council, the Earl of Huntingdon.

Subsequently the tradition of civic 'pastimes' lived on in two secondary developments: the visits of travelling theatrical companies (again as in *Hamlet*) enjoying the patronage of noblemen and courtiers like Shakespeare's Earl of Southampton; and, as at York and Chester, in fragments of the old religious drama preserved in what otherwise became purely secular midsummer shows and pageants, unconnected with any religious feast and lacking in meaningful symbolism. At Chester one of the figures in the annual summer procession was the Devil, in feathers supplied by the butchers. This can only have been a relic of the play of the Temptation of Christ in the Chester cycle. However by the early seventeenth century the local vigilantes, and particularly Mayor Henry Hardware, were cleaning up the shows, removing such unacceptable features as devils preceded by women with cups and cans, or naked boys in nets. Running races for silver cups replaced the licensed violence of the traditional Shrove Tuesday football game. In Salisbury the Whitsun festivities were reduced to 'children's dances', which disappeared altogether by 1611. This was 'civility' and itself equivalent, if culture is understood in its broader sense, to a cultural revolution. By this time some towns (but not Coventry) were closing their gates to the strolling players and even paying them to go away. This happened at Stratford-upon-Avon, seven years after the death of a local worthy called William Shakespeare. At Dorchester the leader of a travelling company was imprisoned. In Chester citizens faced fines for going out of town to witness dramatic performances elsewhere. This negative response to the travelling theatre, more or less typical of the Jacobean period, contrasts with the popularity of the players in earlier Elizabethan years, even in towns which were 'forward' in their adoption of the Protestant Reformation. Ipswich was such a town: in the 1560s it had already invested in the institution of a town preacher but in the same decade it opened its gates to many acting companies, whose patrons included the Earl of Leicester, the Duchess of Suffolk, the Earl of Bedford, the Earl of Warwick and Lord Rich, all otherwise promoters of advanced Protestantism. Ipswich also welcomed jugglers, tumblers, flute-players and bear-wards, and continued to make payments to the players well into the 1590s.[12]

Accounts of 'mysteries' end' (to quote the title of Harold Gardiner's standard account)[a] often telescope this story, as if the civic religious drama was a more or less instant and inevitable casualty of the Reformation. But this was not the case. A child at the time of Henry VIII's first divorce could have seen the plays at Coventry as, by the standards of the time, an old man. The first generation of English Protestants and perhaps the second too entertained little hostility towards plays. Nor, for that matter, were they opposed to other cultural forms such as popular music and pictures, at least not *per se*. They objected only to the use of these media to convey false doctrine, what the men of Coventry called 'papistry or any superstition'. It was in no way incongruous for the Coventry martyr John Careless, later a kind of protestant folk hero, to be let out of prison in

Mary's reign to play his usual part in the Corpus Christi play and then to return to confinement, where he later died.[13] At York the change to official Protestantism under Elizabeth was marked by a purging from the play cycle of unacceptable 'popish' elements, such as several scenes featuring the Virgin. But the plays as such survived the Elizabethan Settlement.[14] The essential point is that early Protestantism was troubled by these cultural media as potential vehicles of false religion, not as inherently false or deceptive. There was hostility to mendacious art but not to art itself.

Early Protestantism did better than merely tolerate or bowdlerize the old religious drama. It created a new religious and moral drama of its own for its own propagandist and didactic purposes. These protestant plays and pastimes, the bulk of which have not survived, were written and perhaps directed by the reforming clerics themselves (the last clerical dramatists before this century), most of them obscure figures, but including the learned and vituperative John Bale, ex-Carmelite friar, briefly a Protestant bishop in Ireland and author of self-styled 'comedies' on the Temptation of Christ and the life of John the Baptist, and most notably of the robustly anti-Catholic history play *King Johan*. Bale's dramatic works may be called anti-Catholic rather than positively protestant. But Nicholas Udall's Bible play *Jacob and Esau*, and even more Lewis Wager's *Life and repentance of Marie Magdalene*, are theological plays, proof that the themes of predestination and of salvation through faith alone could be convincingly treated on the stage. The audience which saw the Magdalene play was left in no doubt that the heroine's redemption was effected, not by the moral force of her own repentance, touching though the representation of this was, but by purely unmerited grace:

> There was never man borne yet that was able,
> To perform these preceptes iust, holy and stable,
> Save only Jesus Christ.
> So by faith in Christ you have Justification
> Freely of his grace and beyond mans operation.

So too with the parallel dramatic tradition of the moralities. A run of new interludes on the well-worn 'Prodigal Son' theme, with such titles as *Nice Wanton*, *Lusty Juventus* and *The Disobedient Child*, reworked the devices and conventions of late medieval morality, interlarding heavy-footed protestant moralism with attacks on popery which cast the vices as priestly and prelatical figures: Ignorance, Hypocrisy, Cruelty.[15]

The strategy of the protestant dramatists, one which was as characteristic of primary protestant culture as it would have been inconceivable a generation later, was to encase the bitter pill of these moral lessons in the sweet coating of 'mirth', including popular songs of the time like 'Come oer the bourne Bessie' (these were musicals) and plenty of bawdy. Both the Bible plays and the moralities are, even to a modern ear, startlingly explicit in their treatment of sex. 'Lusty Juventus' gets into a tight clinch with Little Besse – 'such a gyrle' – and is observed by Hypocrisie: 'What a hurly burly is here, Smicke smacke and thys geare, You will to tyck take I feare.' Moros in *The Longer Thou Livest* is incited by Idleness 'to kiss, to clip, and in bed to play. O with lusty girls to singe and dance.' The stunning blonde Mary Magdalene, whose vital statistics are dwelt upon in loving detail, is an accomplished musician. So Infidelitie urges her, most suggestively, to play upon his recorder. 'Truely you have not sene a more goodlie pipe, it is so bigge that your hand can it not gripe.' Evidently these clerical playwrights would have agreed with Prynne's opponent Sir Richard Baker in a later generation: 'To expect, therefore, that plays should be altogether without obscene passages, were it not to expect that Nature should make bodies altogether without privy parts?'

If the protestant dramatists stole the opposition's costumes and scenery, protestant ballad-mongers anticipated the question put by the nineteenth-century Salvationist William Booth: 'Why should the Devil have all the best tunes?' Just as important as the sermon as a vehicle of propaganda and indoctrination, and more important than the play, because potentially more universal and pervasive, was the so-called 'scripture song'. Scripture songs included the Psalms, rendered in popular ballad metre, but were just as likely to consist of polemical attacks on the Mass or of anticlerical satires with no scriptural content at all. They bore titles like 'The Fantasie of Idolatry', a song of fifty stanzas on the folly of going on pilgrimage, preserved by Foxe 'for posterity hereafter to understand what then was used in England'. (Where should we be without Foxe and his profoundly historiographical instincts?) London merchants encouraged their apprentice boys to 'sing a song against the sacrament of the altar'. In Worcester an eleven-year-old boy composed an anticlerical ballad with the refrain: 'Come down for all your shaven crown.' We may well call these, in the language of our own century, 'protest songs'. They were sung in prison but were also provided as entertainment at wedding feasts, where they were performed by professionals, what Foxe calls 'common singers against the sacraments and ceremonies'. (The evidence of this comes from Essex.) In Mary's days Thomas Rider of Herne in Kent was accused of having conducted a mock procession in an alehouse, 'as it were in derision of the service of the Church'. Rider admitted that 'he hath divers times sung a song both there and in other places', but denied the charge of contempt.[16] Revisionist historians of the English Reformation who deny its popular character should take note of these circumstances.

As with the appropriation of the drama, there was initially no rejection of the medium of balladry,[17] only of the unacceptable uses to which it had hitherto been put. An essential part of this strategy, and one which was quite deliberately populist and appealing, was to make common cause with the popular music of the time, and even with the musicians themselves. Mid-Tudor Bible-readers turning to that Old Testament book, the Song of Solomon, found it entitled 'The Ballet of Ballets'. Secular ballads and psalms were both accompanied in the mid-sixteenth century by music which derived from the late Henrician and Edwardian Court, the cultural milieu of Surrey and Wyatt. For the psalms, no less than ballads, were originally sung to an instrumental accompaniment as galliards and 'measures' (and as to what, precisely, a 'measure' was, no one seems to know). Sternhold's invitation to the boy king to exchange 'fayned rhymes of vanity' for 'holy songs of verity' did not require the monarch to alter his musical taste. And no such agonizing choice confronted the public as both ballads and psalms found their way on to the streets, for both shared the same melodies.[18]

Virtually every successful Elizabethan ballad was immediately paid the compliment of a moralistic parody (and this was in itself a measure of success), employing the same tune to words which preserved the original rhythm and cadence while grossly transfiguring the sense. There were moralizations of 'Go from my window', 'The hunt is up', 'John come kisse me now', 'Maid will you marry', 'Into a myrthful May morning' and 'O sweet

Oliver'. Again we should note that these were not Sunday ballads to complement workaday love ballads, but alternatives and
rivals, intended to see secular ballads off the field. At least so
they were regarded by the religious establishment.

Years later the Suffolk preacher Nicholas Bownd complained
that ballads were everywhere supplanting psalms, which was
to reverse the trend of earlier years. In every country fair and
market they were being sung and sold (a scene made familiar
by Autolycus in *The Winter's Tale*) and country people were
sticking them on their cottage walls for want of anything better
to look at. Bownd assumed that ballads and psalms could never
peacefully coexist ('they can so hardly stand together') and he
contemptuously dismissed the suggestion that minstrels and
ballad pedlars might be engaged to popularize the psalms, as
they had been in the early years of the Reformation. For the
'singing men' were so notoriously ungodly that it would be
better to stop their mouths altogether than allow them to pollute
such sacred songs.[19] This was the end, for the time being, of the
strategy of parody or 'counterfeit', the death of the godly popular song.

To be sure two such puritan writers are not in themselves
evidence of a general cultural about-face. More telling is the fact
that the flood of moralistic parodies of the 1560s and 1570s
dwindled to a trickle in the 1580s and 1590s. 'Greensleeves', the
hit of our critical year 1580 (called in that year *'a newe northern
dittye'* and in 1584 'a new Courtly Sonnet'), seems to have been
a landmark. Its publication was smartly followed by 'Green
Sleeves moralized to the Scripture', and other sacred lyrics
seized upon its infectious tune, among them 'The godly and
virtuous song and ballad' of the Coventry martyr (and player)
John Careless. But both Thoms Nashe and Shakespeare wrote
disparagingly of this 'device', and with specific reference to
'Greensleeves' Mistress Ford in *The Merry Wives of Windsor* complained that Falstaff's words 'do no more adhere and keep place
together than the hundred Psalms to the tune of Green Sleeves'.
In 1597 a Kentish vicar sued his parishioners for slander when
they accused him of leading the congregation in a rendering of
the 25th Psalm ('Unto thee, O Lord, do I lift up my soul') to
the tune of 'Greensleeves'.[20]

Subsequently there was a substantial (if never total) divorce
of secular and sacred music. 'Psalms' came to mean the

Psalms of David and little besides, slow and measured *hymns* mainly designed for congregational singing and no longer enjoying any affinity with that 'small music' of country inns and weddings which George Puttenham sneered at in *The arte of English poesie*. Whereas songs and dances would be published in crotchets and quavers by seventeenth-century musical promoters such as John Playford, psalms were printed in minims and semibreves and sung after the parish clerk, note by note and dwelling as much as two seconds on each. George Wither insisted that to sing the Psalms of David to 'roguish tunes' and 'profane jigs', or to set psalm tunes to profane words, were two equally inadmissible procedures. The implications of this alteration in sensibility can hardly be underestimated.

The year 1580, or thereabouts, was a date equally critical to the history of Protestantism in its relation to the drama, but here it marked an even more absolute and irretrievable divorce. It is well known that the movement conventionally described as the Puritan onslaught on the theatre was a storm which blew up with surprising suddenness in about 1577, its timing apparently linked to the full institutionalization of the drama with the opening of the first permanent public theatres in London. This was the epoch marked by incessant attacks from the pulpit at Paul's Cross and by the sustained polemics of Gosson, Northbrooke and Stubbes, as well as by Sidney's riposte in the *Defence of Poesie*. Among the reasons propounded for this profound antitheatrical reaction some may be described as rational and pragmatic: concern with the unfair competition offered to the pulpit, or fear among the city fathers of the threat to public order and decency posed by the playhouses and their inducements to idleness and casual vice. More interesting for our purposes were motives which might be called instinctive, even subliminal: the rejection of dramatic fictions as lies, with a particular objection to the transvestite lie implicit in the acting of female parts by boys; the revulsion against 'filthiness', that is theatrical eroticism; and the urge to close up what has been called 'the idolatrous eye'. Anthony Munday wrote that 'there cometh much evil in the ears, but more at the eyes'. But all in all the reaction seems to any dispassionate and modern eye one of quite unreasonable and unwarranted severity. As Thomas Nashe insisted in *Pierce Pennilesse*, 'Our players are not as the players beyond sea, a sort of squirting bawdy comedians that have whores and common courtesans to play women's parts and forbear no immodest speech or unchaste action that may procure laughter.'[21]

For the study of protestant culture the most significant and problematical aspect of the antitheatrical reaction was the particular attack mounted by both Gosson and Stubbes on the religious drama, moving in Gosson's case from an initial endorsement of some plays as 'good' and 'sweet' to condemnation of 'divine' plays as the worst of all, an argument which is elaborated in Stubbes's *Anatomie of Abuses* (1581). Stubbes found it intolerable that the glorious majesty of God should be handled in these 'sacrilegious' performances 'scoffingly, flauntingly and jibingly'. The merits of Christ's Passion were not available to be 'derided and jested at, as they be in these filthy plays and interludes', which was as much as to 'mix scurrility with divinity', or, wrote John Northbrooke, 'to eat meat with unwashed hands', a commonplace probably derived from Erasmus's essay based on the classical adage *illotis manibus*.

Stubbes was the victim of what Nashe called a 'melancholic imagination', but in this case he had caught the crest of a wave. Bible plays would continue to be written and performed for a few more years. As many as fourteen can be traced in Henslowe's Diary and other sources of the 1590s. But even Thomas Lodge, who had clashed with Gosson and whose own Jonah play was staged as late as 1594, wrote in 1596 that stage plays based on Scripture were 'odious'. After the Blasphemy Act of 1605 they became illegal, and when William Prynne wrote in *Histrio-mastix* in 1637 that the more sublime the matter of the play the more pernicious its fruits he was expressing a commonplace which commanded widespread assent. The reasoning behind the commonplace can be found in Stubbes and represents a drastic repudiation of centuries of religious culture. This, however, happened not in the 1530s but in the 1580s. To *represent* the Word of God mimetically rather than to expound it faithfully was to turn it into an object of mockery. For, as we read in the opening words of St John's Gospel, 'the word is God, and God is the word'. For Stubbes that was an open and shut case.[22]

The consequence was a divorce of the sacred and secular even more complete than that which we have already observed in the field of popular music and verse. The ambition of the reformers and complainers was to close the theatres, Prynne being willing to allow only the *reading* of a select list of play texts. This ambition was not fulfilled until 1642. While Charles I sat secure on his throne Prynne's vast polemical exercise *Histrio-mastix*, a work of hundreds of pages and thousands of learned citations, was a gesture of impotence. The drama was not suppressed but from the 1580s advanced to its greatest artistic achievement. But having been left to its own devices it became, in the perception of the hyper-religious public, 'filthier', more abandoned than ever. From a more sympathetic and less pejorative viewpoint it must appear that dramatists were now better able to explore the moral and social complexities of the human condition on their own terms and in their own language. After all it would require a singular perversity to prefer *The life and repentance of Marie Magdalene* to *Hamlet* or *Measure for Measure* (where, however, theology is still resonant), or even to the more modest and domestic dimensions of, say, *A Woman Killed with Kindness*. So, unwittingly, the about-face in Protestant cultural attitudes emancipated the English theatre by completing its secularization.

It is possible to identify a similar watershed, and at about the same time, in the pictorial arts, and for this we have been prepared by what Stubbes asserted about the wordiness of God as Word. Mid-sixteenth-century English Bibles were copiously illustrated, as well as being equipped with maps and other visual aids. And, very famously, Foxe's 'Book of Martyrs' incorporated a stunning range of varied graphical material. This included the dumb show of an array or 'pageant' of popes and a visual display of the ten great persecutions of the Church. There were historical narrative pictures of the Emperor Henry IV at Canossa and of the poisoning of King John, plenty of stylized martyrs in the flames, which were repeated whenever the text called for them, and a sharply observed caricature of Bishop Bonner caning the bare backsides of protestant prisoners in his orchard at Fulham. This last picture was perhaps Foxe's own work (we know that he drew, from the marginalia of his correspondence), for when Bonner was shown it in prison he is said to have roared with laughter, exclaiming: 'A vengeance on the fool! How could he get my picture drawn so right?'[23] Miss Tessa Watt believes that some of these pictures, especially a number of ambitious folded pull-outs, were also detached from the book and stuck on walls. One set, surviving in Cambridge, has been coloured in, evidently for this purpose.

So up to about 1580 a very positive answer could have been given, and in the protestant tradition of plain sincerity and biblical and historical truth, to the question later put by Francis Quarles. Christ is presented in the Scripture as Sower, Fisher and Physician: 'And why not presented so, as well to the eye as to the ear?' Quarles asked.[24] But from the 1580s Protestants began to direct the eye, that potentially idolatrous eye, inward, rejecting realistic religious pictures as unreservedly as Bible plays and godly ballads. Bibles for the most part ceased to be illustrated. Other newly published works which seem to cry out for illustration, like Thomas Beard's collection of instructive providences, *The theatre of Gods judgments* (1597, 1612, 1631), are totally devoid of pictures. Book illustration in England seems to regress, just when we might expect it to advance. The later editions of Foxe (1596, 1620, 1632) continued to carry the same brilliant illustrative apparatus. But the same old woodcuts were used over and over again (to be replaced in 1641 with copper engravings of the same subjects) and I do not think that these pictures would have been newly commissioned at any time between 1580 and 1630.

'These are certain pictures', wrote the Somerset minister Richard Bernard in 1610, introducing his book *Contemplative pictures with wholesome precepts*. But there *are* no pictures in the ordinary and literal sense, only what might be called word pictures, of God, Goodness, Heaven; the Devil, Badness, Hell. Bernard explains that his pictures are not 'popish and sensible for superstition, but mental, for divine contemplation'. By this time Protestant England had moved from a cultural phase which may be described as iconoclastic, characterized by the attack on unacceptable images but consistent with the enjoyment of good images, to an episode lasting some few decades around 1600 which Karl-Josef Höltgen has called iconophobic, rejecting all material images and implying an advanced and radical application of the Second Commandment of the Decalogue.[25] Wall paintings had been wiped out in many, probably most, parish churches in response to the Elizabethan injunction against 'feigned images of idolatry', even the official church homilies declaring that the seeking out of images was 'the beginning of whoredom'. Much stained and painted glass had equally fallen foul of the Injunctions and of private acts of iconoclasm.

There was later a revision of religious aesthetics which we connect with the anti-Calvinist reaction of Arminianism and, presently, with Archbishop Laud's associated programme of liturgical enrichment, the 'beauty of holiness'. After all, the age of extreme iconophobia was quite short, equivalent to little more than a single generation. As early as 1626 even a conventional provincial preacher, albeit occupying the pulpit in Canterbury Cathedral, 'a wonderful piece of work to the beholder', could articulate a revived apology for images as the books of the ignorant and illiterate. Describing an elaborate stone conduit erected in Canterbury at the expense of Archbishop Abbot and decorated not only with heraldry and inscriptions but also with 'lively images' in the shape of sculpted representations of the Seven Virtues, James Cleland spoke of 'the speaking power of Pictures': 'For herein the gross conceit is led on with pleasure, and informed while it feels nothing but delight. And if Pictures have been accounted the Books of Idiots, behold here the benefit of an Image without Offence.' The sentiment matches George Herbert's near-contemporary lines in 'The Church-porch':

> A verse may finde him, who a sermon flies,
> And turn delight into a sacrifice.

These were modest enough beginnings. But within ten years, and under the mastership of William Beale, the chapel of St John's College, Cambridge, a place not noted for ignorance and illiteracy, was 'dressed up after a new fashion'. It had an altar frontal depicting the deposition from the Cross and large gilt-framed pictures around the walls portraying the life of Christ 'from his conception to his ascension', with a large crucifix behind the altar which was surmounted with a canopy painted with angels and a 'sun with great light beams and a dove in the midst'. By this time the vicar of Sturry, near Canterbury, a man 'famously noted for a forward agent in superstitious and popish innovations', had a large painted crucifix framed and hanging in his parlour. Such were the aesthetics of English Arminianism.[26]

Meanwhile, pending the restoration to 'gross conceits' of images, it is a good question what the mind's eye sees if it has not been fed with pictures, has never been taught to see in that way. Exponents of Renaissance rhetoric and logic and its affinity with the printed book tell us that the educated minds of this generation had their image-forming capacity replaced with the lines and brackets of severely practical Ramist[b] logic, these forming abstract mnemonic patterns which almost literally imprinted the scheme of salvation and other syllogistic arguments on the memory in diagrammatic form. The third Earl of Huntingdon, Queen Elizabeth's lieutenant in the North of England and a top administrator rather than a scholar, had nothing to decorate the walls of his headquarters in York (the enlarged and enriched former mansion of the abbots of St Mary's Abbey) save some maps, a 'table' of the Ten Commandments, and another 'table in a frame, containing the cause of salvation and damnation'.[27]

However, no man can live by diagrams alone. Nor is it clear that the mind which is fed on print alone sees only print. This is to say that Calvinism did not succeed in killing the imagination, even if that was its purpose, which is a dubious proposition. Richard Bernard's *Contemplative pictures* were, he tells us, *mental pictures*, and they exceed in visual power what any country artist could have hoped to achieve in rural Nottinghamshire or Somerset, the counties where Bernard ministered. And yet they are of no special distinction, consisting of language well within the reach of any competent Jacobean preacher: 'The azured sky his comely curtain, his privy chamber, the place of unspeakable pleasure. His face is a flame of fire, his voice thunder, his wrath dread and terrible horror.' This is Bernard's mental picture of God and it recalls Sir Philip Sidney's *Defence of Poesie*, in which the Psalms are called 'a divine Poem', the psalmist 'a passionate lover of that unspeakable and everlasting beauty to be seen by the eyes of the mind'. For David 'maketh you, as it were, see God coming in his Majesty'.[28]

If there was a literary Renaissance there was also a literary Reformation, which affirmed truth in the plain beauty of Scripture, eliciting from the disciples that cry of relief: 'Now thou speakest no parables.' It was to this tradition that Milton was heir when he declared that the rich variety of biblical forms exceeded the pagan classics 'not in their divine argument alone, but in the very critical art of composition', in which 'over all the kinds of lyrical poesy', Scripture was 'incomparable'.

What should be grasped by the social and cultural historian

who may have been too much swayed by recent talk of the growing division of élite and popular cultures in early modern Europe is that all this fertile imagery was as accessible to the obscure and ordinary bible scholar and sermon-goer as it was to the erudite. Indeed this was shared ground. The Geneva Bible[c] advises the reader to 'diligently keep such order of reading the scriptures' as his calling will allow: 'At the least twice every day this exercise to be kept. ... The time once appointed hereunto after a good entry be no otherwise employed.' This was how the imaginative world of the Bible became the mentality of the literate or scarcely literate lay person, whose mental powers are consistently underestimated by those historians who assume that Protestantism was a message which must have passed clean over his head. The proof is in the many tedious but still deeply impressive letters printed in Foxe's book, written by or to the artisan martyrs of the Marian persecution, which suggest minds so steeped in the cross-references and resonant concordances of Scripture as to be incapable of exercising themselves in any other way. As the martyr John Bradford wrote to a certain Joyce, 'a faithful woman in her heaviness': 'You are one of his lively stones – be content therefore to be hewn and snagged at. ... You are of God's corn, fear not therefore the flail. ... You are one of Christ's lambs, look therefore to be fleeced, haled at, or even slain.'[29] This was protestant culture, and while it was the culture of Herbert and Milton, it was also a kind of popular culture.

EDITOR'S NOTES

Patrick Collinson, 1988; reprinted in abridged form from chapter 4 of *The Birthpangs of Protestant England: Religious and Cultural Change in the Sixteenth and Seventeenth Centuries* (New York, 1988), with the permission of St Martin's Press, Incorporated and Macmillan Ltd.

a *Mysteries' End: An Investigation of the Last Days of the Medieval Religious Stage* (New Haven, 1946).
b Named after the French Calvinist dialectician Pierre de la Ramée (1515–72), known for his diagrammatic method and his humanistic anti-Aristotelianism.
c An English translation published in Geneva in 1560 with copious Calvinist marginal notes. Probably the translation in most widespread private use before the Authorized Version of 1611.

NOTES

Further documentation will be found in my *From Iconoclasm to Iconophobia: The Cultural Impact of the Second English Reformation (The Stenton Lecture, 1985)* (Reading, 1986).

1 This is attributed in the *corrigenda* of the *Oxford Dictionary of Quotations* to a character in the Nazi play *Schlageter* by Hanns Johst.

2 C. S. Lewis, *English Literature in the Sixteenth Century Excluding Drama* (Oxford, 1973 edn) p. 43.

3 See most recently Anthea Hume, *Edmund Spenser: Protestant Poet* (Cambridge, 1984) and her 'Spenser, Puritanism and the "Maye" Eclogue', *Review of English Studies*, 20 (1969), pp. 155–67.

4 Barbara K. Lewalski, *Protestant Poetics and the Seventeenth-Century Religious Lyric* (Princeton, 1979), p. 3 and *passim*; John M. King, *English Reformation Literature: The Tudor Origins of the Protestant Tradition* (Princeton, 1982), p. 141.

5 G. D. Bone, 'Tindale and the English Language', in S. L. Greenslade, *The Work of William Tindale* (London, 1938) p. 67.

6 Lewis Wager, *A new enterlude . . . entreating of the life and repentaunce of Marie Magdalene* (1566; modern edn F. I. Carpenter: Chicago, 1940); *A newe mery and wittie comedie or enterlude newely imprinted, treating upon the historie of Jacob and Esau* (licensed 1557/8, printed 1568; Malone Society reprint 1956); *A pretie new enterlude both pithie and pleasaunt of the story of Kyng Daryus* (1565).

7 R. W. Scribner, *For the Sake of Simple Folk: Popular Propaganda for the German Reformation* (Cambridge, 1981), pp. 3–4.

8 Glynne Wickham, *Early English Stages 1300 to 1660*, I (1959), p. 71; C. R. Smith, ed., 'Concordia Facta Inter Regem Riccardum II et Civitatem Londinie' (Princeton University Ph. D. dissertation, 1972); Lawrence M. Clopper, ed., *Records of the Early English Drama* I, *Chester* (Toronto, 1979), p. 75.

9 Alexander F. Johnston and Margaret Rogerson, eds., *Records of the Early English Drama* II *York*, I (Toronto, 1979), pp. 359–62.

10 Robert Laneham, *A Letter* (1575), pp. 33–4.

11 *Records of the Early English Drama* III, *Coventry*, pp. 294, 303, 307–9.

12 *Records of the Early English Drama*, I, *Chester*, pp. 197–9, 234–6, 184; David Underdown, *Revel, Riot and Rebellion: Popular Politics and Culture in England (1603–1660)* (Oxford, 1985), p. 51; E. I. Fripp, ed., *Minutes and Accounts of Stratford-upon-Avon*, II *1566–1577*, Dugdale Society Publications, 3 (1924), p. xxxvi; Ipswich and East Suffolk Record Office, Ipswich Chamberlains Accounts, temp. Elizabeth I, *passim*.

13 *Records of the Early English Drama*, III, *Coventry*, p. 207.

14 *Records of the Early English Drama*, II *York*, I, pp. 331–3.

15 *A pretie new enterlude called Nice Wanton* (1560, written *c.*1547–53); *An enterlude called Lusty Juventus* (1565); Thomas Inglend, *A pretie and mery new enterlude called the disobedient child* (1569, written *c.*

1560); W. Wager, *The longer thou livest the more foole thou art* (*c.* 1559–68, written *c.* 1559).

16 *Acts and Monuments of Foxe*, v, pp. 404–9, 403, 445; viii, pp. 214, 554–5, 416, 578; BL, MS Harley 421, fo. 97ʳ.

17 Full references to what follows on the godly parodic ballad will be found in my *From Iconoclasm to Iconophobia*. See also the article by Tessa Watt, 'Religion and the Broadside Ballad Trade', forthcoming in the *Journal of Ecclesiastical History*.

18 Nicholas Temperley, *The Music of the English Parish Church*, 2 vols (Cambridge, 1979).

19 Nicholas Bownd, *The doctrine of the sabbath* (1595), pp. 241–2.

20 Hyder E. Rollins, *An Analytical Index to the Ballad-Entries in the Registers of the Company of Stationers of London*, Studies in Philology 21 (Chapel Hill, 1924), nos 1892, 1051. Further references are in my *From Iconoclasm to Iconophobia*, notes 65–70. 'Greensleeves' is described as 'a new Courtly Sonet' in its publication in *A handefull of pleasant delites* (1584).

21 Quoted by Sandra Clark in *The Elizabethan Pamphleteers: Popular Moralistic Pamphlets 1580–1640* (Rutherford, N. J., 1983), p. 140. On the appearance and growth of the antitheatrical prejudice see William A. Ringler, 'The First Phase of the Elizabethan Attack on the Stage 1558–1579', *Huntington Library Quarterly*, 5 (1942), pp. 391–418; William Ringler, *Stephen Gosson: A Biographical and Critical Study* (Princeton, 1924); R. W. Chambers, *The Elizabethan Stage*, i (Oxford, 1923), pp. 242–56; Jonas Barish, *The Antitheatrical Prejudice* (Berkeley and Los Angeles, 1981); David Lerenz, *The Language of Puritan Feeling: An Exploration of Literature, Psychology and Social History* (New Brunswick, 1980) ch. 1, 'Why Did Puritans Hate Stage Plays?' I owe the point about 'the idolatrous eye' to Dr Michael O'Connell of University of California, Santa Barbara.

22 Full references to the decline of biblical and religious drama will be found in my *From Iconoclasm to Iconophobia*, notes 43–8.

23 J. F. Mozley, *John Foxe and his Book* (London, 1940), p. 131.

24 K.-J. Höltgen, *Francis Quarles (1592–1644)* (Tübingen, 1978), p. 216.

25 K.-J. Höltgen, 'The Reformation of Images and Some Jacobean Writers on Art', in U. Broich, T. Stemmler and G. Stratmann, eds, *Functions of Literature, Essays Presented to Erwin Wolff on his Sixtieth Birthday* (Tübingen, 1984), pp. 119–46.

26 James Cleland, *Iacobs wel, and Abbots conduit* (1626), pp. 44, 50–2; F. E. Hutchinson, ed., *The Works of George Herbert* (Oxford, 1941), p. 6; Nicholas Tyacke, *Anti-Calvinists: The Rise of English Arminianism c. 1590–1640* (Oxford, 1987), p. 194; L. B. Larking, ed., *Proceedings in the County of Kent in Connection with the Parliaments called in 1640* (Camden Society c, 1862), p. 185.

27 Huntington Library, MS HA Inventories Box 1, no. 1.

28 Philip Sidney, *The Defence of Poesie*, Cambridge English Classics (Cambridge, 1923), pp. 6–7, 9, 14.

29 *Acts and Monuments of Foxe*, vii, p. 232. To be sure, Joyce Hales was no artisan but an educated woman.

3

PURITANISM, ARMINIANISM AND COUNTER-REVOLUTION

Nicholas Tyacke

Before the 1970s, the religious history of Elizabethan and early Stuart England was depicted as a steadily mounting conflict between the conservative, 'Anglican' establishment and radical puritanism, culminating in the Civil War – a 'Puritan Revolution'. In this 1973 article, and more fully in his recent book, Anti-Calvinists, Tyacke turned this model on its head and set the agenda for historical debate on early Stuart religion for the next two decades. First, he argued that the Elizabethan and Jacobean Church was not characterized by conflict at all, but by a consensus based on theological agreement: both puritans and bishops shared a commitment to the Calvinist view of grace, embodied in the Church's official confession of faith, the Thirty-nine Articles, and especially in the Lambeth Articles of 1595. This part of his argument has received strong support from Patrick Collinson's recent work. Only after the accession of Charles I and the ascendancy of William Laud, Archbishop of Canterbury from 1633, did conflict emerge and escalate. This conflict was not, however, between radical puritans and conservative bishops; rather, it pitted radical anti-Calvinist theology (Arminianism, defined more fully below), against traditional reformed predestinarianism, which after 1625 was increasingly identified with puritans. The 'Puritan Revolution' was thus really a Calvinist counter-revolution against Arminian notions of free will and universal grace.

Since the publication of the article reprinted below, Tyacke has shifted on two points: he no longer regards Archbishop Bancroft as anti-Calvinist, and he now acknowledges the puritanism of John Pym. The article stands, though, as the best brief argument for radical Arminianism as the cause of religious war in the 1640s.

* * *

Historians of the English Civil War all agree that Puritanism had a role to play in its origins. Beyond this, however, agreement ceases. For some, particularly the Marxists, Puritanism was the ideology of the newly emergent middle classes or *bourgeosie*, as they are sometimes called. Puritan ideas, it is argued, complemented and encouraged the capitalist activities of 'progressive' gentry, merchants and artisans alike. On the assumption, again made by those most under the influence of Marxism, that the English Civil War was a 'bourgeois revolution', the Puritans are naturally to be found fighting against King Charles and his old-world followers. An alternative and widely held interpretation sees Puritanism as a religious fifth column within the Church of England, and one whose numbers dramatically increased during the first decades of the seventeenth century; by the early 1640s, with the collapse of the central government and its repressive system of church courts, the Puritans were thus able to take over at least in the religious sphere. These two schools of thought, the Marxist and the fifth-columnist, are best represented by the writings respectively of Dr Christopher Hill and Professor William Haller.[1]

In the following essay, however, a different view will be put forward, to the effect that religion became an issue in the Civil War crisis due primarily to the rise to power of Arminianism in the 1620s. The essence of Arminianism was a belief in God's universal grace and the free will of all men to obtain salvation. Therefore Arminians rejected the teaching of Calvinism that the world was divided into elect and reprobate whom God had arbitrarily predestinated, the one to Heaven and the other to Hell. It is difficult for us to grasp how great a revolution this involved for a society as steeped in Calvinist theology as was England before the Civil War. But whether or not we agree with the arguments of Christopher Hill, it is clear that the Puritan ideas to which he ascribes so much importance for the development of modern, capitalist society are in the main predestinarian ones. Similarly with Haller's thesis concerning the growth of Puritanism, the message preached with such success from Puritan pulpits was rooted in the Calvinist theology of grace.

At the beginning of the seventeenth century, a majority of the clergy from the Archbishop of Canterbury downwards were

Calvinists in doctrine, and the same was probably true of the more educated laity. So Puritanism in this Calvinist sense was not then seen as a political threat. Only when predestinarian teaching came to be outlawed by the leaders of the established church, as was the case under Archbishop William Laud, would its exponents find themselves in opposition to the government. Any doubts that the Church of England was doctrinally Calvinist, before Laud took control, can be resolved by reading the extant doctoral theses in divinity maintained at Oxford University from the 1580s to the 1620s. There, year after year, predestinarian teaching was formally endorsed, and its opposite denied. The following are a representative selection of such theses, translated from the original Latin and listed in chronological order: 'No one who is elect can perish' (1582); 'God of his own volition will repudiate some people' (1596); 'According to the eternal predestination of God some are ordained to life and others to death' (1597); 'Man's spiritual will is not itself capable of achieving true good' (1602); 'The saints cannot fall from grace' (1608); 'Is grace sufficient for salvation granted to all men? No' (1612); 'Does man's will only play a passive role in his initial conversion? Yes' (1618); 'Is faith and the righteousness of faith the exclusive property of the elect? Yes' (1619); and 'Has original sin utterly extinguished free will in Adam and his posterity? Yes' (1622). The licensed publications of the English press tell the same Calvinist story, albeit in a more popular vein, as do many religious preambles to wills where the testator confidently affirms belief in his divine election. A good example of this type of Calvinist will is that made by Lord Treasurer Dorset, who died in 1608; George Abbot, future Archbishop of Canterbury, was so impressed by Dorset's claim to be an elect saint that he quoted the will verbatim when preaching his funeral sermon in Westminster Abbey. Calvinism at the time was clearly establishment orthodoxy, and contemporaries would have found any suggestion that Calvinists were Puritans completely incomprehensible.[2]

Puritanism around the year 1600, and for more than two decades subsequently, was thought of in terms either of a refusal to conform with the religious rites and ceremonies of the English Church, or as a presbyterian rejection of church government by bishops. At that date conformists and nonconformists, episcopalians and presbyterians all had in common Calvinist predestinarian ideas. Here, however, we come to the crux of the matter, for Calvinism also helped to reconcile the differences between them. Thus the late Elizabethan Archbishop of Canterbury, John Whitgift, who was a Calvinist in doctrine, regarded Puritan nonconformity in a different light from that of the Arminian Archbishop Laud. This did not stop Whitgift as archbishop from attacking nonconformists, especially with Queen Elizabeth hard on his heels, but it did impose important limits on the extent of his persecution. Before the advent of Laud, nonconformists and even presbyterians were never regarded as being totally beyond the pale; they were seen instead as aberrant brethren deserving of some indulgence. Symbolic of the pre-Laudian state of affairs is that in the 1560s Whitgift had been a nonconformist and Thomas Cartwright, the later presbyterian, a candidate for an Irish archbishopric and, despite a long history of public controversy between them, they ended up on good terms in the 1590s. Calvinist doctrine provided a common and ameliorating bond that was only to be destroyed by the rise of Arminianism. As a result of this destruction, during the 1620s, Puritanism came to be redefined in terms which included the very Calvinism that previously had linked nonconformists to the leaders of the established church, and the nonconformist element in the former Calvinist partnership was driven into an unprecedented radicalism. The Arminians and their patron King Charles were undoubtedly the religious revolutionaries in the first instance. Opposed to them were the Calvinists, initially conservative and counter-revolutionary, of whom the typical lay representative was John Pym.

The first decades of the seventeenth century in England did not witness any straightforward contest between an 'Anglican' hierarchy on the one hand and the serried ranks of Puritanism on the other. This becomes even clearer if we take the case of William Perkins, whom Christopher Hill has described as 'the dominant influence in Puritan thought for the forty years after his death' in 1602. His funeral sermon was preached by James Montagu, shortly to become dean of the chapel royal and subsequently Bishop of Winchester, and the chief critic of Perkins's works was answered in print by Bishop Robert Abbot of Salisbury, whose intellectual position was identical to that of his brother the archbishop. While this blurring of religious differences seems characteristic of the period, a further complicating factor was the religious standpoint of the monarch, as supreme head of the English Church. James I was much more sympathetic to Calvinist doctrine than his predecessor Elizabeth had been, and to that extent those Puritan nonconformists were correct who hoped for better things on the queen's death in 1603. The proof of the king's Calvinist affinities was conveniently published as a pamphlet in 1626, by Francis Rous, who was the step-brother of John Pym and an outspoken parliamentary critic of Arminianism. Two examples of this royal Calvinism must suffice. In 1604 James was officially quoted as saying that 'predestination and election dependeth not upon any qualities, actions or works of man, which be mutable, but upon God his eternal and immutable decree and purpose.' Similarly in 1619 he wrote that 'God draws by his effectual grace, out of that attainted and corrupt mass [mankind], whom he pleaseth for the work of his mercy, leaving the rest to their own ways which all lead to perdition.' Yet having demonstrated James's Calvinism, and therefore the existence of a common and potentially reconciling bond with Puritan nonconformists, one is faced with the problem of his celebrated outbursts against Puritans – as for instance when he described them in March 1604 as a 'sect unable to be suffered in any well-governed commonwealth', and the deprivations for nonconformity which occurred during his first years on the throne. The explanation, however, would seem to lie in *raison d'état*, as that was interpreted by the king. His exposure in Scotland at an early age to Calvinist theology had left him favourably disposed towards its teachings, yet his experience there of religious rebellion had also made him politically suspicious of anything remotely akin to presbyterianism. Whereas for Elizabeth political considerations had complemented her religious antipathies, with James there was thus something of a conflict.[3]

These distinctions would be rather academic had James's fear of Puritan nonconformity continued to dominate him as much as it did during the earliest years of his English reign. Increasingly, however, a countervailing political factor emerged in the shape of an intensified fear of Catholicism. This was particularly the case between 1608 and 1615, a period in which the king himself wrote as many as three works on the subject of the Oath of Allegiance. The latter was a modified form of the Supremacy Oath, enacted by statute during the aftermath of Gunpowder

Plot in an attempt to isolate politically disloyal Catholics. Any chance of success which the scheme might have had was effectively wrecked by strong papal opposition and an ensuing pamphlet war. Almost inevitably Puritanism benefited from this redirection of government energies. Religious differences among the various royal champions who entered the lists were subsumed in a cloud of zeal against the common papist enemy. Catholic charges that Puritans differed on doctrinal grounds from the established church were publicly denied even by emergent Arminians like Bishop Andrewes, and there was a widespread campaign to ban the use of the term 'Puritan' completely. Suggestive also is the fact that from 1611 until 1618 no work directed specifically against Puritanism, either in its nonconformist or presbyterian guises, is recorded in the Stationers' Registers as being licensed for the press.[4]

In part symptomatic of the altered climate was George Abbot's own promotion to Canterbury in 1611. The Jesuit Father Coffin wrote of the new primate as 'a brutal and fierce man, and a sworn enemy of the very name of Catholic'. Certainly his elevation occurred during a two-year period which witnessed a third of all the Catholic martyrdoms under James. The supposition that these events were linked is further strengthened by the terms in which the appointment of Toby Matthew to the archbishopric of York had been canvassed back in 1606. Already at that date there was alarm in government circles over conditions in the North, as an area 'overpestered with popery and not with puritanism'. Cecil was urged to promote the appointment of 'a painful and preaching successor' to Archbishop Hutton and one 'industrious against papists'.[5]

By contrast, the archiepiscopal predecessor whom Abbot least resembled was the man he immediately succeeded. This was Richard Bancroft, whose policies more than those of any other churchman prior to the Arminian Laud drove Puritan nonconformists to extremes. Bancroft's loathing of Puritanism amounted almost to paranoia, and his espionage methods threatened to make real the Puritan conspiracy which originated largely as a figment of his own imagination. He was also among the first Protestant churchmen in England to disassociate himself from the predestinarian teachings of Calvinism, and therefore lacked the restraining influence of a theology shared with his nonconformist opponents. Fortunately, from the point of view of political stability, Bancroft's extremism was kept in check by King James. Those who succeeded him in the bishopric of London, a post which administratively ranked second only to Canterbury, were all Calvinists during his lifetime. One of them, Richard Vaughan, who was Bishop of London from 1604 to 1607, became well known for his tolerance of Puritan deviation from the strict letter of the law. Moreover in 1608 Bancroft was forced to acquiesce in the publication of an official Calvinist commentary on The Thirty-nine Articles – the Church of England's confession of faith. After his death in 1610 Calvinist dominance became even more marked, and the combined religious and political atmosphere generally favoured a *modus vivendi* with Puritan nonconformity. In addition to government attacks on Catholicism, which distracted attention from disagreements among Protestants, the chief posts in the Church were filled by men whose views at many important points merged with those of their nonconformist brethren. Both Archbishop Abbot and John King, bishop of London from 1611 to 1621, had been lecturers in the 1590s, and the former expressed the hope during a parliamentary debate in 1610 that he would die in the pulpit. They were also sabbatarians, Abbot successfully intervening in 1618 to preserve the Puritan Sunday from the threat of the royal Declaration of Sports. A third very powerful Jacobean cleric was Bishop James Montagu of Winchester, editor of King James's collected works and a Privy Councillor. He had been the first master of Sidney Sussex College in Cambridge, where he had not enforced conformity, and we have noted his connection with the 'Puritan' theologian William Perkins. In Montagu's view the period since the accession of King James in 1603 had on the whole been one of 'harmony' with the Puritans.[6]

This impression of comparative calm receives some statistical confirmation from a recent study of Puritan lectures in London by Dr Seaver. Between 1604 and 1606 out of twenty identifiable Puritan lecturers only six came before the church courts, and of these six only one was permanently suspended from preaching. From 1607 to 1609 the pattern was 'much the same'. During the second decade of the seventeenth century prosecutions for nonconformity were even fewer and Seaver conjectures that 'at a time when controversy was at a minimum, when no great issues divided public opinion ... some puritanically inclined ministers might have found little cause for militancy and small reason not to conform'. A situation similar to that in London existed in the northern province, under Archbishop Toby Matthew, where citations for nonconformity were rare despite the existence of many potential offenders. According to Dr Marchant's account of Puritanism in the diocese of York, a 'general policy of toleration' prevailed there until the late 1620s. Matthew was a Calvinist and employed at least one moderate nonconformist, John Favour, as his chaplain, as well as being an indefatigable preacher himself. With archbishops like Matthew and Abbot in command, Puritanism presented no real problem.[7]

There was, however, an element of uncertainty in the situation, since much could depend on the vagaries of international politics and the shifting sands of court favour. Just as the Oath of Allegiance controversy, and its associated anti-Catholic attitudes, had worked to the benefit of Puritan nonconformity, so with plans for marrying Prince Charles to a Catholic-Spanish infanta the process seemed about to go into reverse. By 1618 there was talk of tolerating Catholicism, as a condition of the Spanish marriage. The concomitant of this would be a slump in demand for polemic against the popish Antichrist, and tighter government control over the diversity of Protestant practice. That this threat did not materialize was mainly due to a political crisis in the Low Countries, which was deemed to affect England's foreign policy interests. In the United Provinces, Oldenbarneveldt and Prince Maurice were engaged in a struggle for power, and had enlisted on their respective sides the rival Dutch church parties of Arminian and Calvinist. King James, for reasons which included theology, supported Maurice and the Calvinists, and in late 1618 sent a delegation, under Bishop Carleton of Llandaff, to participate in an international synod at Dort. This gathering proceeded to condemn the Arminian theology of grace, and affirm its Calvinist converse, and was an event which has never received the emphasis it deserves from students of English religious history. For the Calvinist doctrines at issue in the United Provinces were fundamental to English Puritanism before the Civil War, in a way that ceremonies and discipline were not. Calvinist predestinarian teaching was, as we have indicated, a crucial common assumption, shared by a majority of the hierarchy and virtually all its nonconformist opponents, during the Elizabethan and Jacobean periods. Indeed, it is not too much to say that for many people in the early seventeenth century the basic issue between Protestantism and Catholicism was that of divine determinism versus human free will. Calvinist affinities between the bishops and their critics lent substance to claims that rites and ceremonies were matters of indifference. Accordingly the assertion of predestinarian Calvinism made by the Synod of Dort, with English delegates participating and its published proceedings dedicated to King James, served to emphasize afresh the theology binding conformist and nonconformist together, and the limits which that common bond imposed on persecution.

Hindsight is often the curse of the historian, and none more so in the attempt to reconstruct the religious history of the pre-Civil War era. The battle lines of 1640–2 were not drawn by the early 1620s in this any more than other spheres. The parliaments of 1621 and 1624 were remarkable for a dearth of religious grievances. 'Godly reformation' was limited to allegations of corrupt practices by certain ecclesiastical officials and requests that the recusancy laws be more strictly enforced. When therefore the Spanish marriage negotiations finally collapsed in 1624 it was natural for the favourite Buckingham to cultivate closer relations with John Preston, at that date 'leader of the Puritan party', again to quote Christopher Hill. Two years before, Buckingham had secured for Preston the mastership of Emmanuel College, Cambridge, and now held out promises of further preferment. Preston was a Calvinist conformist and the Cambridge protégé of John Davenant, who had been a delegate to the Synod of Dort and was now Bishop of Salisbury. Far from being an untypical eccentric, Davenant was in the mainstream of Calvinist episcopalianism, and that Preston also found favour was of a piece with Jacobean religious developments. Indeed Preston might well have ended up adorning the episcopal bench. This was the context in which John Pym, during the parliament of 1621, rejected 'that odious and factious name of Puritans' which a fellow member had tried to fasten on the promoters of a bill for the better observance of Sunday. Pym thought that the speech was especially reprehensible in that it tended to 'divide us amongst our selves ... or at least would make the world believe we were divided'. As it turned out, however, Preston died in the ecclesiastical wilderness in 1628, and a doctrinal revolution took place within the established church which shattered the Jacobean dispensation. The two events were intimately connected, for during the 1620s the Calvinist heritage was overthrown and with it the prerequisite of English Protestant unity. The result was a polarization of extremes unknown since the Reformation, and one which rendered earlier compromises unworkable. It is this triumph of Arminianism, and its divisive consequences, which we must now consider.[8]

England in the early seventeenth century was doctrinally a part of Calvinist Europe, and it is within this ambience that the teachings of the Dutch theologian Arminius at Leyden have to be seen. During the first decade of the century, Arminius elaborated a critique of doctrinal Calvinism so systematic as to give his name to an international movement, namely Arminianism. He was concerned to refute the teachings on divine grace associated with the followers of Calvin, but he spoke as a member of the fully reformed and presbyterian Dutch Church, whereas his doctrinal equivalents in England were part of a different ecclesiastical tradition. There the most notable survivor of the English Reformation, apart from episcopacy, was the Prayer Book, which, as its critics were pleased to point out, was an adapted version of the old Catholic mass book. Consequently Arminianism in England emerged with an additional, sacramental dimension to that in the United Provinces. Arminius was read with approval by anti-Calvinists in England but adapted to the local situation. English Arminians came to balance their rejection of the arbitrary grace of predestination with a newfound source of grace freely available in the sacraments, which Calvinists had belittled. Hence the preoccupation under Archbishop Laud with altars and private confession before receiving communion, as well as a belief in the absolute necessity of baptism.

By the 1620s the Church of England had been Calvinist in doctrine for approximately sixty years. There had, however, always been a minority of dissidents, who led a more or less clandestine existence; in so far as these had a collective designation in the Elizabethan period they were known as 'Lutherans', after the second-generation followers of Luther who had rejected Calvinist predestinarian teaching. Not until Bancroft did the English 'Lutherans' find a champion holding high office and, as we have noted, not even he was strong enough to swim against the Calvinist tide. But after Bancroft's death in 1610 other lesser figures emerged to lead what it now becomes proper to call the Arminian party within the Church of England. The most powerful member of this early Arminian leadership was Bishop Richard Neile, although it also included Bishops Andrewes, Buckeridge and Overall; Laud was still a relatively obscure figure, dependent on Neile's patronage. They were not allowed to air their Arminian views in print, but managed to register them in a variety of covert ways. For example, in 1617, Neile, on his translation to the bishopric of Durham, had the communion table transformed into an altar at the east end of the cathedral and supported Laud in a like action the same year at Gloucester, where the latter was dean. A few years later Overall and Andrewes can be found advocating the novel practice of private confession before receiving the communion. As Laud was to say, during the 1630s,

> the altar is the greatest place of God's residence upon earth, greater than the pulpit; for there 'tis *Hoc est corpus meum*, This is my body; but in the other it is at most but *Hoc est verbum meum*, This is my word.

Such a view involved the replacement of preaching as the normal vehicle of saving grace, and one restricted in its application to the elect saints, by sacraments which conferred grace indiscriminately; baptism of all infants, without qualification, began the process of salvation, and this was to be followed by the regular receiving of communion as a result of which all partakers, provided they confessed past sins, were renewed in grace. This flank attack on predestinarian Calvinism has misled historians into thinking that the Dutch and English Arminian movements were unconnected. In fact both Arminian parties considered themselves to be engaged in a mutual duel with Calvinism; as early as 1605 the views of Arminius were being cited with approval by anti-Calvinists in Cambridge, and the Dutch Arminians can be found from 1613 until the eve of the Synod of Dort appealing for help to Arminian bishops like Andrewes and Overall. But the latter were powerless to intervene in the United Provinces, engaged as they were in their own English struggle for survival.

If the situation was ever to alter in favour of the English Arminians, their best hope lay in trying to capture the mind of the king or at least that of the royal favourite. This was the course on which they embarked during the aftermath of the Synod of Dort. Neile was the chief intermediary between the Arminians and King James, while Laud came to play an equivalent role in Buckingham's entourage. Apart from direct theological argument in favour of Arminianism, one powerful lever was to suggest that Calvinist conformists were Puritans at heart and as such politically subversive, or again that predestinarian Calvinism lent itself to so much popular misunderstanding that its widespread propagation inevitably led to religious conflict. By 1624 arguments of this kind seem to have affected adversely James's attitude towards Calvinism. Fear of approaching death may also have helped sap his confidence in deterministic teaching, for should doubt as to whether one was an elect saint ever become unbearable, there was always the Arminian possibility of denying that the predestinarian scheme was true. As regards Buckingham, opportunism was the most effective argument for his listening sympathetically to the Arminians. In 1624 he was identified with war against Spain, and was temporarily the hero of the parliamentary and ultra-Protestant camp. Buckingham was well aware, however, that the situation could rapidly change and a need arise for new allies. His willingness to support the Arminian Laud, while at the same time patronizing the 'Puritan' Preston, was part of a double insurance policy for the future.

It was in this more hopeful atmosphere that the Arminian party decided on a test case. This took the form of publishing a book in 1624, by the Arminian Richard Montagu, which, while ostensibly answering Roman Catholic criticisms of the Church of England, also rejected predestinarian Calvinism, on the ground that this was no part of the teaching enshrined in the Thirty-nine Articles. The interpretation of these articles was and still is debatable, but not only were Bishop Neile and his chaplains able to get Montagu's book, the *New Gag*, past the censor; they also managed to prevent its subsequent suppression. In terms of previous Arminian experience in England this was a dramatic breakthrough. Outraged Calvinist clergy appealed to Parliament; John Pym took up their cause in the House of Commons, and Archbishop Abbot made representations to King James. The only result was a royal request that Richard Montagu clarify his views by writing a second book. Yet it soon became clear that the final arbiter of England's theological fate would be the heir to the throne, Prince Charles. Prior to his accession some observers considered Charles to be inclined towards Puritanism, but those closer to him, among them the Arminian Matthew Wren, claimed the reverse was true and that on this score his reign would contrast with James's. Wren's prediction was to prove abundantly true, for King Charles became the architect of an Arminian revolution which had at most been dimly foreshadowed in the last year of his father's reign. As the House of Commons was to complain in 1629: 'some prelates, near the King, having gotten the chief administration of ecclesiastical affairs under his Majesty, have discountenanced and hindered the preferment of those that are orthodox [i.e. Calvinist], and favoured such as are contrary.'[9]

The suddenness of James's death in March 1625 seems to have taken most people by surprise. Buckingham survived as royal favourite, but it was now Charles who increasingly made the religious pace. The new king had never apparently been a Calvinist; certainly a decisive bias in favour of Arminianism became clear during the first few months of his reign. Calvinist bishops were excluded from the royal counsels, and in July 1625 the Arminian Richard Montagu was placed under Charles's personal protection. In February of the following year Buckingham, clearly acting with the approval of Charles, chaired a debate at York House on the subject of Montagu's writings, in the course of which he made plain his Arminian sympathies. The Arminian Bishop Buckeridge was pitted against the Calvinist Bishop Morton, and during their exchanges the question arose as to how predestinarian doctrine could be reconciled with Prayer Book teaching on the sacraments of baptism and communion. 'What,' exclaimed Morton, 'will you have the grace of God tied to sacraments?' Buckeridge's seconder, Dean White of Carlisle, replied that all baptized infants were 'made the sons of God by adoption', and Buckingham told Morton that he 'disparaged his own ministry, and did ... debase the sacrament'. White further argued that the Synod of Dort, by limiting Christ's redemption to the elect, had overthrown the sacrament of communion; he asked how on such predestinarian assumptions could ministers

> say to all communicants whatsoever, 'The Body of Our Lord which was given for thee', as we are bound to say? Let the opinion of the Dortists be admitted, and the tenth person in the Church shall not have been redeemed.

This clash of interpretation underlines the sacramental emphasis of the English Arminian rejection of Calvinism, whereby the Prayer Book was thrown into the scales against the Calvinist interpretation of the Thirty-nine Articles which had been so prevalent in Elizabethan and Jacobean times.[10]

The York House conference was, however, far from being a mere wrangle among theologians. It had been called at the request of Viscount Saye and the Earl of Warwick, who were two of the government's most prominent critics and subsequently leaders of the parliamentary party in the Civil War. Moreover, Bishop Morton's seconder at the conference was the 'Puritan' John Preston, and their ability to collaborate in this fashion exemplified the sixty-year-old shared Calvinist assumptions which were now at risk. Immediately after the conference, the Arminian John Cosin was reporting that the king 'swears his perpetual patronage of our cause', and the rebuff that Calvinism received at York House was the signal for the House of Commons to begin impeachment proceedings against Buckingham for alleged gross mismanagement of the government. The fiction was maintained by the opposition that Buckingham's policies were distinct from those of the Crown, but this became increasingly unconvincing especially as regards religion. In June 1626 Buckingham was foisted on Cambridge University as chancellor, and all predestinarian teaching was forthwith forbidden. This was backed up by a royal proclamation which effectively outlawed Calvinism on a national basis.[11]

Reaction in Parliament to this Arminianization of the Church of England became increasingly strident, and the situation was made worse by the readiness of the Arminians to brand their Calvinist opponents as Puritans. We know from Laud's diary that in 1626 he had been promised the succession to Canterbury, and from this date he comes into prominence as the chief religious spokesman of the government. His sermon at the opening of Charles's second parliament in February 1626 was remarkable for its aggressive tone. He conjured up the vision of a presbyterian conspiracy, aiming at the overthrow of church and state.

> They, whoever they be, that would overthrow *sedes ecclesia*, the seats of ecclesiastical government, will not spare (if ever they get power) to have a pluck at the throne of

David. And there is not a man that is for parity, all fellows in the Church, but he is not for monarchy in the State.

The reply of Pym and numerous other Calvinist members of the House of Commons was that, on the contrary, they were the true orthodox loyalists and that the new Arminian religion was both heterodox and the means of introducing Roman Catholicism into England. Some went further and claimed that the denouement would be the murder of the king at the hands of Jesuit-inspired plotters. They took particular exception to Richard Montagu's use of the term 'Puritan' – a use shared by Laud, who in 1624 had written on the subject of 'doctrinal Puritanism'. A Commons committee reported in 1625 that Montagu 'saith there are Puritans in heart' and that 'bishops may be Puritans'; since Montagu also defined predestinarian Calvinists as Puritans, the committee were quite correct to conclude that 'by his opinion we may be all Puritans'. More generally the Commons appealed to recent history in justification of their Calvinist exposition of English religion.[12]

Arminianism was of course only one among a number of reasons for the breakdown of relations between Charles and his parliaments in the late 1620s, but some idea of its relative importance is conveyed by the last parliament before the Personal Rule, that of 1628–9. The first session was largely taken up with the Petition of Right, in an attempt to prevent any future resort by the Crown to Forced Loans, but the second session saw Arminianism as an issue taking precedence over other questions; charges of heterodoxy were levelled at Neile and Laud, who had both been made Privy Councillors in early 1627, and it was claimed the path of ecclesiastical preferment was blocked to all but men of their persuasion. The debate on Arminianism was opened on 26 January 1629 by Francis Rous. The issue he said was 'right of religion . . . and this right, in the name of this nation, I this day claim, and desire that there may be a deep and serious consideration of the violation of it'. The violations, he thought, reduced to two, consisting of a growth of both Catholicism and Arminianism, the latter being 'an error that maketh the grace of God lackey it after the will of man, that maketh the sheep to keep the shepherd, that maketh mortal seed of an immortal God'. Moreover, he claimed that the two phenomena were biologically connected, 'for an Arminian is the spawn of a Papist', and it was now high time for the Commons to covenant together in defence of true religion. Arminianism and the more mundane subject of tunnage and poundage were the main items of the session until it was forcibly terminated on 2 March. Rous and all the other contributors to the debate on religion, with one Arminian exception, spoke as Calvinist episcopalians.[13]

The continued failure, however, of Calvinist episcopalianism to withstand the pressures of Arminianism was bound in the longer term to result in its being discredited as a viable church system. Charles's decision in 1629 to rule without parliament brought that time nearer, for it meant there was now no court of Calvinist appeal left. In 1630 died the third Earl of Pembroke, who had been the most influential Calvinist among the king's Privy Councillors. He was, moreover, succeeded as Chancellor of Oxford by Laud, who since 1628 had been controlling the London printing press as Bishop of London. The York primacy had been filled with a succession of Arminians since the Calvinist Matthew's death in 1628, and from 1632 was occupied by Neile. At Canterbury the Calvinist Abbot, in disgrace ever since refusing to license a sermon in support of forced loans in 1627, lingered on until 1633, when he was succeeded by Laud. By this process the Court increasingly isolated itself from Calvinist opinion in the country. Arminian doctrines were now freely published while Calvinism languished in silence.

Theory went hand in hand with practice. In November 1633, three months after Laud became Archbishop of Canterbury, King Charles by act of Privy Council established the precedent that all parochial churches should follow the by then general cathedral practice of placing communion tables altar-wise at the east end of chancels. We have already had cause to comment on the sacramental undermining by English Arminians of the Calvinist theology of grace, and on the basis of this Privy Council ruling Arminianism during the 1630s was made manifest throughout every parish in England, the sacrament of the altar becoming henceforth a propitiation for the sins of all partakers. These were the years, too, which saw an unprecedented onslaught on the lecturing movement.

Hardly surprisingly the 1630s as a whole saw a great increase in the number of prosecutions for Puritanism, an indirect measure of this being the large-scale emigration to New

England. In addition to creating widespread resentment of the episcopal hierarchy, these persecuting activities generated a Puritan militancy which in the early 1640s was to erupt in the shape of presbyterianism and congregationalism.

The Short Parliament of 1640, called to subsidize the suppression of the Scottish rebellion, did not last long enough for the religious question fully to come out in the open, although 'innovations in matters of religion' were high on Pym's list of grievances. The fact that after the dissolution of Parliament the convocation of clergy continued in session and proceeded to enact a series of canons which included a strong statement of royal absolution, all fostered a mounting hostility to the episcopate. Nor was the example of Scotland lost on the English opposition, and increasingly too a presbyterian model in religion became the price of Scottish support. When the Long Parliament assembled later in the year more radical pressures were brought to bear by the London populace, and the Root and Branch Petition of December, which called for the abolition of bishops, in part represented such interests. Even here, however, it was the woeful results of episcopacy, with Arminianism taking a prominent place, that were stressed rather than the essential unlawfulness of the order. Moreover, Calvinists like Archbishop Ussher and Bishop Morton meeting in committee during March 1641 with Puritan ministers such as Marshall and Calamy looked like agreeing on a common reformist platform. But the basic Arminian intransigence of King Charles, combined with the sheer speed of events, made religious compromises of this kind unworkable. Conciliation was overtaken by the drift to war.[14]

In terms of English Protestant history the charge in 1640 that King Charles and Archbishop Laud were religious innovators is irrefutable. The reaction provoked, however, by the Arminian revolution was of such violence that it could be transformed with relative ease into a call for 'root and branch' remedies, and presbyterianism emerge as the cure of Arminian disease. Thus what had begun as a counter-revolution itself became radicalized.

EDITOR'S NOTE

Reprinted in abridged form from Conrad Russell, ed., *The Origins of the English Civil War* (London, 1973), pp. 119–43, with the permissions of the author and of Macmillan Press.

NICHOLAS TYACKE

NOTES

1 C. Hill, *Society and Puritanism in Pre-Revolutionary England* (London, 1964); W. Haller, *The Rise of Puritanism* (New York, 1938).
2 A. Clark, ed., *Register of the University of Oxford* (1887–9), II pt I, pp. 194–217; G. Abbot, *A Sermon preached at Westminster* (1608), pp. 19–20.
3 C. Hill, *Puritanism and Revolution* (London, 1958), pp. 216, 238; R. Abbot, *A Defence of the Reformed Catholic of W. Perkins* (1611); F. Rous, *Testis Veritatis* (1626), pp. 2–3; C. H. McIlwain, ed., *The Political Works of James I* (Cambridge, Mass., 1918), p. 274.
4 L. Andrewes, *Responsio* (1610), p. 123; T. G. Crippen, ed., 'Of the Name of Puritans', *Transactions of the Congregational History Society*, 6 (1913–15), p. 83; E. Arber, ed., *A Transcript of Registers of the Company of Stationers, 1554–1640* (1875–94), III.
5 H. Foley, *Records of the English Province of the Society of Jesus* (1877–83), I, p. 70; M. Tierney, ed., *Dodd's Church History* (1839–43), IV, pp. 179–80; HMC, *Salisbury*, XVIII, p. 21.
6 R. Bancroft, *Dangerous Positions and Proceedings . . . under pretence of Reformation* (1593); M. Knappen, ed., *Two Elizabethan Diaries* (Chicago, 1933). p. 32; T. Rogers, *The Faith, Doctrine, and Religion professed and protected in . . . England* (Cambridge, 1607/8); Elizabeth Read Foster, ed., *Proceedings in Parliament, 1610* (New Haven, 1966), II, p. 78; G. Goodman, *The Court of James I* (1839), II, pp. 160–1; P. Hembry, *The Bishops of Bath and Wells* (London, 1967), p. 211; *The Works of [King] James* (1616), sig. e. For much of the information in this and succeeding paragraphs, see Tyacke, *Anti-Calvinists: The Rise of English Arminianism c. 1590–1640* (Oxford, 1987).
7 P. Seaver, *The Puritan Lectureships . . . 1560–1662* (Stanford, 1970), pp. 224–9; R. A. Marchant, *The Puritans and the Church Courts in the Diocese of York, 1560–1642* (London, 1960), p. 43.
8 Manchester MSS (formerly at PRO), Hughes to Nathaniel Rich, 19 May 1617; L. Hughes, *A Plain and True Relation of . . . the Summer Islands* (1621); C. Hill, *Puritanism and Revolution*, p. 146; I. Morgan, *Prince Charles's Puritan Chaplain* (London, 1957); W. Notestein, ed., *Commons' Debates 1621* (New Haven, 1935), IV, p. 63.
9 W. Notestein, ed., *Commons Debates for 1629* (Minneapolis, 1921), p. 100.
10 J. Sansom, ed., *The Works of John Cosin* (Oxford 1843–55), II, pp. 61–4.
11 Ibid., p. 74; J. P. Kenyon, *The Stuart Constitution* (Cambridge, 1966), pp. 154–5.
12 Kenyon, *Stuart Constitution*, pp. 153–4; S. R. Gardiner, ed., *Debates in the House of Commons for 1625* (Camden Society, NS 6, 1873), p. 49.
13 *Commons Debates for 1629*, pp. 12–15, 27.
14 Kenyon, *Stuart Constitution*, pp. 167–8, 172, 198; W. A. Shaw, *A History of the English Church . . . 1640–60* (1900), I, pp. 65–76.

4

ARCHBISHOP LAUD

Kevin Sharpe

Historians like Collinson and Tyacke have judged Archbishop Laud 'the greatest calamity ever visited upon the Church of England'[a] because he disrupted the reformed consensus of the Church by rigorously imposing theological and ceremonial innovations. In their view, he enforced a theology opposed to traditional English Calvinism, a heightened emphasis on the sacraments and corresponding repression of preaching, and new structures and forms of worship that looked remarkably like a return to 'popish superstition' – railed altars rather than simple communion tables, for instance, and bowing at the name of Jesus. Their judgement is similar to that of seventeenth-century Puritans who were sure that Laud's repressive enforcement of ceremony was misguiding the Church of England right back to Rome.

This view of Laud has provoked a sharp reaction from those historians who take the archbishop at his own word and portray him as the defender of a traditional order of worship, interested not in theological dispute at all, but in uniformity and peace in the Church of England. They find no evidence that Laud was an Arminian at all; he simply wanted to end the disputes over predestination that had upset the unity of the Church. The following two authors represent this newer view of Laud and his associates. Both can be seen as revisionists in their repudiation of the old 'high road to Civil War' and the strict 'Puritan versus Anglican' dichotomy. But you will find that their revision is a far cry from Tyacke's. Remember that revisionists want to revise each other as much as the received version.

* * *

William Laud was a controversial figure from his student days in Oxford in the 1590s to his death on the scaffold in 1645. Laud rose to prominence in a period during which it became clear that the Church of England meant different things to different men. These were decades which witnessed theological wrangles between the Calvinists (who asserted that men were predestined to either salvation or reprobation) and the Arminians who believed in God's universal grace and the free will of man. They were years too of sharper disagreements over the liturgy between those who rejected and those who emphasized the ceremonies prescribed in the canons of the Church and the Book of Common Prayer. Laud's career reflected as well as affected the course of those wrangles and disputes. Not surprisingly he has remained the subject of controversy ever since.

To some a martyr for the Church of England, to others a crypto-Catholic who corrupted it, judgements on the archbishop have too often reflected religious preferences more than careful consideration of the evidence. Those who brought Laud to trial in 1644 charged him with innovation, Arminianism and popery. Recently, after centuries of disagreement, historians have come close to endorsing those charges: William Laud, the historical verdict now has it, was the prelate who introduced novel doctrines and elaborate ceremony, the archbishop who wrecked the Elizabethan and Jacobean compromise – in the words of Patrick Collinson, 'the greatest calamity ever visited upon the Church of England'. Some would argue that Laud thereby fostered an even greater calamity: by exciting fears that an Arminian was but the spawn of a papist, he fuelled the paranoia about popery which kindled the Civil War.

Both the disagreements of contemporaries and the recent unanimity among historians would have puzzled Laud himself. For where he met with controversy, he eschewed it; in contrast to the charge of innovation he asserted his conservatism. How are we to explain this? Not least of the obstacles in the way of understanding is the nature of the evidence. Laud is too often depicted from the standpoint and propaganda of his enemies. His own letters and speeches, even more his sermons and treatises, remain inexplicably neglected. Yet Laud's own words cast a different light upon his intentions and better knowledge of his intentions in turn illuminates his actions.

It seems appropriate now, three hundred and fifty years after his elevation to the see of Canterbury, to allow William Laud to speak for and explain himself. On the supposedly crucial questions of theology, however, he spoke and wrote little. Laud framed no new articles, nor crafted any new catechism for the Church. His silence is itself informative: Laud did not debate doctrine because it was not of great interest to him. Whilst, on royal orders, he entered reluctantly ('I am no controvertist') into theological debate with the Catholics, he never took up the theological cudgel against the puritans. Laud's personal doctrinal beliefs elude us – and probably never taxed him. At his trial, he denied that he was an Arminian and if there is any evidence to question the denial it escaped the searches of his indefatigable prosecutor, William Prynne. Even during the more comfortable days of his ascendency, Laud never attempted to create an Arminian clergy – either as Chancellor of Oxford or as Archbishop of Canterbury. Once again his position is perhaps best explained by his own words – to the Master of Trinity College, Cambridge, who was composing a pro-Arminian treatise on predestination: 'I am yet where I was, that something about these controversies is unmasterable in this life.'

But because he campaigned for no doctrinal position, we should not assume that Laud was loyal to no church. Laud was devoted to the Church of England, that is to a church of apostolic antiquity, that part of the universal Catholic Church which had preserved the purity of the primitive church by casting off the corruptions and accretions of Roman superstition. While the Church of England insisted upon subscription to certain articles of faith, it did not, like the Roman Catholic Church, press what were only opinions or preferences by 'making them matters of necessary belief'. When disputed questions arose, they were to be settled by the Head of the Church and the bishops. Concerning things indifferent, men might hold what opinions they would in private, showing only such public obedience as was necessary for the peace of the Church.

For first and foremost, Laud sought peace and unity, urging that 'in and about things not necessary, there ought not to be a contention to a separation'. It was a philosophy which he practised as well as preached. Laud resolved 'in handling matters of religion to leave all gall out of my ink'. His support for royal proclamations forbidding disputes, his friendship and correspondence with Catholics and puritans, his patronage of divines with whom he probably disagreed are all evidence of the enactment of that resolution. In the one work of theology which he published that men 'may see and judge of my religion', Laud declared a faith in Christ 'as it was professed in the ancient Primitive Church and as it is professed in the present Church of England'. His greatest wish, he maintained, was that theological differences 'were not pursued with such heat and animosity'.

Laud's one work of theology, his *Conference with Fisher the Jesuit*, is not often read. It is ironic that one of the best defences of the Church of England against Rome was penned by a prelate charged with popery. When we read its pages, we are stuck by its moderation and oecumenism, not by denominational zeal or fanaticism. This was the work which, together with Hooker's *Laws of Ecclesiastical Polity* and the works of Lancelot Andrewes, Charles I was to give to his daughter as the corpus of Anglicanism. In the preface to the second edition of 1639, Laud took up the subject which was central to his career as bishop, archbishop and Privy Councillor: a concern for order and decency. To Laud:

No one thing hath made conscientious men more wavering in their own minds, or more apt and easy to be drawn aside from the sincerity of religion professed in the Church of England than the want of uniform and decent order in too many churches of the Kingdom.

External worship was the outward witness and bulwark of the inner faith. And external worship was manifested in and through ceremonies. Ceremonies were not the essence of religion: men should not place 'the principal part of ... piety in them'. But ceremonies were necessary as 'the hedge that fence the substance of religion from all the indignities'. While there was room within the Church for differences of belief and doctrine, the hedge of ceremony, in order to protect the Church, had to be uniform in all its parts: 'unity cannot long continue in the church where uniformity is shut out at the church door'. A belief in uniformity of ceremony as the essential prop of inner spirituality was not new: it had been the policy of Archbishops Parker, Whitgift and Bancroft and of Queen Elizabeth herself. And in the 1630s it was not the concern only of Archbishop Laud, but of Charles I himself.

To the king and his archbishop the external fabric and outward worship of the Church were subjects of urgent concern. Churches with decaying roofs and broken windows, churchyards with wandering swine or open privies, no less services devoid of prescribed ceremonies and canonical vestments, invited the papist to scoff at and the sceptic to suspect a poverty of faith within. In the eyes of Charles I and Laud, those who had laid stress upon the preaching of God's Word had exhibited too little care of his home. Laud did not wish to denigrate sermons: he believed them 'the most necessary expositions and applications of Holy Scripture'; he preached them regularly. But the Church embraced tradition as well as Scripture, the sacrament as well as the word. And so in the detailed articles of enquiry issued for Laud's metropolitical visitation, we find a painstaking concern for the condition of the church, the churchyard and the church furniture and for the diligence of the bishops, the clergy and the parish officers. Like the Statutes which as Chancellor he drew up for Oxford University, Laud's visitation articles, as Archbishop of Canterbury, were intended above all to secure order and discipline.

Order and discipline required effective authority within the Church. Because he believed the Church 'overgrown, not only with weeds within it, but with trees and bushes about it', Laud stressed the authority of the bishops and clergy as the gardeners who might best prune them. If he was concerned to repel the encroachments made by the laity upon the terrain of clerical jurisdiction, it was because only the clergy and episcopacy could enforce the order and uniformity which hedged the Church. Lay patronage to livings or the common lawyers' challenge to the church courts weakened the authority of the Church and undermined the uniformity which was its support. Charles I agreed: 'I will have no Priest have any necessity of a lay dependency.' Behind the attempts to bolster the fiscal independence, quality, power and prestige of the clergy lay their central purpose: the concern for decency and order in matters sacred.

It was a goal pursued with more moderation than fanaticism. Laud preferred persuasion to suppression, believing that the attractions of the 'beauty of holiness' would soon become self-evident. In answer to the charges of his enemies, Laud boasted that he had deprived fewer clergy than his predecessor, the latitudinarian Archbishop Abbot. There is much evidence to support the claim. Laud proceeded 'tenderly' with a mad lecturer at Leicester who had been expelled by the Dean of the Arches; with the foreign congregations at Canterbury, even in 1638, he believed it 'fitting to keep a moderate hand'. In visitation articles, he enjoined upon the clergy 'mildness and temperance' in order to win over recusants. With regard to receiving the communion at the altar rails, he left it as a matter of conscience, maintaining that 'the people will best be won by the decency of the thing itself'. Laud made painstaking efforts to win over the refractory. Only those who could not be won, those who would not subscribe to the articles and ceremonies prescribed by the Prayer Book and canons, were forced from the Church and, in some cases, the country. Concerning such refractory nonconformists, Charles I himself issued the orders: 'let him go; we are well rid of him'.

Throughout his archiepiscopacy Laud remained very much the king's man. A monarch obsessed with order and uniformity, in church as in state, Charles I had elevated Laud not for his theology (he was no theologian) nor even primarily for his counsel (Charles knew his own mind) but for his concern with ceremony and his pertinency as an administrator. Laud was not always 'master of this work, but a servant to it'. The king by letters, instructions, audiences, by marginal comment on visitation reports, chivvied the archbishop, who in turn harried the episcopacy and clergy. Often Charles proved more intransigent than Laud. It was Charles I who, after hearing the St Gregory's case at the Council board, recommended the altar be set at the east end of the church; Laud enquired only whether it was placed in 'such convenient sort within the chancel or church as that the minister may be best heard'. But on most matters the architect and his patron shared a common vision of the final edifice: a church built from the fabric of decency and ceremony – the place for worship in peace and uniformity.

It is an irony that it was Archbishop Laud (and King Charles) with whom the puritans went to war. For both in his policies and in his personality, Laud had much in common with them. Like the puritans he sought an upright and well-educated clergy; like them he was virulent against popery, hard against clerical failings and intolerant of lay profligacy. Like the puritans he urged harsh measures against drunkenness and incontinency – be it in the counties or colleges of England. Personally too, Laud, like his royal master, was an intense, ascetic and self-disciplined figure. His diary, a record of dreams, omens and insecurities, of the application of scriptural text to everyday life, has been aptly described as a Puritan document. His portrait, a dark brooding figure, suggests a sombre demeanour and stern determination which even the flamboyant romanticism of Van Dyck failed, or never attempted, to soften. It was their tragedy – and that of the Church – that Laud and the puritans shared a mutual fear, a common paranoia. To him, the nonconformists, in undermining the uniformity of external worship, threatened the fabric of church and state. To them, after years of laxity, an insistence upon ceremony and an emphasis upon the position of the clergy smacked of popery. By examining Laud's words, we have seen that, had they known more of his intentions, the fears of the puritans might have been calmed. Those who knew Laud well neither feared nor suspected him. Philip Warwick, a Gentleman of the Bedchamber, thought his 'grand design was no other than that of our first Reformation'. But it was that Reformation which others felt Laud might reverse. As Clarendon was astutely to reflect, he failed to make 'his designs and purposes appear as candid as they were'.

EDITOR'S NOTES

Reprinted with permission of the author and *History Today*, which published the article in August of 1983. The absence of notes is the policy of the journal. For a fuller view of Sharpe's understanding of Laud, see his 'Archbishop Laud and the University of Oxford', in *History and Imagination*, ed. H. Lloyd-Jones *et al.* (London, 1981), and references in *The Personal Rule of Charles I* (New Haven, 1993).

a Patrick Collinson, *The Religion of Protestants* (Oxford, 1982), p. 90.

5

THE *VIA MEDIA* IN THE EARLY STUART CHURCH

Peter White

While Sharpe's focus is on Laud and his activities, Peter White's is on theology and liturgical practice. The two agree, however, that blame for the religious division of the 1640s has been wrongly placed on Arminians. White is concerned in his book, Predestination, Policy and Polemic (1992), and in the following essay, to reject altogether the old model of polarity between Calvinist and Arminian, puritan and conformist, in favour of a broad religious spectrum on which no one group had a monopoly of middle ground. He finds that the old version derived less from reality than from seventeenth-century polemic (especially that of the puritan William Prynne). In fact, the middle ground was occupied by people as devoted to 'puritan' sermons as to 'Laudian' sacramentalism. To the extent that tensions existed over the doctrine of election, they were between two predestinarian factions and were primarily concerned with the centrality of the doctrine and whether it should be preached. White finds that the royal directives of the 1620s against preaching on predestination were not anti-Calvinist decrees, as Tyacke thought, but genuine attempts to silence the controversy about the doctrine that had grown in the wake of the Synod of Dort and the outbreak of the Thirty Years War. Enforcement of the policy, moreover, was even-handed, not biased towards Arminians. The peace of the Church was the central goal for the early Stuart kings and their bishops. They were determined to maintain the Church of England on its traditional 'middle way' between the extremes of puritanism and popery. When White turns to the 1630s, he identifies a newly rigorous enforcement of ceremonies and altar placement as the more divisive religious issue, and one not correlated to theological position. By 1640 he finds Arminianism no longer a real point of contention, even in Parliament. Predestinarian theology thus appears to have had nothing to do with the Civil War, the causes of which, for White, 'remain elusive'.[a]

The essay below is a sustained attack on the position of Nicholas Tyacke and is best read in the context of Tyacke's essay and the response to both by Peter Lake in Part III of this volume. Tyacke and White exemplify revisionists who heartily disagree not only with the received version, but also with each other.

* * *

Sometime in 1630 Richard Johnson, a layman of the parish of St Laurence in Reading, left in his will £15 to buy 'a silver flagon and two bread plates of silver' to be used at the communion. 'And more I give unto them a fair pulpit cloth of silk and a fair cushion . . . and more I give unto them forty shillings in money towards the making of a wood fence for the communion table.'[1] Johnson can no doubt be added to the list of 'Arminians' who crept out of the ecclesiastical woodwork after 1625, for in that year, we are led to understand, the accession of Charles I destroyed a previously harmonious 'Calvinist' consensus in the English Church. By that revolution, it is claimed, the teaching of predestination was 'outlawed' and an alternative, sacramentally centred theology of grace enforced, the outward sign of which was the remodelling of church interiors by railing off altars at the east end. The enforcement of this policy, and the doctrinal novelty that lay behind it, are held to be crucial in explaining the English Civil War.[2]

All this, we may be sure, would have caused Johnson himself, whose will is one of the many examples of spontaneous lay initiative in the improvement of church furnishings, much astonishment. He fits awkwardly into current historiography, preoccupied as that is with the polarities necessary if church history is to be the tool of political explanation. That Richard Johnson was innocent of any preference of churchmanship is suggested by his bequest of ten shillings for the minister if he preached on the day of St John the Evangelist, for 'Arminians' (we are told) preferred prayer to sermons. Current historiography, however, has no interest in those churchmen it cannot categorize, and is bound on its own premises to ignore, if not altogether to deny, the existence of a middle ground. This should occasion no surprise, for in this as in so many other respects it reflects the outlook of William Prynne. It was Prynne who first claimed an Elizabethan 'Calvinist' consensus, evidenced both by the output of the printing presses and by university commencement theses; and it was Prynne who identified 'Arminian' novelty in the works of Richard Montagu.[3] It is from Prynne's perspective that establishment churchmen, conservative to the core, can be metamorphosed into revolutionaries.

An attempt will be made in the present chapter to offer an alternative matrix. It will be suggested that a spectrum offers a much better model, and that the doctrine of predestination was far from being a crucial determinant of that spectrum. While not of course denying the existence of polarities, it will attempt to balance them by exploring the limits of consensus, identifying some of those churchmen who pursued a moderating role under Elizabeth and James I, and who drew inspiration from the notion and practice of a *via media*. An attempt will thereafter be made to suggest in what senses, if any, the accession of Charles I disturbed the equilibrium.

The polarities in the early Stuart Church did not replace an earlier consensus, but were inherited from the earliest stages of the Reformation. The tension was between a protestantism of the right and a protestantism of the left, and it ran right through Europe. It was particularly acute in England because under both Henry and Elizabeth the Reformation impulse was carefully controlled by the Crown, and conservatism was sustained first by the succession of Mary Tudor and thereafter by the claim of Mary Queen of Scots. Largely as a result, 'Elizabethan England was unique, in trying to find room within the borders of a single state, for the conservative (provided he were not too conservative) and the radical (provided he were not too radical).'[4] Underlying the argument of the present chapter is the view that the Elizabethan Settlement was intended to be as inclusive as possible of a people whose allegiances ranged from Marian conservative to 'the hotter sort of protestants'. The political pragmatism of the queen and her advisers set frustrating limits to the enthusiasm of clerical reformers. The result was a church that stood in an unmistakably intermediate position between the more 'precise' churches of the Continent and the Church of Rome. The Thirty-nine Articles, the Book of Common Prayer and the Homilies represented a settlement of religion that was significantly different, liturgically, doctrinally and in its church polity, from other Protestant churches. The royal supremacy, and a diocesan episcopacy, both distinctive, guaranteed a fundamental continuity with the past, while a widespread conservatism, combined with the preferences of the queen, dictated the retention of rites and vestments elsewhere dispensed with. For similar reasons, the settlement of doctrine was less precise, the extent of permissible *adiaphora* (things indifferent) correspondingly wider, than in the continental reformed churches.[5]

This contrast between the Church of England and the continental reformed churches, above all with Geneva, was far from being, as has recently been claimed, the invention of Richard Hooker. It was widely recognized from the earliest years of the Elizabethan Settlement. The reformers themselves were in no doubt about it, Calvin's gift of his commentaries on Isaiah to Elizabeth in January 1559 being coldly received, and Beza lamenting to Bullinger in 1566 that 'as to our own Church, it is so hateful to that queen . . . because we are accounted too severe and precise'. Some of the returned exiles were correspondingly apologetic about their church in letters to their continental mentors. Others drew the same distinction only to applaud it.[6]

There were many clerics early in the reign of James I whose churchmanship reflected above all their awareness of the special character of the Church of England, and whose loyalties were above all to her polity and liturgy as established by law. Provided no more than that is read into the word, they are most appropriately described as 'Anglicans'. Although they were quite ready to accept an underlying unity of doctrine among the protestant churches, it did not tie them to a particular doctrine of predestination, and they cannot adequately be categorized as either 'Calvinist' or 'Arminian'. A brief study of two of them will enable the reader to construct a model of their central Jacobean churchmanship.

The first is John Boys (1571–1625), a Dean of Canterbury patronized in turn by Whitgift, Bancroft and Abbot. 'From my youth up, I did ever esteem as a second Bible the Book of Common Prayer.' 'Every tittle' was grounded upon Scripture. The liturgy was threatened on both sides, 'crucified between two malefactors: on the left hand the papists, on the right schismatics'. 'Against the Romanist I use a sword, against the novelist a buckler.' His published works were commentaries on the Book of Common Prayer, and he was a staunch supporter of the establishment. 'Except we have the Church for our mother, we shall never have God for our father.'

There is no doubt of Boys's protestantism. He made many references to the elect and the reprobate, but offered no formal treatment of the doctrine of predestination, affirming that exact knowledge to discuss curious points is not required of a Christian. On the doctrine of justification, he recommended Luther on Galatians and Robert Abbot's Defence of Perkins's *Reformed Catholic* – 'my conscience was never more quieted than in reading the one, and my curiosity never satisfied more than in examining the other'. He strongly believed in preaching, and wrote of 'ministers', 'pastors' and the 'Lord's table'. Yet 'we protest, and that unfeignedly, that no Church ought further to depart from the Church of Rome, than she is departed from herself in her flourishing estate'. Grace was conveyed both by the preaching of the word and by the administration of the sacraments, of which there were only two, baptism and the Lord's Supper. The former is a sacrament of initiation, and therefore the font is placed at the church door; the latter is a sacrament of confirmation, and therefore 'the Lord's table by good order is placed in the best and highest room of the church'. Boys was not afraid to use the word 'priest', or to speak of the Communion as in some respects a sacrifice (above all as representative and commemorative of Christ's).[7]

Another important moderate was Arthur Lake (1569–1626), a Bishop of Bath and Wells admired both by the Dort delegate Samuel Ward and by Laud's biographer Peter Heylyn. Like Boys, he was exercised equally by threats from the right and the left. On the one hand, the papists had 'bred up the people in an ignorant devotion and bid them rest content with an implicit faith, and rest their souls upon the authority of the Church; they offend *in Parum* [by asking too little] in overscanting the people's knowledge'; on the other, 'the separatists run to the other extreme, they offend *in Nimium* [by asking too much], attribute too little to the Church, and exceed in knowledge, or fancies, which they suppose to be divine knowledge'. Lake was an assiduous preacher, but his preachings often had a sacramental emphasis. He preached at St Paul's Cross at the beginning of James's reign that 'God's mercy is double to his justice', and that 'the first grace that fails us is a good conscience'. Far from predestination being the foundation of his view of Christian doctrine, he invariably expounded it in the light of the Church's teaching about the sacraments. In an attempt to include him within the 'Calvinist consensus' he has been described as a 'hypothetical universalist', but his universalism was in reality pragmatic or sacramental, as in a notable sermon in which he identified the 'elect' with members of the Church through baptism, and in which the whole emphasis is on the need for prayer 'or else they [the elect] shall not have what God doth purpose them'.[8]

Jacobean churchmen, it has been said, can be divided into 'two sides, the members of which knew who each other were and disliked each other heartily',[9] but Boys and Lake do not naturally fall into either category; nor do many others. Printed works are not necessarily adequate evidence, for by definition moderate churchmen were less likely to enter the lists of Jacobean polemical theology. Nor should we be too influenced by competition for preferment, which has always tended to sharpen rivalries and provoke abrasive churchmanship. Even the model of a spectrum should not be taken too literally. Both conservative and radical Protestantism were heterogeneous. Doctrinal preference did not necessarily correspond with liturgical taste. Men, especially thinking men, develop. For all these reasons it is not always possible neatly to categorize individual churchmen. As the Church developed, moreover, the defence of the existing settlement required a flexible response to new challenges. The *via media* was exactly that, implying movement as well as moderation.

The foundations of the Jacobean *via media* were laid at the Hampton Court Conference. Lay observers had no difficulty in identifying two sides, but there is no reference in the contemporary records to the 'Calvinists' and 'Arminians' of modern historiography. On the contrary, the disagreement was between the 'prelates' unwilling to contemplate even moderate reforms and 'puritans' who arrogated to themselves the names of 'zealous' and 'reformed' and whose chief passion was the imitation of foreign churches. As Francis Bacon wrote, 'The truth is, here be two extremes: some few, would have no change; no, not reformation. Some many, would have much change, even with perturbation', and Dudley Carleton observed 'these two companies as they differ in opinions so do they in fashions, for one side marches in gowns and rochets, and th'other in cloaks and night-caps'. Bacon rejoiced that the king was 'disposed to find out the golden mediocrity in the establishment of that which is sound, and in the reparation of that which is corrupt and decayed'.[10] Accounts of the conference repeatedly suggest moderation and equilibrium. It was evident, even before it started, in the proclamation of 24 October 1603, where the Church of England was claimed not only to be 'near to the condition of the primitive Church' but also to be 'agreeable to God's word': the appeal to antiquity was deliberately balanced by an appeal to scripture obviously mindful of the Puritan emphasis on holy writ.[11]

There is no real substitute for Barlow's account of the proceedings,[12] and it too repeatedly offers variations on the theme of balance. In the discussions on baptism, for example, there was no question either that the king doubted the necessity of the sacrament, or that private baptism would not continue: yet James was firm that the sacrament should be administered by a lawful minister, and that the rubric should be made explicit to rule out baptism by midwives and laymen. Similarly, in the discussions on predestination, the king

wished that the doctrine might be very tenderly handled, and with great discretion, lest on the one side, God's omnipotency might be called in question . . . or on the other, a desperate presumption might be arreared, by inferring the necessary certainty of standing and persisting in grace.

When Rainolds suggested that the 'nine orthodoxal assertions concluded at Lambeth' be added to the Thirty-nine Articles, the king made it clear that he was against any extension of doctrinal tests. 'Curious questions' should be determined only in the universities, and avoided 'in the fundamental instruction of the people': it is clear that for King James, predestination was not part of that basic doctrine.[13]

The agreement to arrange for a new translation of the Bible was a further state in the evolution of the *via media*. It was agreed that the new version should be the joint work of the flower of English linguistic scholarship, irrespective of churchmanship. As a result, it has been deservedly said that the Authorized Version is 'even in the minutest details the translation of a church and not of a party.' That the catholicity of design was no accident is demonstrated by the notes left by one of the revisers, which suggest that the translators deliberately sought a rendering which left the version open to a range of meanings.[14]

James I's comments at Hampton Court show how seriously he took the claim to true catholicity. That claim went back to Jewel's *Apology*. The *Apology* was republished in 1609 and a copy ordered to be in every parish church. A preface by Overall emphasized that the object of Jewel's works had been to show

> that this is and hath been the open profession of the Church of England, to defend and maintain no other Church, Faith and Religion than that which is truly Catholic and apostolic, and for such warranted, not only by the written word of God, but also by the testimony and consent of the ancient and godly fathers.[15]

The claim to true catholicity was given a contemporary significance by James's relations with the Roman Church. In his speech to the first parliament of his reign he revealed his hopes for a reconciliation. Again, the concept of the *via media* made its appearance:

> I could wish from my heart that it would please God to make me one of the members of such a general Christian union in religion, as laying wilfulness aside on both hands, we might meet in the midst, which is the centre and perfection of all things. For if they would leave, and be ashamed of such new and gross corruptions of theirs, as themselves cannot maintain, nor deny to be worthy of reformation, I would for mine own part be content to meet them in the mid-way.

Such a union, James believed, might be achieved through an ecumenical council summoned by the pope, and he let it be known that if the pope agreed he would use his influence with heads of state in northern Europe.[16] He stressed his reverence for antiquity, and said he was even prepared to contemplate a common order of divine worship. Although Pope Clement VIII received James's proposals coldly, they were not altogether lost sight of in the controversy which followed over the Oath of Allegiance. James defended his orthodoxy and that of the Church of England in the *Premonition* addressed to European heads of state in 1609. 'I will never refuse to embrace any opinion in divinity necessary to salvation which the whole Catholic Church with an unanimous consent has constantly taught and believed even from the apostles' days.'[17]

Theologians from both home and abroad supported the king's defence of his orthodoxy. Lancelot Andrewes was engaged to write against Bellarmine. 'Our appeal is to antiquity yea even to the most extreme antiquity. We do not innovate; it may be we renovate what was customary with some ancients but with you has disappeared in novelties.' The Church of England was in the position of an appellant, waiting for a genuinely general council, but meanwhile she had not cut herself off from Catholicism, for she had preserved the apostolic succession, and her faith was that of the universal church. She trod a middle way. 'We follow neither Calvin nor the pope, where either has forsaken the footsteps of the fathers.'[18]

Foreign theologians who had visited the Jacobean court added their defence of the Church of England to that of Andrewes. Isaac Casaubon, who had come to England in 1610 because he was attracted by the reputation of the English Church for patristic studies and because it offered a middle way between Rome and Geneva, echoed Andrewes and Overall. 'The authors of the Reformation here, had no purpose to erect any new Church (as the ignorant and malicious do cavil), but to repair the ruins of the old', and Casaubon instanced that was no denial of auricular confession, merely a concern to guard against abuses and dangers. Casaubon praised the 'godly moderation' of the Church of England on the real presence, the eucharist as the commemoration of a sacrifice, prayer for the dead and invocation of the saints. It was only abuses, like private masses and communion in one kind, that the king rejected.[19]

It would be hard to overestimate the importance of this Jacobean apologetic against Rome. It is there we should look (and not to Arminius) if we are seeking the theological basis of Laudianism. The centrality of the apologetic of true catholicity also helps to explain the relations between the English Church and the Netherlands. The king was under strong pressure from his archbishop, George Abbot, to take the lead in condemning the Remonstrant followers of Arminius. Supporters of the Remonstrants, however, were convinced, on the basis of the king's patronage of Andrewes, Casaubon and Overall, and his known moderation on the doctrine of predestination, that they could secure his support against the Contra-Remonstrants (the extreme Calvinists).[20] The full story of James's involvement in the events which culminated in the condemnation of the Remonstrants at the Synod of Dort cannot be told here,[21] but the primary aim of the king and of the British delegates was the preservation of peace. James would not allow either side to monopolize his support without qualification. In 1613 he wrote that 'we find neither the one nor the other so wide of the mark that they cannot be reconciled both with Christian truth and the salvation of souls'.[22] In 1614 he suggested that a ban on polemical preaching was preferable to a national synod, provided that it was acceptable to both parties, and the resulting draft was submitted to him for approval. Only after the ban had failed to resolve the dispute did James become reconciled to the need for a synod.[23]

The conduct of the delegates at Dort demonstrates that throughout their aim was to bring peace if they could. They saw themselves as representatives of the king and as apologists of the English Church rather than as defenders of 'Calvinist' orthodoxy. In the debates on doctrine, their influence was invariably towards moderation.

However eirenic the role of the British delegation, one result of the condemnation of the Remonstrants at Dort was to polarize opinion in the English Church. Tensions were further inflamed by the outbreak of the Thirty Years War. Abbot hoped that James would intervene to secure the denouement that militant protestant theology expected. Instead he had to stomach the opening of negotiations for a Spanish match for Prince Charles, a development which shocked even moderate protestant opinion abroad. A number of preachers found themselves in prison for protesting against it. Anti-Arminian sermons at Paul's Cross were matched by provocative anti-Calvinist sermons at both Oxford and Cambridge: the debate, it has been rightly pointed out, was 'fully in the public domain long before Montagu appeared on the scene'.[24] The Directions to Preachers of 1622, issued on the king's personal authority, required all under the rank of bishop or dean to restrict their sermons to the Articles of Religion and the Homilies and to avoid predestination altogether. Bitter invectives against either papists or puritans were to be avoided.[25] However unpalatable to the archbishop, this represented no change of view by James, whose dislike of the finer points of predestinarian teaching being aired in popular preaching had been evident since the Hampton Court Conference.

The puritan and parliamentary attack on Montagu's anti-Calvinism has tended to obscure the fact that the *New Gagg* was a piece of anti-Roman apologetic of the type that the king had been long promoting. Aggressive as indeed he was, Montague too believed in a middle way: he said he 'wanted to stand in the gap between popery and puritanism, the Scylla and Charybdis of ancient piety'. Even unsympathetic observers agreed. 'Such', said Fuller, 'was the equability of the sharpness of his style he was unpartial therein, be he ancient or modern writer, papist or protestant, that stood in his way', while Prynne criticized him for being a 'neuter'. Many churchmen, especially those who liked to assimilate the English Church to the reformed churches, were of course incensed at his distinction between the moderation of the doctrines of the Church of England compared with the extreme ones of 'doctrinal puritans', but Montagu did not invent the phrase, for it had been used by Roman writers since at least the turn of the century.[26]

King James provoked not only the writing but the publication of the *Appello Caesarem*.[27] Montagu had throughout been confident of his backing, but he was unsure how Charles would react. Historians content to follow Prynne and Rushworth in associating the 'rise of Arminianism' with Charles and Laud have written that 'the accession of Charles I in 1625 meant the overthrow of Calvinism',[28] but the facts are that the new king did all he could to satisfy Montagu's critics without abandoning the middle way. Although Charles, supporting the right of Convocation to judge doctrine, made Montague his chaplain (to protect him from proceedings in Parliament), he was far from committing himself to approval of his books. Clergy of all shades of opinion pressed him to inhibit further doctrinal debate. Although some (like Ussher) argued that 'Arminianism' alone should be suppressed, others (Laud, yes, but Joseph Hall too) argued that both sides should be silenced.[29] The draft of the 1626 *Proclamation for Peace and Quiet in the Church of England* was in fact anti-Arminian, but the final version, approved by a committee under the chairmanship of Abbot and at least seven other bishops (Davenant and Felton among them) was, as even Tyacke concedes, 'neutral'.[30]

It has been argued that the Declaration prefixed to the Thirty-nine Articles of Religion in 1628 'abandoned the neutrality of the Proclamation' and that 'Charles glossed the Thirty-nine Articles in favour of the Arminians and their doctrine of universal grace'.[31] It did nothing of the sort. It tried to heal divisions by pointing out that 'both sides' appealed to the Articles: it therefore required that in future everybody should accept them 'in the plain and full meaning thereof, and shall not put his own sense or comment to be the meaning of the Article'. The so-called Arminian gloss is a literal quotation from the final paragraph of the article in question.

For the next four years Abbot was responsible for enforcing the Declaration. Montagu's *Appello Caesarem* was withdrawn by royal proclamation early in 1629. Enforcement under Laud was even-handed, but Calvinism was not suppressed. The works of William Perkins were in print throughout the 1630s. There was no alteration to official formularies, no propagation of new doctrines, no promulgation of new definitions. Of course it is understandable that those who were committed to 'Calvinism' feared that their rivals of 'Durham House' (the circle around Bishop Richard Neile) would be given free licence to propagate 'Arminianism', but that is not what happened. Laud was widely recognized to have acted even-handedly. It is not enough merely to concede that he took action against 'extreme' Arminians like Tooker of Oriel College, for even moderates were discouraged from disturbing the precarious harmony. As archbishop, Laud wrote to Samuel Brooke, who had written a treatise which tried to steer a middle course on the disputed points, saying that he doubted whether the king would be willing to have them 'any further stirred, which now, God be thanked, begin to be more at peace'. Yet the notion lingers among historians that in subtle and insidious ways Laud tried to insinuate a new heresy into the seventeenth-century Church. There is simply no evidence to support them.[32]

What happened in 1625–9 then? Not the propagation of Arminianism by the king and Laud, but the redefinition of Arminianism by Pym. From being a particular doctrine of predestination, it became a 'bridge to usher in popery' and a plot to impose arbitrary government.[33] Laud was charged with it not because of any doctrinal statement, but because he was believed (incorrectly) to have licensed Sibthorpe's and Manwaring's sermons. Neile was also accused, but much more for 'popery' than for Arminianism. For the future of the *via media*, the decisive change was the political ascendancy of Durham House, which dates not from 1625 but from 1617. The controversy over Montagu threatened rather than consolidated that ascendancy, but it was reinforced by the appointment of Neile and Laud to the Privy Council and by Abbot's sequestration.

With the rise of Durham House, conservative churchmanship was triumphant. But if in some cases (Wren's and Cosin's, for example) that churchmanship was aggressive, from Laud's point of view it was still determined by the ideal of a *via media*. Like his 'old master' Aristotle, he 'did ever believe that truth lies betwixt two extremes'.[34] The Church of England, as he told Charles, was 'in a hard condition', condemned by the Romans for novelty in doctrine and by the separatist for an anti-Christian discipline. 'The plain truth is, she is between two millstones, and unless your majesty look to it, she will be ground to powder'. Laud justified his preoccupation with the 'external worship of God in the Church' on the grounds that

> no one thing hath made conscientious men ... more apt and easy to be drawn aside from the sincerity of religion professed in the Church of England than the want of uniform and decent order in too many churches; and the Romanists have been apt to say, the houses of God could not be suffered to lie so nastily, as in some places they have done, were the true worship of God observed in them.[35]

Such was the rationale of the 'altar policy', a misleading term unless it is remembered that it was part of a much wider movement of emphasis on the visual and sacramental aspects of Prayer Book worship which had its origins deep in Elizabeth's reign. Churchwardens' accounts demonstrate that parochial religion was marked from the 1570s onwards both by more frequent communions and by improved buildings and church furnishings. There is space here only to remove a few common misconceptions. In the first place, not only the Injunctions of 1559 but also the canons of 1604 envisaged the east end of the chancel as the normal position for the communion table at times other than during a communion.[36] It remains true, however, that it was not *enforced* generally until the 1630s. Second, that programme of enforcement was not, and on the whole was not perceived as, 'anti-Calvinist': some 'Calvinist' churchmen imposed the changes with less hesitation than Laud.[37] A canon imposing the east end position was adopted without protest by the Irish Church under Archbishop Ussher in 1634, by a Convocation which refused to accept bowing at the name of Jesus. Third, the vast majority of English parishes railed their communion tables off at the east end without significant resistance. Destruction of altar-rails in the early 1640s (by no means universal) was often the work of disaffected minorities and it dismayed parishioners.[38] In most parishes the Restoration was followed by their spontaneous replacement and the permanent removal of the communion table to the east end.

It was not so much the novelty of policy but its vigour that distinguishes the 1630s. The canons of 1604 were enforced systematically for the first time.[39] Insistence on the wearing of the surplice, the use of the sign of the cross at baptism, bowing at the name of Jesus and the licensing of lecturers could be contrasted with what seemed the appeasement of papists. 'The neglect of punishing puritans breeds papists,' Charles told Neile in 1634. The thrust of policy was inevitably misrepresented. It is understandable that Sir Benjamin Rudyerd should tell the House of Commons in 1640 that 'under the name of puritans, all our religion is branded ... The great work, now is, their masterpiece, to make all those of the religion to be the suspected party of the kingdom.'[40] It was all so different from the days of Good Queen Bess, when penal laws had been for papists.

There was one sense in which the middle way as it had been understood under both Elizabeth and James I was abandoned under Charles I, and that was in its careful balance of clerical and lay interests. Where James I is reported to have been suspicious of Laud's 'schemes of reformation in his own brain', Charles upbraided his bishops for not giving the Church a higher profile in Parliament, and expressed his readiness to 'promote the cause of the Church'.

The downside was that the very survival of the Church came to depend on the king's own skills as a monarch. James, who understood only too well that politics was the art of the possible, was succeeded by Charles who (more cleric than king) could neither defend a bad cause nor yield in a good one. The difference was evident above all in their respective policies towards

Scotland. James had learned to abandon his scheme for a union, and in church policy finally rested content with the Five Articles of Perth. Charles was determined to do better. James had said 'No bishop, no king'. Under Charles, it was more a case of no king, no bishop.

EDITOR'S NOTES

Reprinted in abridged form from White's essay in *The Early Stuart Church*, ed. Kenneth Fincham (1993), with permission of the author, the Macmillan Press Ltd, and Stanford University Press.

a Peter White, *Predestination, Policy and Polemic: Conflict and Consensus in the English Church from the Reformation to the Civil War* (Cambridge, 1992), p. 311.

NOTES

1 Berkshire RO, Parish Documents, DP 97/5/9, p. 6.
2 N. Tyacke, 'Puritanism, Arminianism and Counter-Revolution', ch. 3 above; N. Tyacke, *Anti-Calvinists: The Rise of English Arminianism, c. 1590–1640* (Oxford, 1987).
3 William Prynne, *Canterburies Doome* (1646), pp. 155–61, followed by John Rushworth, *Historical Collections*, I, *1618–1629* (1659), pp. 62, 173–4, 413.
4 G. Nuttall and O. Chadwick, *From Uniformity to Unity 1662–1962* (1962), 5–6.
5 For a contemporary statement of this view, see Edwin Sandys, *Europae Speculu, or A View or Survey of the State of Religion in the Western Parts of the World* (1605), p. 213.
6 P. Lake, *Anglicans and Puritans? Presbyterianism and English Conformist Thought from Whitgift to Hooker* (London, 1988), pp. 159–60.
7 John Boys, *Workes* (1629), pp. 6, 14, 23, 40–1, 61, 184, 207–9.
8 Arthur Lake, *Sermons* (1629), pp. 81, 531–47.
9 P. Lake, 'Calvinism and the English Church, 1570–1635', *Past and Present*, 114 (1987), pp 49–50.
10 J. Spedding, *The Letters and Life of Francis Bacon* (1861–74), III, pp. 73–4; VII, pp. 36ff, 43–6, 54, 63. PRO, SP 14/6/21, quoted by F. Shriver, 'Hampton Court Revisited: James I and the Puritans', *JEH*, 33 (1982), p. 59.
11 Shriver, 'James I and the Puritans', pp. 53–4.
12 William Barlow, *The Summe and Substance of the Conference ... at Hampton Court* (1605), printed in E. Cardwell, *A History of Conferences ...* (Oxford, 1849), pp. 167–212.
13 Barlow, *Summe and Substance*, 172, 175–6, 181, 185.
14 B. F. Westcott, *A General View of the History of the English Bible*, 3rd edn, revised by W. Aldis Wright (London, 1905), pp. 112–15, 256–7;

G. W. Bernard, 'The Church of England, *c.* 1529–*c.* 1642, *History,* 75 (1990), p. 189.

15 J. Jewel, *Works* (1609), Preface, sig. q2ʳ–3ʳ.

16 W. B. Patterson, 'King James I's Call for an Ecumenical Council', in C. J. Cuming and D. Baker, eds, *Studies in Church History, VII* (Cambridge, 1971), pp. 267–8.

17 C. H. McIlwain, ed., *The Political Works of James I* (Cambridge, Mass., 1918), pp. 110–68.

18 Lancelot Andrewes, *Tortura Torti* (Oxford, 1851), pp. 96; *Responsio and Apologiam Cardinalis Bellarminum* (Oxford, 1851), pp. 25–6, 69, 216–17.

19 Mark Pattison, *Isaac Casaubon, 1559–1614* (Oxford, 1875), pp. 299–300, 328; *The Answer of Mr Isaac Casaubon to the Epistle of the most illustrious and most reverend Cardinal Peron* (1612), esp. pp. 4, 13, 16, 20, 25, 29, 32, 33–43.

20 For Remonstrant hopes, see Grotius to Casaubon, 7 January 1612; *Briefwisseling van Hugo Grotius,* ed. P. C. Molhuysen and B. L. Meulenbroek (11 vols, The Hague, 1928–81), I, pp. 192–3; for Abbot's perspective, K. Fincham, 'Prelacy and Politics: Archbishop Abbot's Defence of Protestant Orthodoxy', *Historical Research,* 61 (1988), pp. 36–64.

21 The best short accounts of British involvement are C. Grayson, 'James I and the Religious Crisis of the United Provinces, 1613–19; in D. Baker, ed., *Studies in Church History, Subsidia 2: Reform and Reformation, England and the Continent, c.1500–c.1750* (Oxford, 1979), pp. 195–219, and J. Platt, 'Eirenical Anglicans at the Synod of Dort', ibid., pp. 221–43.

22 The French text of James's letter is printed in *Praestantium ac Eruditorum Vivorum Ecclesiasticae et Theologicae,* 2nd edn (Amsterdam, 1684), p. 351.

23 Jan Den Tex, *Oldenbarnevelt,* trans. R. B. Powell, 2 vols (Cambridge, 1973), II, pp. 547ff.

24 S. Lambert, 'Richard Montagu, Arminianism and Censorship', *Past and Present,* no. 124 (1989), p. 51.

25 The Directions to Preachers are printed in J. P. Kenyon, *The Stuart Constitution,* 2nd edn (Cambridge, 1986), pp. 128–30.

26 R. Montagu, *A Gagg for the New Gospell? No, a New Gagg for an Old Goose* (1624), p. 179; W. Prynne, *The Perpetuity of a Regenerate Man's Estate* (1626), pp. 250–1.

27 Lambert, 'Richard Montagu', p. 43–4.

28 Tyacke, *Anti-Calvinists,* p. 8.

29 Laud, *Works,* VI, p. 249; *The Works of Joseph Hall,* 10 vols (Oxford, 1863), ed. P. Wynter, IX, p. 498; *The Works of James Ussher,* 17 vols (Dublin, 1847–64), ed. C. R. Elrington, XV, pp. 348–9, 351.

30 For *A Proclamation for the establishing of the Peace and Quiet of the Church of England,* see P. L. Hughes and J. F. Larkin, eds, *Stuart Royal Proclamations* (Oxford, 1983), II, pp. 90–1. The draft is PRO, SP 16/29/79.

31 Tyacke, *Anti-Calvinists,* p. 50.

32 Hughes and Larkin, eds, *Stuart Royal Proclamations*, ɪɪ, pp. 218–19; Laud, *Works*, v, p. 15, vɪ, p. 292.
33 H. Schwarz, 'Arminianism and the English Parliament, 1624–29, *JBS*, 12 (1973), pp. 41–68.
34 Laud, *Works*, vɪ, p. 85.
35 Ibid., ɪɪ, pp. xiii-xvi.
36 R. Bancroft, *Articles to be enquired of, in the first Metropolitical Visitation of the Most Reverend Father in God Richard* . . . (1605), p. 15.
37 As will be evident from J. E. Davies, *The Caroline Captivity of the Church: Charles I and the Remoulding of Anglicanism* (Oxford, 1992).
38 A. Fletcher, *The Outbreak of the English Civil War* (London, 1981), pp. 109–20.
39 Julian Davies, 'The Growth and Implementation of "Laudianism" with special reference to the Southern Province' (Oxford University D.Phil. thesis, 1987).
40 Bodl., Tanner MS 65, fo. 179.

Part II

REVISING POLITICS

6

PARLIAMENT IN THE REIGN OF ELIZABETH I

Geoffrey Elton

Best known for his work on early Tudor government and especially the bureaucratic reforms of Thomas Cromwell, Geoffrey Elton has recently turned to the later Tudor period to replace the old view of conflict between the House of Commons and the queen with a drastically revised version. The following essay provides a preview of many of the themes more fully expanded in his latest book, The Parliament of England, 1559–1581. *You will notice as you read it that for political, as for religious, revisionists the move has been away from an understanding of institutions as conflict-ridden and divided along partisan lines. Elton argues that in Parliament, as in the Church, the old thesis of partisan struggle simply will not bear the weight of the evidence. Instead, he finds relative co-operation and consensus within parliament, and between Parliament and the queen. He finds that disagreements are better traced to factions at Court than to parties in the House of Commons or to the Parliament's attempts to expand its power and liberties vis-à-vis the royal prerogative.*

Elton's work on the Elizabethan period has turned the received version on its head and set the stage for a similarly revised view of early Stuart parliaments. While some historians quarrel with elements of his account, they acknowledge that his efforts have 'breathed new life into the putrefying corpse of Elizabethan parliamentary history' and predict that his new synthesis will become 'standard orthodoxy' – with a little further revision.[a]

* * *

It is at present particularly difficult to give an account of the role and history of Parliament in the reign of the first Elizabeth. The last three generations have seen two well-entrenched interpretations shattered, one after the other, and we are still in the process of putting the new insights together.[1] Until about sixty years ago it was generally held that in the sixteenth century Parliament played very little part in a system of government which centred on an exceptionally strong, even autocratic, monarchy. Parliaments were thought of as 'subservient'; the Tudor period supposedly formed an interruption in what was regarded as the normal and proper development of England – the subjugation of the Crown to the representative assembly. As recently as 1964, this medievalists' view, which treated the Tudor age as a retreat from the position achieved under the Lancastrians, could be defended against the newer theories of Parliament's novel political importance in the sixteenth century.[2]

This newer view, although adumbrated already by A. F. Pollard, became dominant through the work of Sir John Neale and was orthodoxy until very recently. Neale believed in a markedly evolutionary scheme for the history of the Tudor Parliament, a progress from underdeveloped beginnings handed on by the Middle Ages to 'maturity' under Elizabeth – maturity in procedure, privilege and political role-playing. To him, the reign of Elizabeth witnessed the rise of the Commons, just in time to get ready for the battle with the Stuart kings. Indeed, he thought he saw Elizabethan rehearsals for that political conflict. Neale discerned an eager interest (which he thought novel, though it existed in the fourteenth century) among the gentry in parliamentary representation; he argued for a steady rise in education, experience and eminence among the members of the Lower House; and he discovered there a powerful group of assertive men, able and willing to challenge the control which the government normally exercised, directly through Privy Councillors and the Speaker and indirectly through the messages and inspired rumours with which the queen tried to suppress unruly thoughts and actions. For these difficult men he identified an ideology: they were Puritans – that is, men anxious for drastic changes in church and religion who used Parliament to promote their ambitions, attacked the queen's policies when these seemed to threaten the future of the reformed faith, and worked in harness with the Puritan clergy outside. Neale thus presented a coherent story of loyalty and conflict expressed in the workings of an institution which both offered opportunity for opposition and, in turn, learned through opposition to develop

claims and machinery to make it effective. Neale's Parliament –
or, rather, his House of Commons – fitted neatly into the
received story of a growth from the supposedly acquiescent
assemblies of Henry VIII's reign to the supposedly recalcitrant
assemblies of the early seventeenth century.

Of this picture and story so little now remains that I must
first emphasize the need to remember that Neale got some
things right. His narrative of parliamentary events is quite often
correct in detail, though often also falsely slanted in interpretation. His analysis of the expansion of constituencies and election disputes appears to be still acceptable. He was also right
in his analysis of knights and burgesses: the reign of Elizabeth
did witness the final culmination of a process by which the
gentry came to take over a proportion of parliamentary seats
four times larger than under the qualifying laws they should
have held, at the expense of genuine townsmen. However, Neale
misunderstood the political consequences of this by ascribing
the growing independence of the Commons to this influx of
men of standing. It is true that the Commons thus acquired a
social homogeneity which made them more representative of
the political nation as a whole, but the gentry did not so much
free the House from outside influence as introduce into it the
politics of the shire and the royal Court – politics themselves
dominated by the nobility also present in the Lords. It was
the normal political involvements of the age that this influx of
gentlemen carried with them, and those politics had little to
do with parliamentary affairs and nothing with institutional
independence.

The work of major revision is still very much proceeding, and
at present no new comprehensive analysis and reconstruction
presents itself for summary. This account, therefore, must to
an extent rest on unfinished and unpublished labours. It may,
however, make the discarding of the old interpretation more
persuasive if reasons can be shown to explain what it was that
put Neale on so wrong a track. At heart he simply accepted a
highly traditional general scheme which read the history of
Parliament as one of conflict between Crown and Commons,
regarded the Commons' role as pertaining solely to the control
of the Crown, and was always aware of the breach of 1640–2,
which was treated as conditioning all that went before and came
after. Neale's originality lay in his fitting the Elizabethan phase

more neatly into this whiggish outline. Yet of late all the components of this hoary myth have been shown up for what they are: a mixture of political conviction and of tendentious misreadings of selected evidence. Since the notion of an independent, anti-government, opposition has had to be abandoned for the reigns of both Mary I and James I,[3] it is the less necessary to look, as Neale did, for an Elizabethan House of Commons which will not disturb the line of development. Directed by prevalent interpretations to a false approach, to which he adhered throughout his life, Neale then found what he was looking for by three heuristic devices which have little virtue in them. He assumed the role of the Upper House, a part of Parliament on which he did no work, to be that of assisting the monarch against a rising House of Commons; once assumed, the point was never investigated. He took over from Wallace Notestein evolutionary theories according to which developments in procedure helped the Commons to freedom from official control, and he added his own mite to all this evolution by treating the Commons Journals as having developed from primitive to accomplished, a view resting on false assumptions and arguments from silence. Lastly, he identified as Puritans and as members of a consistent and cohesive policy-making group a number of men who were neither of these things.

A word is needed to substantiate this critique. Touching the Lords, the record makes it very plain that they were not only an active part of the Parliament, deeply engaged in the work of legislation, but also by no means united and quite capable of going counter to the queen's wishes. It was members of the Upper House who opposed the religious settlements of 1559,[4] and it was the bishops quite as much as ardent Protestants in the Commons who, in the face of Elizabeth's disapproval, kept trying to use statute for the improvement of church and clergy.[5] The social pre-eminence of the peers, and the close relations between noble courtiers and particular men in the Commons, are well documented in the correspondence of the day, though these things still require the sort of study which factional influences have been receiving in the next two reigns.

With respect to the record – Journals and the rest – what we now have is known to lack some material once extant, and Neale introduced a wrong note when he called the Commons Journal of Elizabeth's first two parliaments more primitive than the later ones.[6] He mistook a change of clerk for a significant change in procedure, compared a fair copy with a rough draft, and supposed that recording speeches in the House proved 'maturing' when it is more likely to be connected with Cecil's[b] move into the Lords and his need for written information. The keeping of parliamentary diaries seems to have begun in 1571, the year of the Lord Treasurer's elevation. Those materials, which have never received really critical attention, need to be studied without the tacit conviction that they reflect a growth in the Commons' self-esteem, powers or procedural advance. Indeed, the whole notion that developments in procedure measure a rise in independence has been convincingly demolished:[7] in so far as procedure developed – and the very term is suspect – it did so under the pressure of business and demonstrably on the initiative of the Council, who were forever seeking ways of speeding the handling of bills; for the queen's distaste for parliamentary meetings always threatened premature prorogation or dissolution. In the Lower House, business was managed not only by the Speaker and clerk, with the assistance of Privy Councillors, but also by 'men of business' – that is, men without official positions but active as Council agents. Thomas Norton, famous in his day as a parliamentarian and to Neale a leading Puritan proponent of the Commons' independence, has turned out to be such a conscientious labourer on behalf of Council and Queen.[8]

Furthermore, the whole notion of a Puritan opposition group rested on two unfounded assertions. Neale supposed that in 1559 more extreme Protestants exercised a powerful influence on the Church settlement; however, ingeniously as he argued his case, it has turned out to be contrary to the facts.[9] And a squib of 1566, listing some forty-odd members of the Commons of very varied views but all active in the succession agitation of that year, was read by Neale to comprise a hard-core body of Puritans, so that whenever men there mentioned afterwards occur in the story he smelled out opposition tactics and manoeuvres employed by a Puritan opposition. He employed a circular argument: without good grounds, leading members of the House were identified as Puritans, so that what leading members did became Puritan activities, and when something happened that might be connected with reformist views in religion the notional Puritan group was alleged to be behind it.

In fact, the members of that 'choir' formed no party and few of them were Puritans; the actions and opinions of those supposedly part of it cannot be assessed from that accidental listing.[10]

One example shall be cited to show how preconceived notions misled this historian. Among the bills for religion put up in 1566 there was one for enacting the Thirty-nine Articles. It is agreed that the queen heard that the bishops had been active in promoting it, read the Riot Act to some of them, was assured that those present had not been responsible, and a few days later received a petition from fifteen bishops (including some involved in that audience) asking that the bill be allowed to pass. The obvious, and correct, conclusion is that the original report told something like the truth, though face to face with their angry sovereign the prelates prevaricated a little. Since Neale, however, had convinced himself that the bill came from a Puritan (anti-episcopal) quarter, he ascribed the report of the bishops' initiative to 'some mischief-maker' (unidentified), accepted their denial before the queen, and could offer no explanation for the subsequent petition, which yet he dutifully mentioned. His one footnote reference does not support the crucial details of his reconstruction.[11]

It has been necessary to spend so much time in discussing Neale's work because, expansive and cohesive as it is, it naturally has a firm hold: denying him outright, as I have been obliged to do, will not be acceptable unless reasons are given. Now that the ground is clear, we must see how the next generation of historians is likely to replant it. As has already been made plain, much of what must be said constitutes a preview of work in progress.

The Elizabethan Parliament was in one way a very ancient institution, in another of quite recent origin. As Tudor antiquarians never tired of pointing out, its history vanished into the mists of time, even if they erred in supposing that it had existed from the beginnings of that time. That history is sufficiently continuous from the late thirteenth century onwards, and the Elizabethan Parliament is in some respects identical with its medieval predecessor. On the other hand, the Parliament had undergone something like a transformation roughly between 1484 and 1540, a time during which the two Houses moved from inferiority/superiority to institutional equality, the Crown turned from the owner of a high court into a member of the parliamentary trinity, legislative procedure was settled, statute acquired both omnicompetence and a kind of legal sanctity as the Crown lost the power to amend it unilaterally, and the keeping of records was systematized.[12] In spite of a paucity of records, enough survives to support the conclusion (also reached by Arthur Hall, Elizabethan burgess for Grantham)[13] that the shape of the Elizabethan (and therefore the later) Parliament was effectively established in the long Reformation Parliament of 1529–36. The better documentation of Elizabeth's reign enables us to trace further changes in practices and attitudes, but nothing happened then to justify talk of transformation. For instance, we can be confident that a record was kept in the Commons before the accidental date (1547) from which the Journal now survives. A 'clerk's book' is mentioned authoritatively in an act of 1515, and no one looking at the seemingly scrappy first surviving volume can fail to note the air of established practice that hangs over that record as it registers bill proceedings, licences for absence and orders touching privilege. Though, naturally, the forty-five years and thirteen sessions of the queen's reign do not depict a static condition, the parliaments of 1559 and 1601 are the same sort of institution and do not testify to institutional development. In all that governed their work, their rights and their accepted claims, 'maturity' – as Sir Thomas Smith's description, written in the early 1560s, testifies[14] – had been achieved by the beginning of the reign. Furthermore, the Parliament was an institution, not just a succession of occasions, and this despite the long gaps between meetings and the less than three years altogether in forty-five that it sat. This shows clearly in the regularity of all the arrangements which governed meetings from the opening day to the close, and in the continuity of business across the gaps. It needed only the push of a button – the writs of summons – to activate this institution in full and familiar detail. Routine, not improvization, governed all the meetings of the Parliament, and while the roots of that routine went back into the fourteenth century its Elizabethan form and substance had been shaped by what had happened under Henry VIII.

The Parliament consisted of three parts – prince, Lords and Commons. By 1559, the King-in-Parliament as a sovereign lawmaker had replaced the King's High Court of Parliament. The new concept was first spoken of round about 1530 and had been endorsed by Henry VIII in 1542. Occasionally the older doctrine of three estates assembled in Parliament to assist the prince can be found, but the dominant doctrine, as stated by Lord Burghley himself,[15] identified the three estates with the three parts of the Parliament, jointly able to make laws. In that respect all parts were equal: unless all consented no law could be made. But, of course, equality is not really the right word for a relationship in which one of the partners alone could decide whether and when the partnership should come to life and again retire into a suspended state. At the same time, it should be remembered that the queen did not have total freedom in her role as the convenor and terminator of parliamentary meetings. Since there were things that she could do only in Parliament, she had to call it when she wanted to tax the realm or have new laws for its defence, and since both needs occurred regularly in the reign it would be a mistake to suppose that the sometimes lengthy intermissions signified the possible end of Parliament. No one in this reign considered a government without it.

The possibility was the more remote because in this reign neither Lords nor Commons constituted any sort of threat to the Crown. We have heard so much about the rising power of the Lower House, or alternatively about the political strength collected in the Upper, with its complement of locally dominant men, that it comes as something of a surprise to discover how little real power the Commons especially possessed. By comparison with such late medieval assemblies as those of Aragon or Sicily, or with the contemporary provincial and general States of the Netherlands, the English Parliament – that is, Lords and Commons without the monarch – was really quite weak; more precisely, it was strong, indeed very strong, only when acting in unison, for of its component parts only the Crown had strength of its own. Each House exercised various constitutional powers over its members, and both at times, with limited success, tried to extend these over outsiders, but the reality is well exemplified in the fact that when the Commons, asserting themselves, sent a man to the Tower they could get him out again only by relying on the queen for his release.[16] What from the first marked the Commons in the Long Parliament as so revolutionary was the manner in which they acted on all sorts of issues by their own authority – actions for which there were no precedents at all. In constitutional fact, the Elizabethan Commons were weak, not strong.

Yet that weakness, in its turn, demonstrated the real strength of those parliaments. Since they could not threaten the rule of the monarch even if they had wanted to, they could but be useful to him – and so they were. In the sixteenth century, as it always had been and nearly always was to be in future, Parliament formed a component in the system of government, not an agent outside and possibly in opposition to it. In order to carry out its role in government effectively and usefully it needed management – instruction, guidance, control. After all, when we speak of co-operation between the three parts we really mean co-operation among potentially more than 500 individuals. These individuals' interests might very easily conflict among themselves, and these individuals were liable to hold widely different views on the issues of the day, large or small; if it is wrong to interpret events from the assumption that conflict between Queen and Commons directed them, it would be as wrong to suppose that general agreement came naturally, perhaps by the dispensation of providence. By the reign of Elizabeth, the techniques of management had become well understood – mainly, it would seem, as the result of the feverish activity of the years 1529–59. During those thirty years the Lords and Commons had again and again been involved in the highest of high politics and very explosive issues: of course they had to be guided, and the standards of managerial practice first established by Thomas Cromwell had become routine in the hands of the Privy Council. They included not only the preparation of official bills (though it is an ancient error to suppose that the bulk of public bills came from the Council) and the steering of them, but also the organization of useful patronage and the reasoned persuasion of doubters. No detail could safely be overlooked: thus Francis Bacon was quite right when in 1615 he ascribed recent failures to the incompetence which had started sessions without providing something for members to do apart from voting money.[17] Much depended on councillors' manners: neither Lords nor Commons contained an 'opposition', but both contained (as all of Elizabethan England did) touchy men likely to stand on their dignity. A parliamentary session meant intensive work for the Council, and the brevity of meetings owed something at least to the difficulties they created for men who had to govern the realm, conduct foreign policy, supervise religious conformity, oversee the administration of justice, not to mention lead private lives and run their own affairs, while giving time and thought to the often capricious behaviour of Lords and Commons in Parliament. There has never been a time when the ministers of the Crown have not welcomed the parliamentary recess with sighs of relief; in the reign of Elizabeth such recesses, while very much longer, were equally welcome.

Ordinary members of either House, not compelled by managerial duties to attend with regularity, avoided the burden of attendance with respectable readiness. For the Lords we possess presence lists, and they are revealing. No peer could ignore the summons without permission, but permission was often granted and every session saw the presentation of numerous proxies. However, the purpose and meaning of proxies, never, apparently, used in votes and occasionally entered by peers who attended, remain very obscure. Generally speaking, the spiritual peers[c] proved more conscientious than the temporal. Take the Parliament of 1571, an averagely busy one which sat for just about eight weeks, an averagely normal length of a session.[18] That year the Upper House consisted of 24 spiritual and 64 lay peers, but of the latter three were under age and thus disqualified from sitting. The total, therefore, was 85. On the formal opening day, with the queen present, 59 attended (17 + 42), some of them persons who had given proxies. Just over halfway through the session, on 8 May, when the much contested Treasons Bill was passed, the numbers, though not the people, were still exactly the same. Attrition set in as the session wore on. A week before the close, when pressure of business compelled afternoon sittings, even the bishops' resolution faltered: in the morning of 22 May there were altogether 53 members present (14 + 39), but by the afternoon they had dwindled to 30 (10 + 20). Even the closing day, when the queen again came into the House, could not restore the original zest: though the 18 bishops present formed the largest spiritual contingent of the session, only 33 lay peers bothered to come, the decline being particularly marked in the higher ranks of the peerage.

Nevertheless, proportionately the Lords did much better than the Commons, whose members notoriously included many for whom Parliament time offered the opportunity to come to London on business or pleasure. While we have no attendance lists for the Lower House, we know that it frequently got so seriously depleted that a call was threatened for the next sitting – a roll-call of the membership which involved fines for absentees if fewer than 40 answered it. Our only figures come from the very occasional divisions which, by definition, occurred on contested matters when one would expect attendance to be larger than usual. In 1571 the clerk lets us down completely. The House divided four times in the session but the only figure recorded is a majority of 36 on the first occasion.[19] That clerk's predecessor – damned by Neale as 'more primitive' – kept a more businesslike record, so that we have information for the very active and allegedly very disturbed session of 1566, during which the House also divided four times. On those four days, 160, 133, 136 and 158 of its approximately 400 members were in the House – the last occasion being the vote that dashed the bill for renewing expiring acts, a move that has been read as expressing the resentment of 'the House' at the blocking of 'Puritan' bills in the Lords.[20] Ordinarily, we may well suppose, even fewer members attended.

A thin presence could work both ways. It might easily assist oppositionist moves by real zealots whom one would expect to be more assiduous, but it could also reduce the burden of management. Our patchy evidence gives grounds for thinking that one feature familiar from later days may well already have been characteristic of Commons' debates: it looks as though just about all the talking was done by a hard-core group of regulars among whom the official element – office-holders and men of business – predominated.

Management was not necessarily concerned with assuaging or suppressing opposition; the task of getting the business through could be impeded by much less spectacular difficulties, such as the whims of private members promoting private causes, or those sudden rushes of blood to the head for very small reasons to which the House of Commons has always had an inclination – a not unnatural result, perhaps, of those 'idle heads' (to use Elizabeth's description) in close proximity and only half aware in all that to-and-fro of what was going on.

The chief purpose of management, therefore, was to smooth the paths of legislation – to get bills through and cut down on speeches. The making of acts, or indeed the blocking of undesirable bills, constituted Parliament's chief function in the administrative and social system of England, and every member of the body politic had or could have an interest in what Parliament produced.

The queen's first interest concerned the granting of supply; she sought and obtained subsidies in all but one of her thirteen sessions, and since each grant was always spread over several collecting years few of her years of rule were entirely free of the activities of subsidy commissioners. The conventional notion holds that Parliament's strength, indeed its chance of survival, rested in this power of the purse, but the facts do not fit the theory very well. Subsidies were always forecast in the opening address and always started early in the session. There were certain decencies to be observed. In form, the initiative lay with the Commons and until 1576 the first move there came from some private member, put up for the purpose and backed up by official members who explained the queen's needs. After that date this rather pointless pretence was abandoned in favour of letting the Chancellor of the Exchequer both lay out the necessity and move for a grant. The House then appointed a committee to draw articles and, after these had been reported though rarely debated, to prepare the necessary bill; in fact, the Council was usually ready with the former and commonly with the latter also. Virtually always the bill passed all its stages without trouble, except in 1566 when the subsidy got involved in manoeuvres designed to force the queen to listen to petitions about the uncertain succession. For the years 1559–81, when the survival of the Journal makes it possible to do the calculations, we can say that the bill was not much used to protract the session, nor did its passage immediately lead to the close. Only in 1566, for the reason just stated, did the bill take a long time; usually it passed in anything between two weeks and four, and only in 1563 were there less than two weeks left of the session when the Commons had done with it. The Lords always dispatched it very swiftly. Thus it would not seem to have been the case that the Lower House tactically exploited the queen's needs or that she took care to end the session the minute she had her money. Nor did anyone seriously invoke the famous principle, 'no supply before redress of grievances', which seems to have been quite unknown in the sixteenth century, or indeed later. The one thing that roused the Commons, always aware of the taxpayers back home, was any attempt to enlarge the customary size of the grant, but the war years after 1588 saw ever larger sums voted readily enough. One really cannot tie any sort of constitutional history, touching the rise of the Commons or the weakness of the Crown, to the history of parliamentary taxation in this reign.

Much the largest part of any parliamentary session was occupied with bills intended to become acts, and, though some of them concerned the queen sufficiently to compel her to call Parliament, the bulk came from the country in one way or another. Far more bills were promoted than seems generally realized. The thirteen sessions of the reign passed 433 acts, an average of just over thirty-three – just under two public acts for every private one. Averages mislead because they do not show the legislative slump between 1584 and 1593, both years of active law-making, or the relatively greater number of private acts in the first three sessions of the reign, but they may be used to assess the fact that in every session anything between sixty and eighty additional bills failed to make it to the statute book. A small number passed in one House only to fail in the other, sometimes by formal rejection and sometimes through lack of time; a still smaller number passed both Houses but were vetoed by the queen.[21] A great many received only one reading in either Commons or Lords, mostly the former: this signifies a kind of kite-flying rather than a proposal seriously meant. Bills that failed in one parliament, having yet got some good way towards completion, not infrequently appeared in another and sometimes passed. Two kinds of bills stood the best chance of success: those promoted by the Council, and private bills for individuals.

Bills could start in either House, though more started in the Lower, and there seem to have been few conventions in this matter. Government bills tended to start in whichever House contained the leading manager of the legislative programme; thus Cecil's transformation into Burghley is reflected by the move of the main official measures from the Commons to the Lords in 1571. Only one thing is quite certain: the ancient supposition that in the sixteenth century almost all legislation originated with the government is totally wrong – except perhaps in the age of Thomas Cromwell.

This very general summary is all that in the present state of research, or in the present compass, can usefully be said. It should, however, suffice to indicate the very heavy burden of potential legislation that occupied these parliaments, as well as the very wide range of people or groups of people who sought to tap the legislative authority of Parliament. When a meeting was announced, interests ranging from the Privy Council, through shire and town authorities, economic pressure-groups, reforming lawyers and reforming Protestants, to the heirs of persons attainted, estate-managing landowners and merchants of foreign origin (to name but a selection) prepared their bills for the Parliament, most of which obtained at least one reading. Private bills could take up an inordinate amount of time because both Houses, anxious to prevent fraud or collusion, encouraged parties to appear with their counsel; very soon these investigations, which usually produced a satisfactory settlement, were transferred to the committee for the bill, but the outcome had still to be reported to the House and sometimes led to further argument there. It is no wonder that the Journals of both Houses are essentially registers of bill-proceedings: that was the main business before them and one so crowded and complex that only a careful record could prevent total confusion.

The history of legislation disposes of the view that an ever-likely opposition in or by the Commons was held in check through the Lords and ultimately blocked by the veto. Both these devices of control did occur, but exceedingly rarely. The normal relations over business are not comprehended in a notion of obstreperousness on the one side and supervision on the other; and the vast majority of bills vetoed had nothing to do with the interests of the Crown. Instead we find private promoting-interests clashing with private opponents and the consequent arguments being fought out at every stage of a bill. In the vast majority of cases, the politics of bills and acts were peculiar to those bills and acts; they rose at local or sectional level, not between Parliament and Crown, between Lords and Commons.

It would, however, be wrong to suggest that those who have spread themselves on great principled conflicts between Queen and Commons – on all those occasions of sharp words, ruffled feelings, high-sounding assertions, elegant pacifications – have talked of only imagined things. Conflicts and arguments, even quarrels close to real rifts, do appear in the record, even if they do not signify nearly as much in terms of time spent or passions roused as the standard accounts might lead one to think.

From the first days of the Parliament, in Edward I's day, the writ of summons had always mentioned the need to consult over the affairs of the realm, and matters other than legislation had regularly been thrashed out in those assemblies, though until the Reformation Parliament the usual venue had been in the Lords. The Lord Keeper drew explicit attention to such wider purposes when, in 1559 and 1572, he mentioned the need to settle religion and to deal with Mary, Queen of Scots. Elizabeth, however, faced the problem that on several hotly debated issues she wished to avoid action while other people wished to see it taken; in particular, this applied to the question of her own succession and marriage, but also to the further reform of the Church. Her sister had set a precedent in 1553 when she furiously rebuffed a petition not to marry a foreign prince, but her father's precedents, which had demanded parliamentary initiatives in the attack on Rome and the settlement of the Crown, worked the other way. She therefore worked out what in effect was a new constitutional rule, according to which issues debated in Parliament fell into two categories – matters of the common weal, to be raised by anyone, and matters of state, which could be discussed only if she invited the Parliament to do so. At this level of principle, this rule clashed with the demands made by Paul and Peter Wentworth for full liberty of speech, meaning the right of the Commons, defined (another real innovation) as themselves a council of the realm, to initiate debate on whatever they wished.[22] Even though on occasion other members of the House recalled forty years of active participation in, for instance, religious changes and wondered how the queen could now inhibit them from talking about those things again, the Wentworths' position met with no general acceptance; on the contrary, when Peter made his great plea for free speech in 1576, he was explicitly disavowed. The House took a much more mundane view of what privilege involved; to them privilege meant the right enjoyed by members and their servants to avoid arrest or summons in a private suit. Liberties to them were the technical rights involved in bill-proceedings – freedom to amend any bill even if signed by the queen, or to refuse an invitation to a conference with the Lords touching a bill in the Commons because such an invitation had to come from the House that held the bill. The history of the Commons' privileges in Elizabeth's reign testifies neither to any growth in power nor to the forging of weapons for a fight; it records only the exploitation of immunities against legitimate claims by persons outside, and a sense of self-importance directed against the Lords.

Second, though this is often forgotten, it is obvious that in matters of high policy, as in commonwealth matters, the House of Commons formed no monolithic entity. Parliaments (both Houses) were entirely the proper place for discussing such issues, whether or not one accepted the queen's insistence on royal initiative, but in that arena all sorts of opinions made themselves heard and agreement for or against the official line was rarely complete. The arguments ran between different individuals, not between institutional components of the Parliament. While debate could signify disagreement it did not always mean conflict, least of all conflicts in which 'the House of Commons' as a body attacked the Queen and Council. Parliament existed for, among other things, the airing of opinion – as a sounding-board to assist government, not as an instrument of opposition endeavours to subjugate the Crown – and only total peace, total absence of argument, would have been a cause for disquiet.

It is against this background that the clashes of the reign need to be judged. They arose over religion, the queen's marriage, the safety of the realm, and prerogative practices allegedly harmful to the subject, but there is room here for only a few words on each. In matters of religion it has now been clearly shown that the 1559 settlement took the form intended by Queen and Council; it was not troubled by opposition in the Commons, and opposition in the Lords failed to modify it. Later moves to improve the manners of the clergy, the government of the Church or the piety of the people came from several quarters but quite as much from the bishops as from ardent Protestants dissatisfied with the established order. Thus the religious bills of 1566, revived in 1571, had episcopal support, though most of them failed because the queen, better gauging opinion in the country, regarded them as too likely to disturb the peace. The appearance in the 1570s of 'the platform' – a coherent presbyterian programme for reform of the Church – did produce a Puritan agitation in the country which tried to exploit the occasions of parliamentary meetings (the 1571–2 Admonitions, and Cope's Bill and Book in 1587),[23] but in neither the country nor the Commons could that agitation gain any significant support. A general disquiet over the state of the Church and the threat to the Protestant religion was not the property of Puritans determined to form an opposition in the Commons; it was shared by concerned men in the queen's government, by councillors and bishops, who deplored the queen's own insouciance and expressed their view in Parliament without dreaming of opposition or seeking power for the Lower House, but rather in the hope that such quasi-public pressure might change Elizabeth's refusal to encourage reform.

The agitation over the queen's marriage and the uncertain succession even more clearly demonstrates the real meaning of protest in Parliament. In 1563 and 1566, led by Councillors despairing of any chance of pressing their policy in Council, both Houses were mobilized to urge the queen to act, and the disapproval that expressed itself in the years when Elizabeth seemed likely to marry a French prince was egged on by Court factions opposed to such a marriage. Similarly, the pressure for the executions of Norfolk and the Queen of Scots (1571, 1572, 1587) exhibits not the opposition of religious extremists but a rift within the government itself, as some courtiers and councillors, having failed at Court, tried to use Parliament to press their policies upon the queen. As for prerogative devices resented by those who did not benefit from them, they could indeed rouse majority protests in the Commons but also tended to reveal differences within the normally dominant element of officialdom in either House. In the best-known manifestations of this grievance – the campaign in the 1590s against monopolies[d] – members in the Commons rightly responded to pressure from their constituents (an element in the equation which, though hard to document, should never be forgotten) while the Crown in Parliament stood in some disarray because too many of its agents there profited from the practices attacked.

The Elizabethan Parliament was a working institution engaged in the manufacture of legislation by agreement and in the sorting out of such matters as might cause disagreement. It was dominated by the Queen-in-Council, who guided business in both Houses and only rarely lost control; apparent loss of control either hid covert Council activity against the queen or resulted from factional divisions among those she expected to act in unison. 'Opposition' is the wrong term to employ, and

'Puritan opposition' an even more misleading concept. But all this still needs a lot of working out.

EDITOR'S NOTES

Reprinted in abridged form with the permission of The University of Georgia Press, from *The Reign of Elizabeth I*, ed. Christopher Haigh (Athens, Georgia, 1985).

a J. D. Alsop, 'Reinterpreting the Elizabethan Commons: The Parliamentary Session of 1566', *JBS*, 29 (1990), pp. 216–17.

b William Cecil, Elizabeth's principal secretary and Lord Treasurer, was made Lord Burghley in 1571.

c Bishops and archbishops sitting in the House of Lords.

d A monopoly was a patent granted by the queen to a favoured courtier or sold for revenue; it gave the holder the exclusive right to manufacture or trade in a particular commodity. Many members of the House of Commons, especially in 1597 and 1601, objected to monopolies as a form a indirect taxation; other members, however, had themselves received monopolies for their services to the queen and were thus caught in the middle, ineffective representatives of both their constituents and the queen.

NOTES

1 The present state of the question prohibits much detailed citing of the evidence.

2 J. S. Roskell, 'Perspectives in English Parliamentary History', *Bulletin of the John Rylands Library*, 46 (1964) pp. 448–75.

3 See J. Loach, 'Conservatism and Consent in Parliament, 1547–59', in *The Mid-Tudor Polity c.1540–1560*, ed. J. Loach and R. Tittler (Totowa, N. J., 1980), pp. 9–28; C. Russell, 'Parliamentary History in Perspective, 1604–1629', *History*, 61 (1976), pp. 1–22.

4 N. L. Jones, *Faith by Statute: Parliament and the Settlement of Religion*, Royal Historical Society Studies in History 32 (1982), esp. pp. 99–103, 140–50.

5 G. R. Elton, 'Arthur Hall, Lord Burghley, and the Antiquity of Parliament,' *Studies in Tudor and Stuart Politics and Government* (Cambridge, 1983), III, pp. 177–8.

6 Ibid., pp. 164–7.

7 S. Lambert, 'Procedure in the House of Commons in the Early Stuart Period', *EHR*, 95 (1980), pp. 753–81.

8 M. A. R. Graves, 'Thomas Norton the Parliament Man: An Elizabethan MP', *HJ*, 23 (1980), pp. 17–35.

9 Jones, *Faith by Statute*, esp. pp. 63–9.

10 Cf. Elton, *Studies*, III, p. 176.

11 J. E. Neale, *Elizabeth and her Parliaments*, i, *1559–1581* (New York, 1953), pp. 167–8.

12 Elton, *Studies*, ii, pp. 34, 54–5, and iii, pp. 58–92, 122–33.

13 Ibid., iii, pp. 268–9.

14 Sir Thomas Smith, *De Republica Anglorum*, ed. M. Dewar (Cambridge, 1982), pp. 8, 78–9.

15 Simonds D'Ewes, *The Journals of All the Parliaments during the Reign of Queen Elizabeth* (1682), p. 350.

16 This is what happened to Peter Wentworth in 1576: *Proceedings in the Parliaments of Elizabeth I*, i, *1559–1581*, ed. T. E. Hartley (Leicester, 1981), pp. 476, 491.

17 Bacon on management, in *Letters and Life of Francis Bacon*, ed. J. Spedding (1869) v, pp. 176–91, offers some very revealing Elizabethan comments on Stuart neglect.

18 These calculations are based on *Lords Journal*, i, pp. 667–702.

19 *Commons Journal*, i, pp. 86 (26 Apr), 88 (7 May), 90 (16 and 18 May).

20 Ibid. pp. 78 (30 Nov), 79 (4 and 9 Dec), 81 (24 Dec). Cf. Neale, *Elizabeth I and her Parliaments*, i, pp 168–9. In the Elizabethan system of voting (ayes went forth and noes sat still) abstention was not possible for anyone actually present.

21 In the seven sessions between 1559 and 1581, Elizabeth vetoed thirty-four bills, of which at most four seem to concern the prerogative (Elton, *Studies*, iii, p. 180).

22 Neale, *Elizabeth I and her Parliaments*, i, pp. 152, 318–34.

23 P. Collinson, *The Elizabethan Puritan Movement* (Berkeley, 1967), pp. 118–21, 307–15. Influenced by Neale, Professor Collinson rather overstates the brief success of Cope's move in 1587, but even so its real futility comes across.

7

ENGLAND IN 1637

Conrad Russell

Revisionist studies of early Stuart parliaments, like Elton's of Eliza-
beth's parliaments, suggest that a majority of members tended to be
'neutrals' on issues of high policy, preferring to focus their attention
on regional interests and to avoid conflict. Beyond John Pym's small
circle, moreover, they did not particularly want to increase the power
of Parliament in relation to the king. Conrad Russell's very important
examination of the 1620s parliaments (Parliaments and English
Politics 1621–1629, 1979) *did find plenty of complaint – that being*
one of the proper functions of parliaments – but he argued in that
book *that the difficulties of the early Stuart kings were not so much*
with *their parliaments as* reflected in *them. The first two Stuarts*
suffered from very real problems, among them inadequate revenue,
ineffective local administration of what revenue there was, and the
inability of unpaid voluntary provincial officials to conscript an army
of their neighbours. None of these problems, however, were created by
Parliament. Even in the areas of revenue, while parliaments voted
subsidies, local governors were responsible for assessment and collec-
tion. Parliaments simply discussed and complained about the problems
of the Crown.

Despite this complaint, Russell found that relations between the
Crown and the parliaments of 1621 and 1624 were fundamentally
good. Only when the demands of war combined with religious fears
in the latter half of the decade did relations deteriorate, and even at that
point, the disagreement was not ideological, but practical. Members of
Parliament in the 1620s evinced no desire to increase the power
of Parliament vis-à-vis the Crown; they simply did not wish to finance
the war with Spain upon which they themselves had insisted in 1624.
Charles would proceed to do so without parliament by means of a
Forced Loan and Ship Money – extraparliamentary levies offensive to

the traditional privileges of both the gentlemen sitting in Parliament and their constituents in the provinces, but necessary to finance the war.

Russell's more recent work builds on these conclusions about the 1620s and seeks to identify other causes of the Civil War than constitutional theory and long-term ideological conflict between King and Parliament. His focus remains instead on long-term structural weaknesses in the bureaucratic and financial resources of the Crown – weaknesses that a foreign war would bring to the point of functional breakdown. Inadequate revenue and military need remained the central problem of Charles I in an era of inflation and a very expensive 'military revolution'. With war conducted on a larger scale and with more sophisticated technology than before, the pressure on England's tax base of a foreign war – on the Continent in the 1620s, and then against Scottish and Irish rebels from the end of the 1630s – would prove the bane of Stuart monarchy. Had Charles not ruled a multiple kingdom, two components of which rose in rebellion when he could least afford it, he would presumably not have needed to summon a parliament in 1640, and the crisis of 1642 may have been averted.

These problems were further exacerbated by Charles's divisive religious policy, which, as Tyacke argued earlier, was perceived as innovative, 'popish', and too rigorously enforced. Still, religion alone would not have brought England to war. In Russell's view, a constellation of contingencies coming together only in the later 1630s was required for war to break out in 1642. In the first of the following essays, Russell argues that England in 1637 was 'a country in working order'; far from a high road to civil war, the history of the 1620s and 1630s had tended in the opposite direction, and co-operation between King and counties was the hallmark of the 1630s, when there was external peace and no parliament. He finds that the political nation was not profoundly alienated from the Crown until the Scottish troubles broke out in 1637.

* * *

'None could expect a Parliament, but on some great necessity not now imaginable.'[1] These words are Sir Roger Twysden's summary of the views of some Kentish gentry on the likely consequences of a victory for the king in the Ship Money trial. They are, among other things, a clear example of the indifference to matters British which left the English gentry to be so often caught by surprise in the long crisis in British relations which ran from 1637 to 1707. Yet they are also an accurate assessment of the situation in England in the summer of 1637: England in 1637 was a country in working order, and was not on the edge of revolution.

Twysden's judgement is one which seems in 1637 to have been generally shared. The massive collection of *State Papers, Domestic* is not the record of a regime which believe it was sitting on a powder-keg: there are frequent irritations at foot-dragging over Ship Money, or at the tedious behaviour of the godly, but there seems to be little sense that this represented more than the trials of a busy man's existence. The Earl of Salisbury was taking advantage of a period between wars, when his duties as Lord-Lieutenant were less onerous, to sort and catalogue his pictures.[2]

In local government, the Crown was still receiving the necessary minimum of co-operation even from some of the most alienated of the gentry. The appointment of Oliver Cromwell as a JP[a] for the Isle of Ely on 20 July 1638, coming as it did in the middle of the purge of the Bench over the issue of Ship Money, seems to be sufficient evidence that he paid his Ship Money.[3] In continuing to co-operate, Cromwell was only taking the same line as most of those who were the king's leading opponents five years later. The names of Pym, Hampden, Warwick, Earle, Harley, Barrington and Masham are enough to sustain the point. In the absence of a parliament, a pretender, or a foreign army, there was very little even the most alienated gentleman could do about his discontent. He could tear up his roots and emigrate, yet it is noteworthy that Winthrop[b] seems to have been almost the only man of JP status who did so. He could retire to his country house and withdraw into his library or the hunting field, but in so doing, he would forfeit any influence he might exert, and also any chance he might have of securing a favourable deal next time he was bothered by a Ship Money assessment or a metropolitical visitation. This was a sensible course only for those who had very little to lose, and few gentlemen believed themselves to come into that category. Rebellion, apart from the fact that it was well known to be a sin, was not a practical option. To have any chance of success, it needed more co-ordination before the undertaking than it was safe to risk. Moreover, in the absence of any pretender to the throne, it was a major problem, and one never solved, what any rebellion would do in the event of success. More alarmingly, rebellion without a proper legal title would create a general threat to property of a sort no gentleman was likely to welcome. Popular riots, if they occurred without gentry support, were likely to be limited and local and easily put down. Even a parliament, as was shown in May 1640, had a limited power to challenge the king while it could exist for no longer than he found it useful. From the failure of the Pilgrimage of Grace[c] onwards, the Crown was never successfully challenged without one of two things: a pretender to the throne, or a foreign army. Charles I put a great deal of skill into avoiding the first of these, but was less success-ful with the second.

This discussion is in the strictest degree hypothetical, and designed only to argue that a zealous resort to 'revolution' was not practical politics. There is very little evidence in 1637 that any significant body of the king's subjects would have wanted to resort to revolution if it had been a practical possibility. Many were offended, often deeply offended, by a number of things the king was doing, but the history of the past century had shown that rebellion was not the cleverest way to tackle these things. Wyatt's rebels[d] had done far less for the survival of Protestantism than William Cecil had, and the Gunpowder Plot-ters[e] had done far less for the survival of Catholicism than the Earl of Northampton or Secretary Calvert.[f] It was a lesson well learnt that a voice at the centre of power was a more effective way to support any cause than futile demonstrations of armed resistance. If such a man as the Earl of Essex ever doubted this, he only needed to remember the fate of his father in 1601.[g]

For those who wished to approach the centre of power in order to influence the king in a different direction, the road was still open. Charles I's Court and Council, for all the rude things which have been said about them, were not mere mirrors to the king's ideas. Men who disagreed with the king's approach, both to questions of politics and to questions of religion, were still able to obtain positions which brought them very near to the centre of influence. The Court in 1637 was no more united in subservience to Charles than the country was united in oppo-sition to him. As Professor Zagorin pointed out, the politics of 1640 to 1642 were not a confrontation between a monolithic court and a monolithic country.[4] Anyone who tries to treat them as one is likely to find them entirely unintelligible.

No one better symbolizes this point than the Earl of Holland. As Groom of the Stool he held the key office in the Bedchamber, giving him more constant and confidential access to the king's person than was enjoyed by any other courtier. Yet, at the same time, Holland as Governor of the Providence Company was acting as leader and patron for a group including such people as his brother Warwick, Saye, Brooke and Pym, many of whom were willing to contemplate emigration rather than come to terms with the king's ecclesiastical policy. For Holland, who was a believer in reconciliation, consensus and freedom of information, there was no apparent inconsistency in these positions. When he was ultimately forced to choose, it was not the king's service which he chose. His case alone should go a long way to show that Charles was not gathering a one-party court.

The case of Holland is not unique. Among the great courtiers who attended the king on state occasions, Pembroke Lord Chamberlain and Hamilton Master of the Horse rank close behind Holland. Neither consistently backed the royal line, and both influenced the king regularly in the direction of reconciliation. The picture is similar in other ceremonial functions. The Chancellor of the Order of the Garter Sir Thomas Roe gave so many perceptive warnings of impending trouble that he deserves to be known as the Stuarts' Greek chorus. Those who held the ceremonial offices at the Garter feasts of 1638 and 1640, though they included hardliners, also included the Earls of Bedford, Essex and Hertford, or, in other words, 25 per cent of the signatories of the Petition of the Twelve Peers which called for a parliament in August 1640. The Gentlemen of the Privy Chamber included, in addition to hardliners like Kynaston and Killigrew, Bedford's son Francis Russell. They also included such unexpected figures as William Coryton, a prominent participant in the tumult in the House of Commons in 1629, and John Crew, later chairman of the Long Parliament's committee on religion.[5] Even the court masques, which used to be presented as the epitome of courtly isolationism, brought together people who would be on different sides in the great divisions of 1640 and 1642. The performance of *Britannia Triumphans* on Sunday after Twelfth Night in 1637 included two of Bedford's sons among the performers as well as the future parliamentarian peer Lord Wharton.

It was not only in ceremonial positions that Charles was capable of selecting people from all round the political spectrum. In 1637, as much as in 1627, Charles still had moderate Councillors, and was capable of engaging in dialogue with them. Among those who had been conspicuous in the moderate faction on the legal issues raised by the Forced Loan, Lord Keeper Coventry, Secretary Coke and the Earl of Manchester were still there in 1637.[6] Sympathy both for Calvinism and for parliaments could be found among newly elevated Councillors too. The Earl of Salisbury in 1636 insisted that his sons spend a season in Geneva 'for the exercise of their religion', and what they learnt there can hardly have been pleasing to Charles.[7]

Whatever may have been wrong about Charles's ability to take counsel (and something clearly was wrong), it was not that he was unable to take advice from those who disagreed with him. He knew that this was one of the things a good king was supposed to do, and he knew, too, that a good king was sometimes supposed to concede to the advice of his councillors. Charles did in fact make major decisions against his own inclination and as a result of the persuasion of his Councillors. The decision to call a parliament in 1628, the Pacification of Berwick in 1639, and the decision to call the Short Parliament in 1640 are all cases in point. Yet what seems to have happened when Charles took the advice of his moderate Councillors is a policy less successful than either he or they would have followed in isolation. This seems to be, in each of these three cases, because Charles did not see (or chose not to see) that the policy being urged on him was not a policy viable in isolation, but part of a wider reversal of policy which he was not prepared to adopt. The assemblies of Parliament in 1628 and 1640 were only sensible proposals if the king would let them at least discuss grievances before insisting on supply, and the Pacification of Berwick was only a viable policy if Charles would let the Scots abolish episcopacy. In none of these cases was Charles willing to make the concession of substance implied by his concession of form, and the result was a policy unsuccessful because inconsistent. Much of the tortuousness which makes Charles's policies so difficult to follow is the result of this sort of unsuccessful dialogue between him and his moderate Councillors. Meanwhile, however, the fact that such reversals happened encouraged those who believed that the insider's route to political change was the right one.

There is very little sign in 1637 that those who were to be on opposite sides in 1642 were divided by any social issues. The two biggest causes of social discontent in the 1630s, forest clearance and fen drainage, were ones which pitted rural protestors against those who were to be the leaders of both sides in the Civil War.[8] One of the Crown's most active agents in forest clearance was John Pym, and one of its leading partners in fen drainage was the Earl of Bedford. The Book of Orders, the main social policy of the Caroline government, seems to have done more to unite the Crown and the godly gentry than to divide them. Its leading draftsman, the Earl of Manchester, was a future parliamentarian.[9] It makes a number of important points about English history that the reason why the Long Parliament's plague orders of 1641 so closely follow the Privy Council's Book of Orders is that both were drafted by the same man: the Earl of Manchester.[10] These things are much more typical than Oliver Cromwell's somewhat lonely championship of the fenmen against drainage schemes. Neither the history of the 1630s nor the history of the Long Parliament give us any good reason to suppose that social issues were any significant part of the causes that divided the gentry. They were, it seems, a rare example of something the Civil War was clearly not about.

Superficially, then, England in 1637 was still in the age before party politics. Divisions of opinion, however profound, separated people and not institutions, and most criticism, however heated, was still being absorbed within the political system. Yet, though England was not on the edge of revolution, it was a body politic subject to many visible signs of strain. Whenever the king was forced to make a major and unexpected demand on his subjects' goodwill, these strains were capable of becoming very serious indeed. Kings had always had to bargain with their subjects when they wanted exceptional political favours from them, and it was perfectly possible in 1637 for an informed observer to predict that the next bargain was likely to be a very hard one.

In any such bargain, Ship Money was almost certain to become one of the items of negotiation. If for no other reason, this would have been true because of the sheer financial weight of Ship Money, which came to something in the region of three subsidies every year except 1638. As Sir Roger Twysden wrote, 'the common sort of people are sensible of no loss of liberty so much as that which hath joined with it a parting from money'.

Ship Money highlighted two serious and related issues. One was the breakdown of the principle of government by consent, 'the crossing of known maxims of law, of which they held this the chiefe, that a king of England could lay no taxe but by Parliament'.[11] The other was a growing gap between the maximum weight of taxation the king's subjects were likely to consent to and the minimum sum on which a king could preserve solvency and national security. The case for arguing that the king needed to be able to put out a fleet capable of matching the French or the Dutch was one which those who had reproved him for unpreparedness in 1626 could not easily answer. Such a fleet was unlikely to be financed for much less than £200,000 a year, if something was allowed for rigging, victualling, repairs, and other incidental expenses.[12] Yet the maximum amount of subsidies the king could expect on a regular basis in peacetime, assuming compliant and well-satisfied parliaments, may perhaps have been a third of this, and on this sum, there would be many other calls as well. The critics of Ship Money were as likely as anyone else to reproach Charles for neglecting the defence of the kingdom, and Charles was entitled to ask them, as he did after the Short Parliament, in what form they were likely to give their consent. The answer seems to have been none, and it was an answer from which Charles was entitled to draw his own conclusions.[13]

Meanwhile Ship Money was causing a series of administrative difficulties which fill the pages of the *State Papers, Domestic* for 1637–8. It has been pointed out that the vast majority of the protests about Ship Money concentrate on technical issues of rating and assessment.[14] Even if these issues were no more than what they appear to be, they were serious enough. Rating was the Achilles heel of the English taxation system, and was already full of ambiguities and inconsistencies. Some counties, like Devon, had an ancient rate which apportioned any new levy in fixed proportions between the hundreds and parishes of the county. Such rates of course became out of date through the increasing prosperity of some parishes and the decreasing prosperity of others,[15] though, as with modern rating evaluations, we hear much more from those suffering increasing poverty than from those suffering increasing prosperity. It was a regular county convention that rising reassessments, like taxes, were decided by consent, and that the JPs in quarter sessions were the proper body to give consent. The procedure for Ship Money contained a further assault on government by consent, beyond that implied in its very existence, in the fact that the rates were to be fixed, not by the justices in quarter sessions, or by sworn local jurors, but by the sheriff, acting arbitrarily and alone.[16]

There were other points of strain and ambiguity in the rating system. There was a great deal of doubt, inadequately resolved by the 1633 resolutions of the judges, about whether rates should be assessed in proportion to the area of land held or to its value.[17] Where a county-wide rate was being imposed for a new levy, there was dispute which of the county rates should be used as the basis for calculation. The subsidy rate, the poor rate and the purveyance rate[h] were all used, at different times and places, as a basis of calculation.[18] Since the sums were large and a change in the basis of assessment could mean a considerable alteration in the amount paid, the temptation to argue about rating and assessment was considerable. The inhabitants of Tiverton also attempted to bargain, arguing that they would pay their Ship Money when they were repaid the money due to them for billeting rates[i] for 1627–8.[19] In Middlesex, Chelsea protested at being rated equally with Acton, though it paid less for the subsidy. The sheriffs replied saying Chelsea ought to pay more than it did for the subsidy because it had so many peeresses, who were assessed separately for the subsidy.[20] In Cambridge, the town complained that it found it hard to meet its assessment because so many people were getting exemption as privileged persons of the University. The Council, ever willing to oblige, then tried to assess privileged persons of the University, only to receive an outraged defence of the liberties of the University from the Laudian Vice-Chancellor.[21] The scope for such arguments was almost infinite: such questions as whether the Hundred of Bath Forum should be assessed with Bath or with Somerset provided scope for endless ingenuity. The game was one which any Stuart could play: anyone who sees Ship Money refusal as a 'county' cause should remember the instruction to distrain on Ship Money refusers living in Windsor Castle.[22] Other assessments which were unquestionably legal created lengthy rating disputes: the plague rate, though imposed by the legally impeccable method of a parliamentary statute, led to many protests and disputes, while the attempts to raise rates for the repair of Fisherton Anger bridge may have made the assize judges feel that the place was sadly appropriately named.[23] It is possible, if no legal issue had arisen, that these rating disputes could have crippled the service.

As Dr Morrill and Dr Sharpe have pointed out, the vast majority of known protests about Ship Money concentrate on these issues of rating and assessment.[24] It cannot be presumed that rating disputes cloak legal objections to the payment of Ship Money, since some were patently made by people who fully accepted the legal principles of the levy. Yet, granted the silence, we are left with the central question of the 1630s: what weight can be placed on the *argumentum ex silentio?* Dr Lake has argued that our sources are the wrong place to look if we want to find objections of constitutional principle: the vast majority of them, coming as they do from the *State Papers, Domestic*, are documents addressed to the Privy Council and its associates.[25] These are not the places to look for what the Council would have taken for seditious words: it was far better to play according to rules the Council itself accepted, under which petitioners might actually win some relief from their burdens.

It is also very doubtful how far people felt free to express their feelings even in the most private of letters. The number of letters in which the writer says he will not express himself freely for fear the letter might fall into the wrong hands is beyond count.[26] This is not necessarily a fear of deliberate interception, though the list of letters now surviving in *State Papers, Domestic* is sufficient proof that such interception might take place. It is much more a fear of accidents to an undeveloped postal system. Even where there was no fear of interception, good manners often dictated a restraint in letters which was not needed in more impersonal public pronouncements. Viscount Saye and Sele, for example, was not one of the most mealy-mouthed seventeenth-century Englishmen, yet the letters he wrote to the Marquess of Hamilton during 1641–2 are much less freely expressed than his parliamentary speeches during the same period.[27] The convention of free speech in Parliament did matter, and if we want to know what a man really thought, his parliamentary speeches may be a better guide than even the most private of his letters.

When we find those objectors to their Ship Money assessments including such stalwarts of the 1628 Parliament as Sir Robert Phelips and Walter Long, we should not assume that they had forgotten all the things they said in Parliament because it was not at that time expedient to repeat them.[28] It is the balance of probability that these people, at least, objected to Ship Money because they saw it as an arbitrary and illegal tax imposed without consent in Parliament. When we find the comparatively short list of outright refusers including other parliamentary stalwarts such as Sir Francis Seymour,[29] their actions are so clearly consistent with the views they expressed in public both before and after that it would be a perverse use of the *argumentum ex silentio* to argue that their convictions went into an eleven-year abeyance.[j]

The depth of English attachment to the principle of taxation by consent is clear in the views of the only twelve people in England able to discuss Ship Money freely and in public: the judges. These were, from the king's point of view, a hand-picked sample: he or his father had appointed all of them, and some influence was brought to bear on them during the trial. Yet even in this sample, five out of twelve did not uphold his case. Even in the judgements of those who judged for the king, there are a number of ideas which show the depth of attachment to the notion of taxation by consent and to parliamentary statute as the ultimate source of law. There are, it is true, numerous high-flown and provocative utterances as well, especially Finch's claim that the right to levy Ship Money was something which no Act of Parliament could take away.[30] Yet their principle argument, that in cases of necessity law could be overridden, was one which, in its proper context, their opponents accepted. In cases such as the outbreak of fire, they admitted the principle to be valid. Berkeley and the others also devoted great effort to arguing that Ship Money was legal *because* it was not a tax: the effort put into trying to prove that Ship Money was a form of conscription and not of taxation shows the need to offer at least a powerful lip-service to the principle of taxation by consent.[31] The Ship Money judgements suggest, among much else, that the notion of parliaments as the ultimate source of law was so deeply settled in legal thinking that it was going to take a very long time without parliaments to get it out. All this argument was conducted before a packed courtroom, in which Oliver St John's arguments against Ship Money were applauded by the crowd.[32] It is not to be imagined that such discussion did not continue outside the walls of the courtroom.

We get occasional tantalizing hints of such debate. At Kilsby, Northamptonshire, the vicar took instructions to preach obedience seriously, only to find that he had turned the church into a debating society. On one occasion, 'when I exhorted the people to pay his Majesty's dues', the vicar said they owed both suit and service, only to be told from the congregation that Ship Money was neither 'which did not a little harm in the country'. He was left to face the parish constable saying that the king's taxes were more intolerable than Pharaoh's on the Israelites.[33] Dr Fincham has made the most valuable contribution to the debate on public reactions to Ship Money: he has saved us from discussions of the *argumentum ex silentio* by penetrating the wall of silence. The extract he has published from the commonplace book of Sir Roger Twysden shows us the debate on Ship Money as conducted by the Kentish gentry. As a sample, the Kentish gentry, and particularly Twysden's friends among them, may be unusual in their scholarship, but there is no reason to think them unusual in the depth of their convictions.

The Kentish gentry seem to have agreed that 'this was the greatest cause according to the general opinion of the world was ever heard out of parlyament in England'. Perhaps the most significant conclusion from Twysden's report was that what took place was not a universal protest, but a *debate*. Some, he reported, said that 'the king had full right to impose it, and all concluded that if a kingdom were in jeopardy it ought not to be lost for want of money if it were within it, which these men sayd wee were to beleeve the king affirming'. As his words suggest, Twysden was not one of 'these men'.

That Twysden became a Ship Money refuser will cause little surprise to readers of his commonplace book. What may cause more surprise is that by March 1642, he had also become one of the key figures in the group which became the Kentish royalist party. In following this course, Twysden was by no means alone. The Ship Money refusers included Sir Francis Seymour; the Earl of Peterborough, an ex-Catholic; and Sir Marmaduke Langdale, a Catholic who was to command a wing of the king's cavalry at Naseby.[34] Opposition to Ship Money seems to have been a cause which united most of the English gentry, rather than dividing them, and belief in the rule of law, taxation by consent, and future meetings of Parliament, however passionately held, are not necessarily marks of a future parliamentarian. It is, after all, hard to see how a principled attachment to legality can explain a decision to undertake the ultimate illegality of fighting a war against the king.

Probably most Englishmen looked forward to a time when there might be another parliament. Garrad, Lord Deputy Wentworth's newsletter-writer, took the chance, when sending him good wishes for his Irish Parliament in 1634, to add: 'I wish as heartily to see an happy one in England.' The king, on the other hand, was much less encouraging when he wrote to Wentworth about his Irish Parliament: he said: 'as for that hidra, take good heed; for you know, that here I have found it as well cunning, as malitious'.[35] This passage seems to express a settled hostility, but one based on political, rather than constitutional, objections.

These were serious tensions, but ones whose resolution was not beyond all conjecture. They are not necessarily marks of impending catastrophe, though they did mean that the next parliament, whenever it might come, was likely to be an unusually difficult one. For Charles, any restoration of trust would have had to include a new-found willingness to supply him with adequate finance, and before that could happen, the English gentry would need to go through a financial education. Had Charles seen Sir Roger Twysden's commonplace book, the passage which would, perhaps, have made the deepest impression on him was the assertion that it was possible to defray the charges of a navy for £30,000 a year.[36] This statement is a mark of either strategic or financial illiteracy. £30,000 a year, it is true, was the amount of the ordinary estimate for the navy, but this would suffice only to keep the navy in port and to send out a few ships for a guard. To those who believed, as most of the gentry probably did, that the English navy should be capable of matching the continental navies, such a sum was laughably small.

Yet financial education, difficult though it may be, is easier than theological conversion. Charles had more chance of making his peace with gentlemen who believed Ship Money merely represented the insolence of office than he had of making his peace with those who believed, like the author of an anonymous squib of 1639, that Ship Money was wanted for the setting up of idolatry.[37] This was a crudely parodied form of the thesis which had been developed by Pym, Rous and Rudyerd at the end of the 1620s. The key to this thesis was that the king, or some of those about him, wished to dispense with parliaments because they were an obstacle to a plan to alter the country's religion. As Rous had put it in 1629, the object of these people was 'to set a distaste between prince and people, or to find out some other way of supply to avoid or break Parliaments, that so they may break in upon our religion, and bring in their own errors'.[38] The statement that Ship Money was wanted for the setting up of idolatry is a good caricature of this position. For those who thought this way, something more than a mere reaffirmation of the law was needed. For them, there would be no security for property, any more than for religion, until the theological tendencies associated with the name of Laud had been removed from the king's counsels. By the middle 1630s, this way of thought was widely disseminated. In 1636 one Raphael Britten of Olney, lace-buyer, was repeating a rumour that the king had fallen out with Laud, and there would be a parliament. He added that Laud was a papist, and there was no need to read the Book of Sports in favour of Sunday recreations. In his mind, at least, the indissoluble association between religious and constitutional change was firmly established.[39]

The chief justification for this view was the fact that Charles had changed the Church of England in a way many in his parliaments found profoundly uncongenial. If Arminian clergy feared the prospect of a future parliament, they had every excuse for doing so, since they were often threatened with one. That Charles's church was profoundly different from James's is a case which it is fortunately unnecessary to argue here, since Dr Tyacke and Dr Lake have argued the case fully and convincingly.[40] In transferring dominance in the Church from Calvinists to Arminians, Charles operated under a Declaration of December 1628, forbidding controversy, confirming the 'literal and grammatical sense' of the Thirty-nine Articles, and, 'out of our princely care that the churchmen may do the work which is proper unto them', putting into the hands of the bishops and clergy in convocation the power to 'do all such things, as being made plain by them, and assented unto by us, shall concern the settled continuance of the doctrine and discipline of the church of England'. Meanwhile, these 'curious and unhappy differences' were to be 'shut up in God's promises', and not openly discussed.[41] This Declaration is sometimes ignorantly discussed as if it were an exercise in impartiality. The assertion that it was not does not merely depend on the way it was administered, though a case may easily be based on that.

As Bishop Davenant discovered in 1629, when he preached before the king what he believed to be 'the received doctrine of our church established in the 17th article' on predestination, the most controversial thing about this Declaration was its assessment of what was controversial.[42] To a Calvinist, speaking from a position of established dominance, predestination did not appear controversial. It was the Arminians, coming from behind, who benefited from a ruling regarding these questions as controversial. Moreover, the questions which were not to be discussed were ones an Arminian could safely regard as peripheral: it was no great hardship to most of them to do what they were in any case inclined to do, and move other questions into the centre of debate. To one of the firmer Calvinists, on the other hand, this Declaration was tantamount to a command not to preach the gospel of salvation, and that was a command no Christian preacher could obey without sin. For some of them, a command not to preach Christ crucified would hardly have been a more severe restriction.[43]

Charles's Declaration also conferred the power to interpret the Thirty-nine Articles on the bishops and clergy in Convocation, that is to say, on a body whose upper ranks were handpicked by himself. This was, in effect, to confer the power to interpret the Thirty-nine Articles on the Arminians. In conferring a power to take enforceable religious decisions on the clergy alone, the Declaration also offended many of the deepest prejudices of English lawyers and gentry, including many, such as John Selden, who could not by any stretch of the imagination be classified as Calvinists. The century after the Reformation was an anxious one for gentry, facing constant changes in the list of things they could not do or say without offence. One of the reactions to this anxiety was a growing stress on a creed which went back to Christopher St German, that the clergy had no legislative power, and nothing could be enforced on the laity but what had received general assent in Parliament. Edward Littleton, later Charles's Lord Keeper, said in the Parliament of 1629 that 'the convocation house hath noe power to make any cannon of the church or to put it upon the state but by the assent of the state, what the convocation house hath made for a cannon hath beene rejected by the Parliament'.[44] This Erastian, parliamentary version of the Royal Supremacy seems to have grown in popularity during the 1630s. This dislike of clerical attempts to impose new things on the laity deprived Charles and Laud of the support of many who were no friends to Calvinism, and also meant that any future parliamentary battle to abolish Arminianism was likely to become merged in a struggle to impose parliamentary limitations on the Convocation and the Royal Supremacy. It was thus likely to come into the area where Charles was least flexible: the area where his religious convictions and his sense of his 'authority' merged.

Among Calvinists, there was a considerable difference in their reactions to the changes of the 1630s. It may safely be assumed that none of them liked these changes, but there seems to have been a considerable difference between those who regarded them as antichristian and those who merely regarded them as undesirable. Those in the second category seem to have been able to remain in attendance on Charles. For those in the first category, there was nothing necessarily new about a gulf between them and the ecclesiastical authorities. On the other hand, the gulf which separated them from Charles and Laud was a great deal wider than any previous gulf. It was also a gulf of a different order. This fact follows from the doctrine of the marks of the true church. The Thirty-nine Articles, which on this point follow Calvin exactly, set out that

> the visible church of Christ is a congregation of faithful men, in the which the pure word of God is preached, and the sacraments be duly ministered according to Christ's ordinance in all those things that of necessity are requisite to the same.[45]

For those who followed Calvin, so long as they could find these two things in their church, it was their duty to remain within it without separation. No matter what else they might find wrong in the church, it was theirs, and they had a duty to belong to it. Even if they could only find these things in some part of their church, it was their duty to attend and worship in that part of it. Failure to do so was schism, which was only a slightly lesser sin than heresy.

On the other hand, if they could not find these two things, the church to which they belonged was no true church, and it was their duty not to worship in it. Until the 1630s most had been able to find them without too much difficulty. In and after the 1630s it was rapidly becoming a very different matter. For many Calvinists, the preaching of the pure Word of God was very nearly a synonym for predestination. For Henry Burton, for example, the fundamentals of true Protestantism were 'predestination, election, freewill [sic] justification, faith, perseverance in saving grace, certainty of salvation, and the like'.[46] None of these could he find anywhere where Charles's Declaration was duly observed, so he was reduced to finding the Church of England in those unobserved corners where it was not. The sacraments duly administered, for many, could not be found anywhere where there was an altar, since an altar by definition implied a sacrifice, and therefore some change in the consecrated elements. For many, of whom Pym was the most prominent, bowing to the altar compounded this particular felony by introducing an element of worship of the altar. Worship of any created thing was idolatry. In the debate on the Grand Remonstrance, Pym said that 'altar-worship is idolatry, and that was injoyned by the bishopps in all there cathedrals'.

Sir Robert Harley, whose household prayed for the conversion of the queen and against Arminianism, seems to have been another of the same stamp.[47] Such people were opposed to the Crown in a sense in which almost no Jacobean gentleman had been. They enjoyed national, as well as county-wide, contact with each other, and came regularly to each other's support. In fact, by 1640 they had come to constitute something very close to a party. As such, in a society most of which still hoped to restore consensus, they could enjoy an advantage out of all proportion to their numbers. This was not only because, both in England and in Scotland, their congregations could help to get them ready and organized first. It was also because the political fixers, the Vanes, Hamiltons and Hollands, would make big sacrifices in the hope of reuniting them with the political community and eradicating their party, and therefore potentially disloyal, character. In 1640 it was not necessarily too late for this technique to be practical, but it was a great deal harder to use than it would have been eleven years earlier.

This unwillingness to compromise was fuelled, for many of the godly, by the sense that they, and not their opponents, were the truly orthodox and conformable part of the Church of England. In 1639 one of the Oxford proctors replied to an instruction to bow to the altar, professing his conformity, and asking, if anything 'besides what is established' were to be required of him, for an explicit order from Laud.[48] He was in the right of it: the argument for conformity to established practice worked neither for Laud nor for his opponents.[49] Much of what Laud was requiring was genuinely novel. A correspondent of John Winthrop's, reporting deprivations in East Anglia, distinguished perceptively (and honestly) between deprivations according to the 'new conformity' and deprivations according to the 'old conformity'.[50]

There is a small but persistent undercurrent in the seditious words of the 1630s charging Laud, and sometimes Charles also, with popery. It is so patently clear that Charles and Laud were not papists that modern readers have been unable to take this charge seriously. Yet it is possible that this failure is because we have not quite understood what was being said: 'popery', as much as 'Puritanism', may be in the eye of the beholder. Both were terms of abuse, and both might vary in meaning according to the prejudices of the abuser. In the mouth of a man like Sir Francis Seymour, a charge of 'popery' is straightforward: it means, as it does now, a simple, plain adherence to the Church of Rome. By this definition, Laud was no papist, and it is worth nothing that those who used this definition did not accuse him of being one. For others, the word had subtler meanings. For them, the real challenge was to understand the force of sin which had led most of the western world into apostasy for several centuries. They were always trying to identify the sins, and the spiritual principles, which had proved powerful enough to tempt so much of the world from its allegiance. It was these underlying spiritual principles which constituted the true forbidden fruit of popery.[51] For many, it seems that the Arminian belief that a man might do something to be saved seemed to be the true popish principle on which the apostasy had been based. When Sir Thomas Roe referred to the Palatinate as 'the only clear Protestant church of Germany', what he meant was that it was the only clearly Calvinist church of Germany.[52] For Peter Smart, canon of Durham, a key principle of popery was the belief in organizing worship to 'ravish . . . eyes'.[53] For John Dod, a key sin of popery was the belief that men could devise worship of their own invention. This, at least, was something Laud did believe, and if this was a correct definition of 'popery', then it would be right to call Laud a papist, and the king also. This definition is that of the man who was acting in 1637–9 as Pym's minister.[54] At the end of 1640, a group of Herefordshire and Shropshire ministers wanted to define papists to include all who would not take an oath against popery and Arminianism, or any who refused to subscribe to the doctrinal parts of the Thirty-nine Articles, the Irish Articles of 1615, and the Lambeth Articles of 1595.[55] Again, if refusal to subscribe to the Lambeth Articles made a man a papist, it was perfectly fair to call Laud one. Perhaps, instead of dismissing charges of 'popery' out of hand, we ought to use them as a key to unlock the mystery of what each individual speaker meant by 'popery'. Not all charges of popery have any meaning, but some, at least, are perfectly correct according to their own lights. It is our task to discover what those lights were.

It would be wrong to paint too unrelievedly black a picture of the position of the godly gentry during the 1630s. They often enjoyed far better opportunities to worship as they chose at home than other people, in some cases because they owned the advowsons of their home livings, in some because, unlike lesser people, they could move to another house if it became impossible for them to worship where they were, and in others because of a plain seventeenth-century respect for rank. Sir Nathaniel Barnardiston, one of the leading gentlemen of Suffolk, succeeded in preserving the incumbent of his home living from deprivation by a long series of returns to the effect that, because of a great fall from his horse, he was unfit to ride to court. It perhaps shows something of the compromises which still held society together, that though Barnardiston saved his home vicar by these means, his nominee to another parish where he owned the advowson was deprived without any fuss. These two ministers were guilty of the same offence, which was refusing to read the Book of Sports in favour of Sunday recreation.[56] When the Barringtons were invited to move to Watertown, Massachusetts, the letter of invitation hopefully offered them the inducement of good hawking and hunting and fowling and fishing.[57] It is not the sort of letter which is written to the truly desperate. Had Barrington and his like been truly cowed, they would not have reacted in 1640 as authoritatively as they did. The particular reaction that came is a reaction to being on the losing side, felt by people who had not yet lost all the habits of mind resulting from seventy years of being on the winning one.

* * *

If even the puritan Barringtons were not desperate, and if England was really 'a country in working order' in 1637, how can we explain the resort to arms in 1642? Russell's Causes of the English Civil War *paints a complex picture of many different elements that just happened to come together at the wrong time. The pressures of foreign war (the Bishops' War with Scotland in 1639 and the Irish Rebellion of 1641) head the list of immediate causes, but these pressures were brought to bear on an already overburdened administrative and fiscal system ill-equipped to rule multiple kingdoms and further divided by mishandled religious quarrels. In the following excerpt from his conclusion, Russell summarizes how these contingencies came together to ignite war in 1642.*

* * *

The Civil War should be ascribed to a conjunction of seven events and non-events: why there were Bishops' Wars, why England lost them, why there was no political settlement in England, why the Long Parliament was not dissolved in 1641, why England divided into parties, why there was no serious negotiation to avoid war, and why respect for majesty came to be so deeply diminished. It is now time to face the question how far this conjunction was fortuitous. It clearly contains a fortuitous element; if the Irish Rebellion had been postponed three weeks, it would not have kept the Long Parliament in being, and there would have been no parliament to participate in a civil war.

Yet, though the fortuitous element cannot be ruled out, the conjunction was not entirely fortuitous. It was the result of three long-term causes of instability, all of them well established before Charles came to the throne, and all of them ones which can be observed to have troubled European, as well as British, monarchies. There is nothing particularly British (still less English) about any of them: they were not even exceptionally acute in England. What is peculiar to the two cases of England and the Netherlands is that all of them came to a head at the same time. These three long-term causes were the problem of multiple kingdoms, the problem of religious division, and the breakdown of a financial and political system in the face of inflation and the rising cost of war.

The problem of multiple kingdoms was always a likely cause of instability from 1603 onwards. The temptation to press for greater harmonization was always there, and was always likely to produce serious trouble. In 1603 England encountered what Britain confronts in the 1990s, the shock of subjection to a supra-national authority. That shock was the less, but also the less adequately dealt with, because the English always tried to pretend it was not there, and wished to treat both James and Charles as if they were only kings of a single nation-state called England. Since this was patently not the case, and the kings could not help knowing it, the English were always likely to misread royal actions, and in particular to press their kings to do things which, in British terms, they could not do. When, as in 1637, a British king fell victim to a similar misapprehension, and attempted to govern all Britain as king of England, he found this was something he could not do. In 1988, when an opinion poll shows 35 per cent of Scots in favour of full independence,[58] and the security of the Ulster plantation is still in daily doubt, can we yet say that the British problem has safely receded into history?

It is fortunately easier to say so with the problem of religious division, since it was a problem which derived its explosive force from the belief that religion ought to be enforced. It was a problem of a society which had carried on the assumptions appropriate to a society with a single church into one which had many churches. In the century after the Reformation, this adjustment was a cause of instability in every country where it happened, and was avoided only in countries where persecution was too successful to allow it to arise. In this, England was by no means peculiar. The fact that England was so incompletely and ambiguously reformed was not necessarily a disadvantage, but what it bought was time and not improvement. If the problem had been postponed another thirty or forty years, it might perhaps have been enough to allow temperatures to cool, but August 1640, when the Scottish army, by entering England, merged the religious problem with the British problem, was too early for it to have cooled enough. One might say of the English Calvinists what Machiavelli said of the pope in Italy: they were too weak to unite the country, but too strong to allow anyone else to do so. When the Scots entered England, they were able to join forces with a large group of people who preferred Scottish religion to what was coming to be taken for their own.

The strains caused for monarchies by the combination of inflation with the massive increases in the cost of wars known collectively as 'the military revolution' is also a European theme. The financial difficulties faced, after the conclusion of the long wars of the 1590s, by James VI and I, Philip III of Spain, and Henri IV of France have too much in common to be entirely coincidental. The changes following the regular use of gunpowder, especially the trend to larger-scale fortifications and to larger armies, much increased the economic drain of war. The resulting financial pressures put strain on the principle of consent to taxation everywhere in Europe, and perhaps only the Netherlands, with the advantage of a visible enemy at the gate, were able to combine consent with the levying of taxes on the scale needed. England, because the principle of consent to taxation was so particularly well entrenched, was perhaps put under more constitutional strain by this process than some other powers. Yet kings' impatience with legal forms which restricted their capacity to wage war is not confined to England: Philip IV and the Conde Duque of Olivares, facing the constitution of Catalonia, felt all the same frustrations as Charles I.[59] The similarity of their remarks on 'necessity', and the rights it gave to a monarchy, perhaps suggests that they were facing a common problem, and that the pressure on constitutional forms in both countries did not result from a theoretical drive to 'absolutism', but from the simple fact that legal forms no longer permitted the king to carry on the necessary business.

No one, or even two, of these forces was in the event enough: it took the conjunction of all three to drive England into civil war. To ask whether any one or two of them could have created civil war is to ask a question which is unanswerable because hypothetical. Yet it is a fact that no one or two of them did create civil war, and they had a long time in which to do it if they were capable of it. Both the religious and the financial problem had been plainly visible by the 1550s, and they had not created civil war in ninety years since then. England in 1637 was, no doubt, a country with plenty of discontents, some of them potentially serious, but it was also still a very stable and peaceful one, and one which does not show many visible signs of being on the edge of a major upheaval.

EDITOR'S NOTES

Reprinted in abridged form from the first chapter of *The Fall of the British Monarchies 1637–1642* (Oxford, 1991), with an appended selection excerpted from *The Causes of the English Civil War* (Oxford, 1990), with the permission of the author and the Oxford University Press.

a Justice of the Peace: see Glossary.
b John Winthrop emigrated to Massachusetts in 1630.
c 1536 rising in the North against the dissolution of the monastries, easily put down by Henry VIII.
d Thomas Wyatt lead an abortive attempt in 1553–4 against the Catholic Queen Mary.
e 1605 attempt by Catholic zealots to blow up the Parliament building and replace James I with a Catholic ruler.
f Northampton and Calvert were Catholics whose loyalty to the protestant monarch kept them in positions of power despite their faith.
g The second Earl of Essex, Robert Devereux, was executed by Elizabeth's order for an abortive attempt to seize the government and replace Elizabeth's advisers with his own faction.
h All taxes were based on landholding, but the rate varied according to the type of tax being levied – a parliamentary levy to aid the king (subsidy), a tax for the relief of poverty, or a tax to pay for food for the army or the royal household (purveyance).
i Billeting was compulsory lodging of soldiers in private households during time of war. Reimbursement for charges thus incurred by householders was not always forthcoming in the 1620s, and this was an item of complaint in the 1628 Parliament.
j Phelips, Long and Seymour had all argued vigorously and on principle against unparliamentary taxation in the 1628 Parliament. They did not repeat these arguments when they contested their Ship Money assessments a decade later, but as Russell here suggests, they would hardly need to do so.

NOTES

1 Kenneth Fincham, 'The Judges' Decision on Ship Money in February 1637: The Reaction of Kent', *BIHR*, 57, (1984), pp. 236.

2 *HMC Salis*. XXII, pp. 250–2.

3 Birmingham Reference Library, Coventry MSS, Commissions of the Peace, no. 457.

4 Perez Zagorin, *The Court and the Country*, (London, 1969), p. 305.

5 PRO LC 5/134, pp. 256, 439, 245, 218, 265; PRO E 403/2813, fo. 3a.

6 R. P. Cust, 'Charles I, the Privy Council and the Forced Loan', *JBS*, 24 (1985), pp. 208–35.

7 J. S. A. Adamson, 'The Peerage in Politics 1645–1649', (University of Cambridge Ph. D. thesis, 1986), p. 93 n. I am grateful to Dr Adamson for permission to quote from his thesis.

8 R. Buchanan Sharp, *In Contempt of All Authority* (Berkeley, Calif., 1980), pp. 8, 223, and *passim*.

9 Paul Slack, 'Books of Orders: The Making of English Social Policy 1577–1631', *TRHS*, 30 (1980), pp. 1–22; Brian Quintrell, 'The Making of Charles I's Book of Orders', *EHR*, 95/376 (1980), p. 558.

10 Paul Slack, *The Impact of Plague in Tudor and Stuart England* (London, 1985) p. 221; *LJ* IV, p. 391.

11 Fincham, 'Judges' Decision on Ship Money', pp. 234, 237.

12 I am grateful to Andrew Thrush for numerous discussions on the complex issues involved in navy finance. The amount of money the navy needed depended on the strategic objectives allotted to it.

13 *His Majesties Declaration* (1640), BL E. 203(1), pp. 13–14.

14 J. S. Morrill, *The Revolt of the Provinces* (London, 1976), pp. 24–6.

15 *CSPD 1635*, vol. CCCI, no. 76.

16 *ST* III, 1208. Chief Baron Davenport said the procedure 'is as it were to make a rape'. He was not using the word in its Sussex sense.

17 *CSPD 1635*, vol. CCCI, no. 39; Alnwick MSS, vol. 13, fo. 302; KAO, Sackville MSS U 269/0 273/13.

18 *CSPD 1638–9*, vol. CCCXCVIII, no. 51; *CSPD 1634–5*, vol. CCLXXVIII, no. 100.

19 *CSPD 1634–5*, vol. CCLXXXI, no. 14.

20 *CSPD 1635–6*, vol. CCCXVII, no. 94.

21 *CSPD 1635*, vol. CCXCVII, no. 23; vol. CCCXCVIII, no. 29.

22 *CSPD 1638–9*, vol. CCCXCVIII, no. 4.

23 Paul Slack, *Impact of Plague*, pp. 267–8, 301; *Western Circuit Assize Orders 1629–1648*, ed. J. S. Cockburn (Camden Society, 7, 1976), pp. 23, 31, 68, 80–1, 165, 203.

24 Morrill, *Revolt of the Provinces*, pp. 24–6; Kevin Sharpe, 'Personal Rule of Charles I', in Howard Tomlinson, ed., *Before the English Civil War* (New York, 1984), p. 72.

25 Peter Lake, 'Collection of Ship Money in Cheshire during the 1630s', *Northern History*, 17 (1981), p. 71.

26 *HMC Eighth Report*, II, p. 58; *Winthrop Papers*, ed. R. Winthrop (Massachusetts Historical Society, Boston, 1931), III, p. 139; *CSPD*

1635, vol. ccxcvii, no. 39. It would be easy, but I hope unnecessary, to extend this list into double or even treble figures.

27 Hamilton MSS 1505, 1506, and other refs.

28 T. G. Barnes, *Somerset 1625–1640* (Cambridge, Mass., 1961), 214 and many other refs. *CSPD 1639*, vol. cccxxii, no. 45.

29 Mary Frear Keeler, *The Long Parliament, 1640–41* (Philadelphia, 1954), p. 337.

30 J. P. Kenyon, *The Stuart Constitution* (Cambridge, 1966), p. 116.

31 *ST*, iii, 1090, 1095–6: 'the ships and arms to be provided are to continue the subjects' own in property'.

32 *HMC Ninth Report*, ii pp. 496–7; also *The Notebook of Sir John North-cote*, ed. A. H. A. Hamilton (1877), pp. 85–6. Sir Thomas Knyvett, although he was up 'by peepe of the day', could not get into the courtroom: *The Knyvett Letters*, ed. B. Schofield (Norfolk Record Society, 20, Norwich, 1949), p. 91.

33 PRO SP 16/438/92.

34 Above, and *CSPD 1638–9*, vol. cccc, no. 27; J. S. Morrill, *Revolt of the Provinces*, p. 25.

35 W. Knowler, ed., *The Earl of Strafforde's Letters*, (London, 1739), i, pp. 267, 233.

36 Fincham, 'Judges' Decision on Ship Money', p. 234.

37 PRO SP 16/438/93.

38 Russell, *1621–9*, pp. 404–8; id., *Pym*, pp. 161–4.

39 *CSPD 1636–7*, vol. cccxxvii, no. 140.

40 Nicholas Tyacke, *Anti-Calvinists* (Oxford, 1987); Peter Lake, 'Calvin-ism and the English Church, 1570–1635', *Past and Present*, no. 114 (1987), pp. 32–76, and ch. 10 below. Their works are complementary and, it is to be hoped, definitive.

41 S. R. Gardiner, *The History of England 1603–1642* (London, 1884–6), vii, pp. 21–3.

42 Lake, 'Calvinism', p. 65. Davenant was immediately told that the king was much displeased.

43 Tyacke, *Anti-Calvinists*, pp. 188, 182.

44 *1629 Debates*, pp. 117, 120.

45 Article xix; John Calvin, *Institutes*, iv i. 8–12.

46 Tyacke, *Anti-Calvinists*, pp. 187–8.

47 Jacqueline Levy, 'Perceptions and Beliefs: The Harleys of Brampton Bryan' (University of London Ph. D. thesis, 1983), 62, 164, and *passim*. I am grateful to Dr Levy for permission to quote from her thesis.

48 PRO SP 16/400/7.

49 For a complaint of innovation from an unexpected quarter, see *CSPD 1629–31*, vol. clxxiv, no. 64, and vol. clxxxvi, no. 107, John Howson, Bishop of Durham to Laud, apparently supporting the dissident canon Peter Smart against the liturgical innovations intro-duced by John Cosin as Dean. See also Mervyn James, *Family, Lineage and Civil Society* (Oxford, 1974), pp. 120, 168.

50 *Winthrop Papers*, iii, pp. 380–1.

51 I am grateful to Peter Lake for many interesting discussions of this

question. See Lake, *Moderate Puritans and the Elizabethan Church* (Cambridge, 1982), pp. 171–80, from which our discussions began.

52 *CSPD 1633–4*, p. 439. Roe, perhaps provocatively, was writing to Laud. See also John Dod, *Plaine and Familiar Exposition of the Ten Commandments* (1624), p. 20.

53 Peter Smart, *Vanitie and Downfall* (Edinburgh, 1628), p. 8.

54 John Dod, *Ten Commandments*, p. 12; Russell, 'Pym', p. 249n.

55 BL Loan MS 29/172, fo. 364^v. I am grateful to Dr Levy, who discovered this MS, for helpful discussion of it. It is possibly one of the drafts from which the Ministers' Remonstrance of Feb. 1641 was put together.

56 J. T. Cliffe, *Puritan Gentry* (London, 1984), pp. 176–7. See also *CSPD 1634–5*, vol. cclxxvi, no. 35 for John Hampden's success in coming to terms with the metropolitical visitation.

57 *Barrington Family Letters 1628–1632*, pp. 183–4.

58 *The Times*, 1 May 1988.

59 J. H. Elliot, *Revolt of the Catalans* (Cambridge, 1963), *passim*.

8

THE COMING OF WAR

John Morrill

Morrill's focus, unlike Russell's, is on the shires rather than the centre. He argues here that local interests shaped the 'country' response to problems at the centre. Noting how allegiances shifted in the two years after Charles summoned the Long Parliament in 1640, he rejects earlier historians' accounts of a united and principled 'country' opposition to corruption at Court at the outset of the war in 1642. Country gentlemen, he says, did not understand constitutional issues, were ill-informed about central politics, and cared more about regional concerns than national policy and principle. To the extent that Charles's policies in the 1630s threatened local traditions and created practical administrative problems, they drew a conservative reaction from Members of Parliament in 1640. But when accelerating conflict over the next two years and final resort to arms jeopardized stability in the counties, a royalist 'party' finally emerged from the provinces to defend local order and autonomy from what some perceived as an even greater threat than the king had been. At the same time an even stronger neutralist tendency emerged from the fear and uncertainty of local communities. While extremists – especially those committed to religious reform – took up arms, most Englishmen clung desperately to the fence and wished the war would go away.

In Morrill's account, now expanded in a collection of essays, The Nature of the English Revolution, *constitutional theory thus plays a relatively minor part in the conflict. Opting for one side or the other in the 1640s was determined primarily by localist concerns and perceptions of how royal and parliamentary policy would affect the county community. Morrill's revision thus contrasts sharply with the whig view of the Civil War as a struggle for constitutional liberty against attempted absolutism. It will be answered most directly in the final section of this volume by Richard Cust and Ann Hughes.*

There could be no civil war before 1642 because there was no royalist party. The origins of the English Civil War are really concerned less with the rise of opposition than with the resurgence of loyalism; loyalty to a king who appeared to have disregarded the rights of his subjects, and support for a church which had combined the persecution of an old nonconformity (Puritanism) with the championship of another (Arminianism).

Most historians have in effect concerned themselves with the crisis of 1640, with the isolation of Charles I from the great majority of his people. The events of 1640–2 are treated as of secondary importance, the falling away of the faint-hearted as the crisis worked itself out. The royalists are portrayed, even by those without ideological axes to grind, as men lacking both vision and the stomach for a fight – men unable to overcome an inbred respect for authority and the hierarchy of values expressed in the Great Chain of Being.

Furthermore, the events of 1640–2 are still interpreted almost entirely in terms of a succession of crises at Whitehall and Westminster, as though the political convulsions there were neatly counterpointed by parallel crises in provincial communities. It will be the primary task of this essay to examine what was happening in the partially autonomous shires and boroughs of England and Wales during the years 1640–2. It will also attempt to show that while men – above all those prominent gentry families who ran local government – shared many assumptions about the nature of the crisis, their response was largely conditioned by local events and local power structures. It will be about the interaction of national and local politics.

I am not, of course, going to argue that this provincialism excluded concern for general or national political and constitutional issues, but rather that such issues took on local colours and were articulated within local contexts. The gentry did not consider dispassionately such problems as those arising from the Book of Orders, Ship Money or the Nineteen Propositions. They did not attempt to weigh their legality or necessity in the light of abstruse general constitutional principles. Rather, they evaluated the effect such measures would have on the peace and security of their local communities. Only occasionally did county factions adopt positions in relation to national issues based on local opportunism rather than on conviction. However, they did often reshape the points involved and invested them with a more local significance. It is in this light that I accept Professor Everitt's assertion that 'though the sense of national identity had been increasing since the early Tudors, so too had the sense of county identity, and the latter was normally the more powerful sentiment in 1640–60'.[1]

The leaders of the various groups within the Long Parliament maintained an uneasy alliance for almost twelve months. There was agreement about the need to destroy the institutional instruments of royal misrule, the prerogative courts (Star Chamber, High Commission, the Councils in the North and the Marches), and the need for regular parliaments for the presentation and redress of the grievances of the subject (achieved in a Triennial Act which included machinery for elections to be held even if the king failed to issue writs). For the immediate future the king agreed to a bill which allowed the Long Parliament to sit until it agreed to its own dissolution. The advocates of Thorough[a] were removed from power (Strafford by attainder, the judges and Laudian bishops by impeachment), or fled abroad; but there was less agreement about the solution to other problems. Foremost amongst them was the reform of the Church, for although the machinery of Laudian innovation was broken, there were considerable and growing disagreements about what should take its place. The question of further sanctions to limit the Crown had barely been raised, since it was widely imagined that Charles would be forced to take leaders of the opposition into his government.

Meanwhile, the king's credibility had collapsed. Many of the parliamentary leaders had been in close touch with the Covenanters[b] in Scotland since 1638 (it was fear that Strafford would publicize these treasonable designs which prompted the precipitous attack on him in the first week of the parliament), and they were fully aware that the king had adopted tactics towards the Covenanters which were entirely governed by deceit and double-dealing. As Henry Parker said in 1642: 'there was no difference . . . betwixt that case of the Scots and this of ours.'[2] The exact extent of royal involvement in the Army Plots of 1641 to get rid of Parliament and its leaders was dangerously unclear.

Any remaining doubts about the king's ill faith were removed by the attempt on the Five Members[c] in January 1642. All hope of a *rapprochement* had vanished, and out of the atmosphere of suspicion and distrust a new policy had to be forged. At last there emerged an issue on which no compromise was possible. Parliamentary control first of the London militia, then of the provincial trained bands, and finally of the army became the cornerstone of Pym's demand for a radical, though essentially pragmatic, redistribution of executive power. A justification of these claims, newly generated by the crisis of 1641-2, couched in the language of mixed monarchy, was evolved only after the event.[3]

But in the process, the kaleidoscope of power had been shaken and a new pattern found. The moderate, pragmatic reformers around Pym allied themselves to all those who were determined to achieve an immediate and radical revolution in the Church. These religious radicals included political conservatives like Sir Simonds d'Ewes and also the group around Lords Saye and Brooke. But meanwhile the Great Tew group, those men like Falkland and Hyde who had retained a narrowly constitutional-ist and conservative interpretation of the crisis of 1640, were rapidly moving away from those whom they now believed to be challenging the traditional constitution. After working secretly for Charles in the two Houses for several months, they were taken into the government and accepted important posts in the spring of 1642.

Splits in the unity of the opposition had begun to appear midway through 1641. Although the Commons had passed the attainder of Strafford with little opposition, the debates on religion – particularly between the advocates of presbyterianism and of limited episcopacy – had become so heated that the issue had to be temporarily shelved. But it was the debates on the Grand Remonstrance (November 1641), that catalogue of royal misdeeds which adumbrated parliamentary demands for control of royal appointments, which really revealed the divisions within the Commons. The tendentious and aggressive content of the Remonstrance itself led 148 members to vote against it; but the decision to publish it, to appeal directly to the people without offering it to King or House of Lords, led to unpre-cedented scenes of fury in the Commons. It was concern for proper parliamentary procedure which Hyde[d] stressed in his speech against the Remonstrance. This was the great turning-point in the history of the Long Parliament. Pym's decision to press forward with it at all costs was both cause and effect of the breakdown in the unity of the opposition to Charles. Aware of the disappearance of a majority for further change in the Lords, and conscious of the erosion of support in the Commons, he was forced to appeal to forces outside the Parliament, just as he was forced to further the aims of those radicals seeking to overthrow the oligarchy in the government of London and to maintain popular pressure around the doors of the Houses of Parliament. Angry, anxious pickets had earlier lobbied the Lords to secure the attainder of Strafford. They were called on again to ensure the passage of the bill depriving the bishops of their votes in the Upper House and to complete the revolution in city government.

Yet this calculated appeal to the populace could only result in the further alienation of those who saw in such tactics the continuation of the very threats to order and hierarchy which had made them so desperately opposed to the Crown in 1640. The royalist party was born out of the same concern for adherence to law and constitutional propriety which had been the hallmark of the speeches of Hyde, Colepepper, Falkland, Dering and their allies throughout. These men now came to see that it was time to close with the king.

The situation in the provinces was rather different. Men at Westminster were acutely aware of the interplay of personality and politics, had lived through and corporately experienced the great debates and the traumas of 1640–1, above all were subject to forces which tended to polarize and divide. In the counties, on the other hand, the pressures tended to unite the ruling groups and to make them increasingly confused about the nature, and unsure of the importance, of events at Westminster and Whitehall. The central reality for them was the increasing evidence of the collapse of order. It is unclear whether rioting and violence were more extensive than hitherto, but most gentlemen certainly *believed* that they were. Disruption, often with an overt class basis, was certainly widespread. The king's army marching to Scotland had sacked churches or attacked their conductors in at least twenty counties; preachers, unmuzzled and vengeful, had instigated attacks on Laudian ornaments in the churches (altar rails and stained glass windows were prime targets); disruption of religious services and the settling of old scores were widespread. Enclosure riots spread across the country, particularly in the Midlands and North.

Whether or not these riots were more serious than those earlier in the century, they profoundly shocked the gentry, whose overwhelming response was to assert that at such a time the political differences between king and Parliament could not be allowed to continue. The great majority yearned for settlement.

Furthermore, they were confused. It is true that the years 1641 and 1642 saw an astonishing increase in the volume of news and propaganda: the first English newspapers were devoted to English affairs, the publication of many important speeches by leaders of all parties, the concoction of didactic pamphlets appealing to particular interest groups such as the London artisans or the provincial gentry. In a period of indecision men scrambled to read everything they could. Many letters from the capital not only gave the latest news but referred to the enclosure of newsletters and pamphlets, often representing the views of different opinions or parties. But in general the content of the propaganda would only serve to confuse. Both sides were aiming at the middle ground. Both sides emphasized their own moderation and caricatured their opponents as 'schismaticks and atheists' or 'papists and malignants'. No wonder the provincial gentry were confused: Lady Sussex wrote that 'both sides promise so fair, that I cannot see what it is they should fight for'.[4]

Only those in London or with the king knew the extent of the breach, and very few were prepared to admit it.[5] Every communication between the two sides was treated as an olive branch, and the provinces were left unclear as to why no settlement was concluded. And all the time the threat of the collapse of order and local government loomed closer. Incomprehension of the scale of the crisis is exemplified by the comment of Mistress Eure in a letter to Ralph Verney: 'I wish all were well ended, for things stand in soe ill a condition here as we can make noe money of our co[a]lpits.'[6] Lady Sussex too was afraid her rents would not be paid unless a settlement was reached.[7] Most people saw much worse consequences if there was no agreement.

Fear drove some men into royalism; it drove far more into neutralism. Faced by the threat of social disintegration and incomprehension of the course of events at the centre, most counties closed ranks behind county barriers, determined (as they had been in the 1630s) to protect the administrative integrity of their shires as the first line of defence against disorder. Attempts to neutralize whole areas of the country were set in motion which have never received adequate attention from historians.[8] Indeed, I have found evidence of attempted neutrality pacts in twenty-two English counties and in many boroughs. They can be divided into two broad groups: the totally committed efforts of moderate men – usually representing the leading county governors – to raise a third force to put down both sides and keep out all 'foreigners'; and the demilitarization pacts made between the royalist commissioners of array and the parliamentarian militia commissioners in an attempt to prevent bloodshed.

In Lincolnshire, the gentry declared that they would fight neither for nor against the king, and they raised a troop of horse

> only for the preservation of peace within themselves, in that they resolve (having thus discharged their duties both to the King and the two Houses of Parliament) not to embark further by sending any forces out of the county, to aid either side, but as much as in them lies, to endeavour accommodation.[9]

The crisis of 1642, far from demonstrating the limitations of provincialism, marked its triumph. In Yorkshire, for example, where the leading commissioners of array and deputy lieutenants attempted a demilitarization, the aim, according to a local critic, was

> to put the county in a mere neutrality; that is to estate themselves in a civil independency; this is to make every county a free estate . . . to set up an interpretive court above a legislative, and to call the conclusions of England to the Bar of Yorkshire.[10]

Similar attempts by leaders of both sides achieved success briefly in Cheshire, Cornwall, Devon and Wiltshire,[11] and were attempted in several other counties.[12]

Dr Holmes has recently drawn attention to widespread neutralism in all the counties of East Anglia, heartland of parliamentarianism and Puritanism.[13] Neutralism was just as prevalent in

the towns, particularly where ancient walls offered cor-
porations the opportunity of keeping out trouble. Towns like
Chester, Worcester and Sandwich initially refused to implement
the instruction of either side, while elsewhere city militias were
called up to exclude all 'foreigners'.[14] The ruling groups, far
from identifying oligarchy with royalism, identified civil war
with economic disaster. They were keenly aware of the danger
that the requirements of war would lead to the invasion of
borough rights, especially by county interests (several Kentish
boroughs afford good examples of this).[15] Furthermore, local
studies do not in general bear out the assertion that 'progressive'
towns like those in the clothing areas, or the 'middling sort'
elsewhere, declared for Parliament.

There were exceptions, above all London where a social
revolution in 1641–2 made possible the creation of a parliamentarian army, the financing of a rebellion, and the continued
pursuit of a godly reformation. The concentration of Puritan
preachers in such towns as Manchester no doubt made others
zealous for the cause, but they were not the norm.[16] Equally,
there were counties where the neutralist current hardly existed,
such as Lancashire, long divided bitterly between Puritans and
papists, or Shropshire where the zephyrs of peace from Cheshire
were contemptuously ignored.[17] But generally the parties
formed behind, or were restrained by, a barrier of fear and
indecision.

The moment of decision was delayed, for most men, until
they received commissions from either (or both) king or Parliament. Those less prominent in their communities could escape
the worst of these anxieties – at a price. If they were asked not
to take commissions but to obey the commissioners they could
always accommodate both. Thus William Davenport of Bramhall
sent men and horse to a royalist muster and lent £100 on the
parliamentarian propositions.[18] Professor Everitt has traced three
groups of Kentish moderates who illustrate what happened.
One group, faced by personal summonses from the king, moved
off unhappily north to join him. Thus Sir Edward Dering, who
'did not like one side or the other so well as to join myself with
either. A composing third way was my wish and my prayer',
felt obliged to accept the king's order, going 'out of my own
house and from my own country the most unwilling man that
ever went'. Similarly, another group abandoned accommodation

in the face of express orders from Parliament. For the hallmark of the moderate was that he wanted to obey *both* sides, not *neither*, and when one side issued a direct and personal order, he acquiesced. Those not directly charged by either side could and did continue to sit on the fence.[19]

Thus in 1642 men desperately wished to avoid a conflict or, at least, to let is pass them by. The war began despite, yet also because of, the longing for peace. For while the moderates, as always, talked and agonized, extremists seized the initiative.

At times of crisis men look to known patterns of political and social behaviour. Passivity is the simplest way out, the line of least resistance. To obey an order is less of a political act than to reject it. Anyone who claims to stand for the protection of traditional values and the maintenance of order will be widely supported. In this context, localism meant not an indifference to the great issues agitating church and state, but a preoccupation with the way these issues could be harmonized with the restoration of normality. The pre-existent power groupings within each county buckled under the pressures and tensions of national events, but each county retained a distinctive pattern.

In Leicestershire, two implacably opposed gentry factions – both traditionally Puritan – had long struggled for local dominance. Both the leading families, the Greys and the Hastings, had connections with the Court and with the leading members of the opposition. The original cause of their feud had long been forgotten. When civil was broke out, both groups tried to prevent the involvement of Leicestershire. Only haltingly was the county forced into the war. Then the line-up followed the traditional one; the families who had always been attached to the Hastings's interests declared for the king, those who had always supported the Greys declared for Parliament.[20]

In Cheshire, a rather different pattern prevailed. The élite there had been divided for some years over issues of local precedence. Faced by the political crisis of 1640–1 and by the emergence of a radial puritan group amongst the lesser gentry and freeholders, one of these groups gradually moved into an alliance with the Court, prompted largely by their determination to protect a modified episcopacy. The other group attempted to remain neutral, using its influence to keep the peace. In the autumn of 1642 this group petitioned for a national settlement and tried to raise a third force to keep both sides out of the county. After the failure of this scheme, the group divided, its leaders working for a pacification from within the ranks of the royalist and parliamentarian parties.[21]

Where there were no traditional and deeply felt divisions within a county, the élite might act together throughout. Thus in Buckinghamshire, despite the clear preference of men below the highest ranks for keeping out of the conflict, almost all the leading families co-operated closely with John Hampden.[22] In Shropshire, opposition to the solidly royalist front presented by the justices was soon suppressed, and here commitment to the king did mean more than the use of his name and commission for essentially local peace-keeping aims.[23]

The situation in many other counties was more deeply confused. In Devon the royalists were the first to appear but the Commissioners of Array were deeply distrusted. In July many leading gentry had sent petitions to both king and Parliament seeking a peaceful settlement, and the execution of royalist commissions in August led to further demonstrations, for 'the Arraymen . . . are look'd upon as the first instigators of a breach of the peace'. Although a great many of the gentry were later to appear for the king, the overwhelming feeling in the autumn of 1642 was a desire to procrastinate. The majority opposed the Commission of Array as they were shortly to oppose the Militia Commission: it was the same spirit which led them to oppose Ship Money and Coat and Conduct Money.[24] Similarly in Kent, men who were later, in 1643 and 1648 (in response to parliamentary attempts to destroy local autonomy), to fight in the name of the king, stayed at home in 1642. At Westminster in later 1642 any action was a positive one; to stay was to identify with the Parliament, to leave was seen as a declaration of royalism. In the shires, a dogged stay-at-home policy could still be construed as loyalty to both sides.

Side-taking for the great majority was largely arbitrary. Men delayed declaring themselves until forced to do so by the appearance of activist groups on one or both sides. Polarization then usually followed the lines of purely local groupings and although many families were divided, and many friends parted, the prior sub-political divisions within each shire or borough were reflected in the line-up of forces by early 1643. It was not always obvious which group would support each side: it was frequently determined by the attitude of the leaders or simply by the accident of events.

All this emphasis on neutralism and pacifism begs the questions: Why did civil war break out? Who were the activists and how did they break down the pacifism of the majority?

Although the final breakdown between king and Parliament concerned control of the militia, the provincial significance of this issue should not be overrated. Few petitions from the provinces referred to it, or to the constitutional amendments called for by Pym in the Nineteen Propositions, or to the general question of trust. All petitions, royalist and parliamentarian, assumed that the political and constitutional differences were negotiable. The concept of mixed monarchy was universally acclaimed in the counties. What emerges quite clearly from a study of the activists in the summer of 1642 (those who pushed themselves forward) is that, for them, religion was the crucial issue. Quite simply, in most countries the active royalists are the defenders of episcopacy who saw in puritanism a fundamental challenge to all society and order, and the parliamentarians are those determined to introduce a godly reformation which might, for a few of them, leave room for bishops, but in most cases did not. What the puritan activists did agree on, however, was the need to go beyond a restoration of traditional pre-Laudian Erastian Anglicanism to create a new, militant evangelical church. It may well be that amongst the peerage and ancient gentry, the tug of honour, indoctrination into the values of a patriarchial society, a reflex obedience to the anointed king, were finally decisive in committing them to fighting with their monarch, but the great majority of royalists in 1642 are more likely to have agreed with Thomas Holles, the ex-puritan ('truly I love religion as well as any man, but I do not understand the religion of rebellion') than with the Earl of Cumberland ('the same loyal blood of my ancestors runs still in my veins which they were never sparing of when their sovereign commanded them to fight').[25] While the great majority of men dithered or wrote petitions and talked of raising a third force for peace, it was the men who felt most strongly about religion who began the war.

EDITOR'S NOTES

Reprinted in abridged form from *The Revolt of the Provinces: Conservatives and Radicals in the English Civil War, 1630–1640*, 2nd edn (London, 1980), with permission of the author and the Longman Group UK Limited.

a Policy associated with Thomas Wentworth, the Earl of Strafford, to make royal control more efficient (or, as opponents thought, absolutist) and with Archbishop Laud's efforts to implement Caroline ceremony and uniformity, and to enhance clerical authority in the state church. Strafford was executed in 1641, Laud in 1645.

b Scottish rebels who in 1638 took an oath of association to defend the presbyterian Kirk (Church) of Scotland against English encroachments, and especially attempts to impose the Prayer Book. The National Covenant claimed to bind the nation together and to God.

c Charles attempted the illegal arrest of five opposition members of the House of Commons (Pym, Hampden, Haselrig, Holles and Strode). Forewarned by friends at Court, the five were hidden by sympathizers in London.

d The royalist Edward Hyde later became Earl of Clarendon.

NOTES

1 A. M. Everitt, 'The Local Community and the Great Rebellion', in *Historical Association Pamphlet*, G. 70 (1969), p. 5. He has also written a brilliant case study, *The Community of Kent and the Great Rebellion* (Leicester, 1966).

2 Quoted by M. J. Mendle, 'Politics and Political Thought', in C. Russell, ed., *The Origins of the English Civil War* (London, 1973), p. 231.

3 For the essentially pragmatic nature of the Militia Ordinance, see now L. W. Schwoerer, 'The Fittest Subject for a King's Quarrel: An Essay on the Militia Controversy, 1642', *BS* (1971), pp. 45–76.

4 J. Bruce, ed., 'The Verney Papers', *Camden Society* (1845), II p. 90.

5 For example, B. Schofield ed., *The Knyvett Letters* (London, 1949), pp. 75–6, 91, 103, 107–8.

6 Verney, II, p. 90.

7 Ibid., II p. 83.

8 The pioneering work in this field is B. S. Manning, 'Neutrals and Neutralism in the English Civil War', (University of Oxford D. Phil. thesis, 1957); I cannot accept Dr Manning's starting-point that neutralism was 'a temporary stopping place for men of moderate views', and must record that his almost total dependence on printed sources has led him to confuse different types of neutralism. It is still an original and important work.

9 BL, Thomason Tracts, E 113/7.

10 BL, Thomason Tracts, E 240/30.

11 For Cheshire, see J. S. Morrill, *Cheshire, 1630–1660* (Oxford, 1974), pp. 66–9. For Devon and Cornwall, see E. Andriette, *Devon and Exeter in the Civil War* (Newton Abbot, 1972), pp. 82–4; M. Coate, *Cornwall in the Great Civil War and Interregnum* (Oxford, 1930), pp. 36–7, 54–6; Manning, 'Neutrals', pp. 103ff. For Wiltshire, see G. A. Harrison, 'Royalist Organisation in Wiltshire, 1642–1646' (University of London Ph.D. thesis, 1963), ch. 2.

12 For example Lancashire, Dorset, Leicestershire.

13 C. Holmes, *The Eastern Association and the English Civil War* (Cambridge, 1974), pp. 31–62.

14 For Worcester, see J. W. Willis-Bund, ed., 'The Diary of Henry Townshend of Elmley Lovett, 1640–1663', 3 vols, *Worcestershire Historical Society* (1915–1920), I, p. xxvii; II, p. 87; for Sandwich, see M. V. Jones, 'The Political History of the Parliamentary Boroughs of Kent, 1642–1662' (University of London Ph.D. thesis, 1967), ch. 1, particularly pp. 63–4.

15 Jones, 'Political History', pp. 71–96.

16 V. Pearl, *London and the Outbreak of the Puritan Revolution* (Oxford, 1961).

17 B. G. Blackwood, 'The Lancashire Gentry, 1625–1660' (University of Oxford D.Phil. thesis, 1973), ch. 4; E. Broxap, *The Great Civil War in Lancashire* (Manchester, 1974), ch. 2; R. C. Richardson, *Puritanism in North-West England* (Manchester, 1972), ch. 1 and 5.

18 Morrill, 'William Davenport and the "Silent Majority" of Early Stuart England', *Journal of the Chester Archaeological Society* (1974).

19 Everitt, *Kent*, pp. 119–24.

20 A. M. Everitt, 'The Local Community and the Great Rebellion', *Historical Association Pamphlet*, G. 70 (1969), pp 10–18.

21 Morrill, *Cheshire*, ch. 1 and 2, *passim*.

22 A. M. Johnson, 'Buckinghamshire, 1640–1660' (University of Wales M.A. thesis, 1963), pp. 70–8.

23 H. Beaumont, 'Events in Shropshire at the Commencement of the Civil War', *Transactions of the Salop Archaeological Society*, 51 (1941–3).

24 Andriette, *Devon*, pp. 55–65.

25 See J. G. Marston, 'Gentry Honour and Royalism in Early Stuart England', *JBS*, 13 (1973), pp. 21–43.

Part III

RESPONDING TO REVISIONISM

9

THE EARLY EXPANSION OF PROTESTANTISM IN ENGLAND 1520–1558

A. G. Dickens

Having sustained more than a decade of vigorous criticism, A. G. Dickens in 1989 responded with a revised edition of his classic work, The English Reformation which reaffirmed his view of the Reformation as successful within its first generation in converting English people dissatisfied with late medieval Catholicism to the protestants' religion of the Word. The article that follows was published shortly before the book; it offers a direct, point-by-point response to his critics, drawing heavily from detailed local studies. Dickens points out here that limitations on our surviving sources should not be allowed to obscure the massive protestant iceberg below the surface. He grants regional diversity, as he always has, but he argues that protestantism encountered resistance mainly in the less populous and less politically significant areas of the realm. Local evidence shows that for London and the heavily populated South and East, an 'expansionist' view of pre-Elizabethan protestantism remains more credible than Haigh's 'minimal picture'. Protestantism grew slowly 1530 to 1547, but blossomed under Edward VI, and by the beginning of Mary's reign in 1553 it was 'seemingly ineradicable' in much of England. Dickens maintains throughout his work that popular belief and opinion are the legitimate focus of a historian's efforts and can be deduced from the evidence that remains to us.

* * *

I THE TIMING OF THE ENGLISH REFORMATION

The present article concerns the strength, expansion and geographical distribution of Protestant convictions among the English people during the early Reformation period, the thirty-eight years which separate the first incursion of Lutheranism from the accession of Elizabeth. To some extent it will react against the conclusions attained recently by certain original and respected scholars such as Dr Christopher Haigh and Professor Jack Scarisbrick, who envisage a very slow growth of the movement, sometimes suggesting that, apart from very limited areas of the South-east and certain large towns elsewhere, few English people became convinced Protestants during this early period.[1] Without setting forth much local evidence, they insist that English society did not want the Reformation and remained substantially Catholic until the new beliefs captured many areas in the middle decades of Elizabeth. In 1983 Dr Haigh referred to the area studies summarized in my own book *The English Reformation*, published in 1964 and now (1986) in process of updating by reference to more recent researches:

> And in the area of enquiry which Dickens drew to our attention, the progress of religious change at the popular level, the Dickens picture has been substantially redrawn. From the area studies which sought to chart the pace of reform in the provinces, only Kent has appeared to give unequivocal support for a rapid and popular Reformation while Cambridgeshire, Cornwall, Gloucester, Lancashire, Norfolk, Suffolk, Sussex and York city have yielded at best only small pockets of advanced opinion and a general impression of conservative attachment until the reign of Elizabeth.[2]

More recently Dr Haigh has enlarged somewhat upon this picture, rightly suggesting a differentiation between the towns and the countryside, but then taking snapshots of several counties, from some of which I still find myself bound to differ.

> Though there is a substantial body of opinion, led by Professors Dickens and Elton, which holds that Protestantism spread rapidly in early Tudor England, there is a growing 'slow Reformation' school, composed partly of historians who have conducted local studies of religious

change. Protestanism did make early progress in towns such as Bristol, Colchester, Coventry, Ipswich and London, but elsewhere, and especially in the countryside, the reformist breakthrough came much later. In Cambridgeshire, Cornwall, Gloucestershire, Lancashire, Lincolnshire, Norfolk, Suffolk, Sussex and Yorkshire, the Protestant Reformation was an Elizabethan (and often mid-Elizabethan) event.

In more general terms Professor Scarisbrick appears to accept this scheme, stressing (with good reason) the survival of the parish fraternities and other forms of Catholic piety until the Edwardian dissolutions.[3]

With less justification, he does not proceed to analyse either the slow development of popular Protestantism between 1530 and 1547, or its much swifter, more ascertainable development under Edward VI. He attaches no positive significance to Protestant resistance and martyrdom during the Marian persecution, that crucial episode to which he devotes only seven words in his book *The Reformation and the English People*.[4] My differences from Dr Haigh are somewhat more complicated, though less wholesale than he appears to suppose. For many decades I have been agreeing with the view that Protestantism always had to fight hard, and that throughout some considerable parts of the realm Catholic beliefs did in fact maintain their preponderance until the middle decades of Elizabeth and beyond. From the early 1930s to the late 1940s I worked mainly upon reactionary rebellions and Elizabethan Catholic recusancy, the forces in strong opposition to the Reformation. This early preoccupation has remained explicit in my later works. In 1959 I remarked that the ethos of Anglicanism was not widely understood before the period of Hooker, and that Puritanism had to struggle for a following until the late Elizabethan period.[5] In 1964 I stressed the 'gradual consolidation' of the Anglican Church under Elizabeth and its slowness to convert remote areas, adding that the growth of new movements during the seventeenth century 'might almost be regarded as a second English Reformation'. I also drew attention to the role of Elizabethan Puritanism in converting the so-called 'dark corners of the land'. In view of such oft-repeated conclusions I remain at a loss to understand why Dr Haigh continues at such frequent intervals to label me as a champion of quick and easy 'Reformation from below'.

In fairness it must be added that I have also maintained a converse yet wholly compatible proposition. I believe in territorial diversity, and that one should carefully study regional contrasts before venturing upon generalizations concerning the realm as a whole. I applaud Dr Haigh when he concludes his historiographical review with the words, 'we must show the past in all its variety and irreducible complexity, no matter how far art has to be sacrificed to accuracy'. Yet having widely surveyed the evidence so far presented, I still conclude that by 1553 Protestantism had already become a formidable and seemingly ineradicable phenomenon in fairly large and very populous areas of marked political importance. After all, the regions of England were not of equal influence upon the history of the nation; and the seat of government could not be transferred to Lancashire or the centre of the economy to Wales. Where was this heartland of the early Protestant movement? As I shall shortly demonstrate, it was far more extensive than Kent; it embraced all the coastal counties from Norfolk to Sussex and had sizeable westward extensions. The heart of this heartland was of course London. Moreover, the remainder of the country did not in 1553 consist wholly of what the Puritans regarded as the 'dark corners' of the land. Much of it represented what might be called intermediate or mixed areas, in which the new beliefs had already spread widely rather than intensively, yet where they cannot be adequately characterized as 'small pockets' of Protestantism.

Thus in regard to several specific areas my scheme does show some radical differences from that of Dr Haigh, while overall I take the inherent vitality and expansive achievements of pre-Elizabethan Protestantism far more seriously than either he or Professor Scarisbrick. I cannot imagine, for example, how Dr Haigh can bring himself to class Suffolk – by any criteria one of the three or four most heavily converted counties in England – along with Lancashire, Lincolnshire and Cornwall in a 'conservative' group. Likewise the view of Sussex as a highly conservative county may have been deduced from Professor R.B. Manning's emphasis upon the strong group of Catholic gentry there in Elizabethan times. Yet this later spectacle is far from obliterating the weighty and varied evidence more recently produced by M.J. Kitch and G.J. Mayhew, and showing a heavy infiltration of Protestantism in Edwardian East Sussex. Indeed the thirty-five local Marian martyrs burned in Sussex should have prepared us for these latter discoveries.[6] Again, both Gloucestershire and Norfolk have also been differentiated from the conservative counties by Ralph Houlbrooke, Elaine Sheppard, Ken Powell and others.[7] Least of all can I understand Dr Haigh's omission of Essex from the above passages, since here we are enormously well-informed regarding a county which rivalled even Kent in the intensity of its popular convictions, despite the small but resolute group of local gentry who helped their diocesan Bishop Bonner to carry out the Marian reaction.[8] It is nevertheless true that neither Dr Haigh's minimal picture of pre-Elizabethan Protestantism nor my own more expansionist view can be proved outright by precise statistics. For the most part our broader conclusions must perforce consist of probabilities though often strong probabilities – rather than fully demonstrable facts. This irritating situation one can only explain by a rapid glance at the nature of our source materials for the period 1530–1558.

II THE MAJOR SOURCES AND THEIR LIMITATIONS

Of course it would be easy to begin with some much simpler rejoinders. For example, Dr Haigh elsewhere regards puritanical Elizabethan clergy as producing an anticlericalism among the laity far more violent than any experienced by the pre-Reformation clergy.[9] If this be the case, one finds it difficult to see how the Puritans accomplished even a partial conversion at a time when the people are alleged to have hated them and their teachings so strongly. Again, if England really remained 'a Catholic country' in the autumn of 1558, does this not make a mad gambler or else an imperceptive fool of William Cecil,[a] who within a year of that date ventured to erect a fully-fledged Protestant settlement in England? Revisions which imply a caricature of this most cautious of ministers must surely be in need of reconsideration. Though these may be judged rather more than debating-points, the problems of religion in Tudor society nevertheless demand far more fundamental approaches. We need above all to attack the local history of the Reformation in detail and to explore its regional aspects with sensitive antennae.

These situations cannot, however, be appreciated without grasping the grave limitations which beset our sources. Their coverage, at first sight so voluminous and revealing, is nevertheless far too meagre to allow us to minimize the early Reformation by reference to what they do not tell us.[10] The demonstrable incompleteness of these sources should forbid such arguments from negative evidence and compel us to beware of all overconfident generalization. After all, during these decades we have nothing remotely resembling a contemporary census of early Protestants or a poll of religious opinions. There can be little prospect of establishing tolerably hard statistics concerning the number of these people, or even the rough percentage of the English population which at any stage they attained.

Let us briefly observe six main factors which make our information about early Protestantism so incomplete, and thus so incapable of supporting negative deductions and arguments minimizing the extent of the movement.

1 The loss of ecclesiastical archives has been severe, especially in regard to court books likely to have contained proceedings against numerous heretics.

2 Despite the devotees who believed that God would mitigate their sufferings at the stake, and that their reward would be incalculable and immediate, ordinary people of this period are unlikely to have ignored the prospect of extreme physical pain. The element of fear and the natural urge to survive and avoid notoriety must have operated to keep the vast majority of Protestants out of the fire – and so in most cases out of the records. Convicted heretics were normally granted one recantation, after which a second conviction in the ecclesiastical court meant the delivery of a defendant to the sheriff for burning. Thus martyrdom became a voluntary calling for heroes and heroines only. For humble prisoners who lacked the means to placate their gaolers, even a stretch in a Tudor prison could prove a harrowing trial of their steadfastness, especially if they were manacled for long periods. To the 58 Henrician martyrs and the 291 Marian martyrs we should add at least 40 people who died in prison.[11] Needless to say, these figures, though forming a phenomenon unique in English history, can have constituted but a tiny minority of the Protestant body during the early decades.

3 Quite apart from these severe physical and mental deterrents, the English population was far from dividing itself neatly into convinced Protestants and convinced Catholics. In the reign of Mary the letters and speeches of the heroes denounce their unheroic followers who saved themselves by pretending to be Catholics, while still known to their close associates as Protestants at heart. The martyr Ralph Allerton told Bishop Bonner that in England there were not two but three religions, 'and the third is a neuter, being indifferent – that is to say, observing all things that are commanded outwardly, as though he were of your [i.e. Bonner's] part, his heart being set wholly against the same'.[12]

4 The body of 'neuters' was swollen not merely by terror but by a secular spirit. Contemporary moralists and church officials often complained that many of the people cared little for any sort of religion and 'roistered' in the alehouses even during the times of divine service.[13]

5 A further important deprivation of evidence has arisen from the fact that most of the Marian bishops, diocesan chancellors and local gentry failed to institute rigorous enquiries and prosecutions, or at most selected a few ringleaders. Such methods have apparently reduced the record in those counties like Sussex and Gloucestershire where the recorded offenders now occur mostly by ones and twos per village. This would suggest a minimizing illusion, since under Tudor social conditions it seems highly improbable that most actual offenders were solitaries, thinly spread over the countryside. Yet further distortions occurred because John Foxe[b] patently received better reports from some areas than from others.

6 Moreover there is ample reason to suppose that numerous Protestant groups existed in places unmentioned by Foxe, by ecclesiastical records, or indeed by any of the standard, coherent sources of information. Quite often we detect such groups only through the fortuitous survival of personal letters or other detached and fleeting documents, which in any less fortunate instances must long since have perished. For example, only a letter from the militant wheelwright John Clement has revealed the existence of three otherwise unrecorded groups at Nutfield, Merstham and Chaldon, all near Redhill in Surrey.[14]

The perils of judging from negative evidence become lurid when we realize how few local events and situations can ever have been recorded in an age with no real equivalent to the newspaper, and how impermanent personal correspondence has always been. Only when armed with a realistic view of the extant sources, of their defective coverage and their silences, should we assess the local development of the English Reformation.

III WHERE DID PROTESTANTISM MOST READILY TAKE ROOT? [c]

So far as concerns the role of the largest towns, Dr Haigh's emphasis appears wholly justified. England's five most populous provincial cities of that day, each likely to have contained from ten to twelve thousand inhabitants, were Norwich, Bristol, Coventry, York and Newcastle upon Tyne. In the first three of these, Protestantism appears strong by 1558. At York, with its relatively huge and influential clerical population, the movement remained weak compared with its success in neighbouring Hull, a maritime and merchant-dominated place, about half the size of York, where the few clergy were closely controlled by the civic oligarchs.[15] Newcastle lay within a frontier zone little touched by the new beliefs, which were just being introduced by Bernard Gilpin. The city itself began its conversion under the preachers John Knox and John Rough, who nevertheless moved south before the onset of the Marian reaction.[16]

Even so, to close the urban list with these places, or even with Colchester, Ipswich and the other major towns correctly cited by Dr Haigh, would restrict the picture, since without any doubt another special *locus classicus* of early English Protestantism was the minor urban or near-urban community: the smallish weaving town, the even smaller market town, the large, semi-industrialized village. Foxe was well supported by the evidence when he chose Hadleigh in Suffolk as the prime exemplar of a godly Reformation community. Urged on by its rector Rowland Taylor, both its men and its women studied the Scriptures, so 'that the whole town seemed rather a university of the learned, than a town of cloth-making or labouring people'.[17] In the mid-Tudor years, other places of similar size seem also recognizably proto-Puritan.

To the big towns and the cloth-towns we must add English ports of all sizes, and of these, few of any significance along the eastern and southern coasts fail to reveal a Protestant presence between 1530 and 1558. Beginning with Hull and moving southward, this presence is recorded at Boston, King's Lynn, Yarmouth, Dunwich, Aldeburgh, Oxford, Ipswich, Harwich, Dovercourt, Gravesend and Dartford. In the extended port of London, English and foreign businessmen, sailors, ship-builders and publicans formed a heretical *demi-monde* over which the Church exercised a very tenuous authority.

I shall now briefly survey the more debatable regions of England, saying little about those where the essentials are generally agreed, and without unnecessarily duplicating the relevant and still viable summation of the early advances of Protestantism by Professor Palliser,[18] which should be read alongside the following pages. I shall not be so contentious as to dispute all Dr Haigh's verdicts. There can be no doubt that he is justified in placing Cornwall, Lancashire and even Lincolnshire among the slow developers. Wanting to be offensive, Henry VIII upbraided the Lincolnshire rebels of 1536[d] as 'the rude commons of one shire, and that one of the most brute and beestelie of the hole realme'.[19] With the broad Humber to the north and the broader fens to the south, it was subject to a topographical isolation almost rivalling that of Lancashire. This feature applied less to the more southerly shires within the huge diocese of Lincoln, which latter embraced most of the east Midlands from the Humber to the Thames. Though most parts of the diocese were distinctly slow to adopt new ideas, it should not be dismissed in purely negative terms, especially when we recall the depletion of its ecclesiastical records after 1547, and the fact that little pertinacious and revealing persecution occurred. Including Northamptonshire, detached in 1541 to form the new diocese of Peterborough, I have located – and again without prolonged seeking – activist Protestant groups in rather more places than might be expected.

From this unsensational scene, we move across the Midlands to their south-western areas, where the Cotswolds extend southward to the Avon and the Bristol Channel. Though not to the same degree as Kent, Essex and Suffolk, Gloucestershire proved receptive to the Reformation. The rather spectacular manifestation of Protestantism at Bristol had tended to obscure its diffusion throughout the many towns and villages long since made prosperous by sheep-farming and the cloth-trade; places like Wotton, Dursley, Tetbury, Chipping Campden, Stroud, Stonehouse, Newent, Lydney, Tewkesbury and Gloucester itself.[20] Not so many decades earlier Lollardy had spread across the country and into the industrial Forest of Dean, but from the mid-1530s the expansion of Lutheran ideas had obvious debts to Latimer's preaching and to the labours of people like Richard Webb, the busy distributor of Protestant books in Bristol.[21] By way of a climax there came in 1551 the appointment of the Zurich-trained Hooper to the new see of Gloucester, followed by his vigorous assault upon a parish clergy as yet ignorant of the new biblical theology, and in many cases of the most basic documents of Christianity. Despite his angular disciplinary zeal, Hooper maintained good relations with the civic authorities of Gloucester and also with the common people, who gathered in great numbers to deplore his execution for heresy.[22]

Yet again, both Wiltshire and Berkshire resembled Gloucestershire in their dependence upon the clothiers, whose mobility and social coherence helped them to propagate Reformation doctrines. The activism of this otherwise neglected area has been usefully chronicled by Mr I. T. Shield in an unpublished thesis of 1960, which deserves more attention than it has received. Not a few of the grandchildren of the pious West Country builders, patrons and parishioners of 'wool-churches' embraced Protestant ideas without waiting for safe times. Apart from the Gloucestershire martyrs, eleven other leaders suffered execution at Windsor, Salisbury, Devizes and at the productive cloth-town of Bradford on Avon. Under Mary some seven more burnings followed at Salisbury, Collingbourne and the former Lollard metropolis of Newbury.[23]

Apart from Bristol, Gloucestershire, Coventry and a few lesser places in Warwickshire and Staffordshire, religious changes came very gradually in the western Midlands and along the Welsh Marches. In Coventry, it is true, the new beliefs vigorously invaded even the ruling civic hierarchy and occasioned some martyrdoms, together with the expulsion and replacement of a heretical mayor by the Marian government.[24] Once a city of demonstrative piety, yet also an important Lollard centre, Coventry always held great importance for the reformers. Writing to Bullinger in July 1560, Thomas Lever recalled it as a place where there had always been 'great numbers zealous for the evangelical truth'. He then describes the burnings and banishments. Returning there shortly after Elizabeth's accession, Lever had found 'that vast numbers in this place were in the habit of frequenting the public preaching the Gospel', and so he had consented to settle in Coventry with his family and to serve as one of its preachers.[25] It can be safely assumed that this marked propensity was not suddenly created between Elizabeth's accession and July 1560.

In other parts of Warwickshire the cautious Protestants were probably numerous, at all events among the people who appear here as substantial testators. An analysis of about six hundred Warwickshire wills proved in the Prerogative Court of Canterbury shows that during the reign of Edward VI the number in that well-off class, who deliberately omitted the hitherto almost universal formulae indicating saint-worship, exceeded the traditionalist Catholic wills by nearly three to one. Naturally, under the Marian reaction many such testators nervously reverted to the traditional forms, yet even then the number of traditional wills does not much exceed that of the Protestant type.[26]

While the Tudor religious history of Staffordshire, Shropshire, Derbyshire and Cheshire has not yet been exhaustively investigated, it has been shown that the literary and devotional culture of that region remained on the whole conservative and slow-moving until and beyond the accession of Elizabeth.[27] Certainly, however, some locally sensitive enquiries need to be conducted within such areas, which were by no means homogeneous in spirit. So far, for example, we have been content to regard Lichfield as a quiet, backward-looking cathedral city,[28] yet to stage a local revision one need go no further than Foxe's *Acts and Monuments*, supported by items from his manuscript collection now in British Library Harleian MS 421. The more spectacular episodes occurred at Lichfield in the reign of Mary: they affected not only the population of the city but a number of people in the neighbouring places, especially within the nearby northern tip of Warwickshire. As usual, a local persecution reveals the facts.[29] Ralph Baines, a Catholic exile under Edward VI and a professor of Hebrew at Paris, returned to England at the accession of Mary and in November 1554 was consecrated as Bishop of Lichfield and Coventry. Along with his chancellor Anthony Draycot – another energetic Marian regarded by Foxe as notably cruel – Bishop Baines took strong action in September 1556 by compelling various Lichfield people to do penance as heretics. Joyce Lewis, daughter of a squire at Tixall and wife of another at Manchetter, refused. She was spared for a year, but only to be condemned and burned at Lichfield in September 1557. At her execution many members of the large crowd joined in drinking with her and showing other marked signs of admiration. There and then her numerous backers joined in open prayers for the abolition of the mass and 'papistry'. Even the officiating sheriff Nicholas Bird cried 'Amen' with the rest, while an unsympathetic priest compiled a list of the main demonstrators, many of whom (including Bird) were afterwards arrested and forced to do public penance. From the records of these transactions we derive the actual names of about sixty local Protestants, mostly from Lichfield itself. The other local martyr also came from the gentry. He was Robert Glover, who took his M. A. at Cambridge and inherited considerable lands at Baxterly and elsewhere. Having been examined at length by Bishop Baines at both Lichfield and Coventry, he was burned at the latter in September 1555. His younger brothers John and William Glover both suffered severe persecution; John, well known to Foxe, being an introspective Puritan who often despaired of his own salvation. Foxe also observes that John Glover had become the chief spiritual adviser to the martyr Joyce Lewis.

The annals of early Protestantism in Shropshire are much slighter, though as early as May 1528 Richard Cotton, curate of Atcham near Shrewsbury, abjured his heresies in Lichfield Cathedral.[30] He had been accused of reading Lutheran books and holding frequent disputations and conversations with disciples of the Lutheran sect 'and mainly with a certain George Constantine in the towns of Whitchurch and Atcham'. This reference is to Tyndale's well-known agent, who at Antwerp had been assisting the Reformer to set forth his edition of the New Testament and to prepare tracts for dispatch to England.

However debatable some of Dr Haigh's general theories may appear, it would be difficult to over-praise his authoritative work on the Reformation in Lancashire: it remains the most comprehensive and scholarly survey of any English region in Tudor times.[31] He describes a shire largely isolated between the Pennines and the Irish Sea.

Under Edward VI two devoted Protestant clerics, born Lancastrians and destined to martyrdom, conducted preaching tours. They and the few lay zealots like Geoffrey Hurst and Roger Holland found an exceptionally resistant clergy and people, with a reputation for rough manners and licentiousness. This primitive conservatism lingered until the advent of Jesuits and Seminary Priests during Elizabeth's later years, by which time Puritanism was also initiating that process whereby Lancashire became a museum of Protestant sects[32] as well as the most heavily Catholic county of the realm.

East of the Pennines we find this intensely provincial history by no means closely mirrored. Though late Elizabethan Yorkshire preserved several limited Catholic enclaves, its social and economic situation had long differed from the Lancashire model.[33] It had maintained direct seagoing contacts with the Continent for centuries. Alongside a few advanced squires and clerics, Yorkshire developed some major pockets of early Protestantism, as at Hull, Leeds and Halifax, while even conservative York did not wholly lack devotees, some of them from Continental background.[34]

In the far South-West of England, modern research is indicating situations more varied than that impression of uniform religious reaction one would derive from Frances Rose-Troup's classic narrative, *The Western Rebellion of 1549*. By far the most detailed analysis of religious change among the people is that by Dr Robert Whiting, who concludes that the Henrician and Edwardian changes rapidly shattered the old pieties, and that modern historians have indeed exaggerated the elements of religious resistance in mid-Tudor Devon and Cornwall. While Catholicism revived only with the coming of the Seminarists, the general popularizing of Anglicanism also occurred during the reign of Elizabeth.[35] Though the majority of the Western rebels doubtless followed their priests in demanding a return in religion to the last years of Henry VIII – though not to the Papal Supremacy – the old label 'Prayer Book Rebellion' ignores a well-documented complex of secular discontents in the South-West. That Cornwall, still largely Celtic-speaking, must be classed among the slower movers goes without saying, yet any claim that it was uniformly Catholic and 'medieval' until after 1558 would remain a simplification. It can be challenged by several references to Protestant opinion.[36]

Through discoveries and eliminations we are now close to defining the heartland of the English Reformation, the area wherein society was deeply permeated by Protestant doctrines before the accession of Elizabeth. It should certainly not be envisaged as consisting merely of London and Kent: rather should we think in terms of a great crescent running from Norwich down to Hove and beyond. Its most intensive sections were Suffolk, Essex, London and Kent. Despite the strength of Protestantism in Norwich and the long tally of martyrs in East Sussex, the two extremities of this crescent may have been somewhat less intensively involved. Yet in addition a western offshoot ran up the Thames Valley embracing not only the old Lollard centres in Buckinghamshire but also places in Oxfordshire and Berkshire, thus linking the crescent with the Protestant communities in Gloucestershire and Wiltshire. The few remaining districts of the South-East appear to have been far less affected than those already mentioned: for example, the inland areas of the diocese of Winchester, comprising most of Hampshire and Surrey, where, in the depleted episcopal records, little beyond a sparse succession of heretics and martyrs may be documented from 1530 onwards.[37] So much for our geographical survey, which has said little about the relatively undisputed areas, such as London and Kent at the Protestant extreme, or conversely those little-affected north-western counties, Cheshire, Derbyshire, Westmorland and Cumberland, which seem even more isolated than Lancashire itself.

It need scarcely be added that such a survey of early Protestant expansion would achieve more significance were it accompanied by an objective survey of Catholicism among the English people during this same period, c.1530–1558. In what senses was the old religion developing under the stresses of the Henrician and Edwardian state reformations? Was Catholic belief and observance in temporary decay? Had it fallen into the danger implied by Thomas More at his trial:[38] the deprivation of its international sustenance? Did the people 'of both religions' really 'detest the Pope', as the Venetian envoy Daniel Barbaro, a future Patriarch of Aquileia, reported from England in 1551?[39] Did the hapless Mary Tudor succeed in fusing Spanish Inquisition with Roman Papacy in the popular mind? How do we explain the collapse in 1559 of the hitherto conservative parish clergy? Why, apart from crass self-interest, did the great majority of them abscond so readily to the Elizabethan Settlement? On these mid-Tudor Catholic problems the evidence may prove somewhat rarefied, yet it seems strange that so very few historians have seriously attempted to explore in close detail this tract of religious history, the importance of which now seems so obvious.

IV CONTINUING RESEARCH: THE STUDY OF WILLS

Can we hope to extend our present imprecise notions as to the relative strengths of the Protestant and non-Protestant populations at the various stages of the period 1530–1558, and in particular counties and towns? Here our only hope of progress seems to lie in a mass study of the many thousands of contemporary wills still extant in ecclesiastical archives and probate registries. Already begun in certain places, this task needs to be pursued with caution, and without the expectation that refined statistics will emerge. Yet provided they are used in considerable numbers, wills seem broadly acceptable as indicating trends of opinion.[40] While individual testators quite frequently outline Protestant doctrines or give other direct evidence of religious beliefs, a mass survey must attach special importance to the pious preambles with which almost all wills of the period commence. Traditional Catholic wills begin with the testator leaving his soul to the company of the saints in heaven, while Protestant-type wills naturally discard this practice and show the testator bequeathing his soul to God or to Christ. In view of the still huge popularity of the saint-cults on the eve of the Reformation, a real significance can be attached to this differentiation, even though we certainly cannot presume that every will corresponds precisely with the personal religious standpoint of the testator. It is known that parish priests and notaries often gave advice on such points. The former and perhaps most of the latter, were people of conservative views, and if their pressures did in fact distort the picture, this would be by enhancing the prevalence of traditionalist, Catholic wills.

A number of scholars have pursued such enquiries in regard to various counties and towns, though classifying them under somewhat differing schemes. It has now become possible to make a provisional statement on the results so far obtained. The available localities are varied and together they may constitute

a fairly representative sample of the country as a whole. The
counties include Kent, East Sussex, Yorkshire, Warwickshire,
Lincolnshire and Nottinghamshire, together with the arch-
deaconry of Northampton and the urban communities of York,
Hull, Leeds and Norwich.[41] The trends indicated in these various
areas have a good deal in common. As Professor Scarisbrook
discovered after reading very numerous early wills, the great
majority continues to make traditional bequests to the Church
throughout the 1530s.[42] In the above group of places, apart from
London and Kent, signs of change are indeed by no means
common until around 1545, while the notable period of Protestant advances occupies the whole of Edward VI's reign. Soon
after the accession of Mary there occurs a predictable decline of
Protestant forms, though nowhere does this partial reversion
restore the Henrician situation. Then in 1559–60 a swift
resurgence of Protestantism supports my conjecture that many
crypto-Protestants, doubtless accompanied by mere opportun-
ists, emerged into the open as soon as it became safe to do so.

As one would anticipate, such fluctuations occur at somewhat
later dates and lower numerical levels in Yorkshire, Lincolnshire
and other conservative areas, as compared with 'advanced'
Kent, where we observe already an annual increase in Protestant-type wills from 1532 to 1542. By the years 1542–46 about
half the Kent wills were showing Protestant inclinations, which
then heavily predominated throughout Edwardian years, and
even – though in lesser degree – under Mary. As elsewhere, the
Protestant figures in Kent rise dramatically in 1559–60.

In Yorkshire a high proportion of the numerous extant wills
remain in manuscript: I have assessed 750 of them dated from
1538 to 1558, but this figure is far from exhausting the surviving
deposit of Yorkshire wills; it needs to be amplified and to be
split regionally, since patterns were far from uniform over so
large and varied a territory. Yet somewhat to my surprise, I
found that more than a third of these wills rescinded the saints,
while for the years 1547 to 1553 there occurred 139 traditional
wills, as opposed to 153 of Protestant type, with 31 'neutral'.

Throughout all these groups of wills the local evidence on
religious opinion corresponds to a reassuring extent with the
miscellaneous information derived from other sources. It attests
not only the advanced situation of Kent but also some of the
more localized situations, such as the Protestant tenor of belief at

mercantile Leeds and Hull, as compared with the conservative, clerical ethos of York. Future progress with these admittedly rough and ready indicators may perhaps produce some surprises, yet so far the results strongly argue that we must not take lightly the substantial advances made by the English Reformation before 1558. they also clearly indicate that neither Lancashire at one extreme nor Kent at the other should be accepted as a national norm. Yet statistics and maps apart, the present writer comes away from all these sources with the distinct impression that, by the advent of Elizabeth, Protestantism had not only surmounted the harshest threat to its survival but had for the time being attained a greater psychological vitality and cohesion in English society than had the cause of conservative Catholicism. At all events this impression would seem fully applicable to the large south-eastern heartland and its westward extensions, the regions which by mere area comprised less than half of England, though constituting the wealthiest, most populous and best-educated portion of the realm.

V SOME RESIDUAL PROBLEMS

In conclusion I desire to set the record straight regarding some general issues which have arisen directly from the problems discussed in the foregoing pages. As already remarked, some readers may have derived the impression that I hold a simplistic belief in 'Reformation from below', as distinct from 'Reformation from above', as an act of state.[43] Writing fifty or even thirty years ago, I certainly did hope to modify the excessive preoccupation of English historians with the statute book, with the mechanisms of church and state, with the top people who manipulated both. It then seemed high time to reiterate that, in England as elsewhere, the Reformation also involved personal conversions and convictions. In particular, should modern observers become too coolly enlightened to perceive the supreme propaganda value of martyrdom, they would lose contact not only with the Tudor mind, but with all Christian history. Even so, our modern concern with popular religion and grassroots mentalities must not for a moment be suffered to obliterate our interest in the familiar theme of 'Reformation from above'. The greater part of my book *The English Reformation* did in fact continue to treat this old theme in detail, since 'from above' and 'from below' remain inseparable and equally essential elements of the story. After all, even the Henrician government abolished the monastic life, brutally despoiled the saints' shrines, forbade 'superstitious' cults, provided English Bibles in the churches and allowed Cranmer to experiment with a vernacular liturgy. Such masterful acts of state powerfully affected, though they never totally dictated, popular belief and opinion. Their continuance and expansion by the Edwardian government gave Protestant convictions the necessary breathing space to attain that degree of recruitment, integration and confidence needed to survive the Marian counter-assault, which must still be regarded as the major crisis of the Reformation in England.

EDITOR'S NOTES

Reprinted with the permission of the author from the *Archiv für Reformationsgeschichte*, 79 (1988), pp. 187–221.

a William Cecil was Elizabeth's principal secretary, and Lord Treasurer 1572–98.
b Foxe was the author of the *Acts and Monuments* (1563, abridged as the 'Book of Martyrs'), a very Protestant martyrology and history of the 'true church', especially in England. After the English Bible, his book was the second-best seller of the sixteenth century.
c You may find it useful to refer to the map on p. xiii as you read this section.
d The 1536 Pilgrimage of Grace was a northern Catholic rebellion primarily against the new religion and particularly Thomas Cromwell's efforts to dissolve the monasteries. Some historians identify secular motives for the rebels as well.

NOTES

1 C. Haigh, 'The Recent Historiography of the English Reformation', chapter 1, above, and other works cited below, notes 2, 3, 10, 11; J. J. Scarisbrick, *The Reformation and the English People* (Oxford, 1984), especially p. 137.
2 *EHR*, 98 (1983), p. 371.
3 C. Haigh, ed., *The Reign of Elizabeth I* (London, 1984), p. 196; J. J. Scarisbrook, *Reformation*, ch. 2.
4 Scarisbrick, *Reformation* p. 136.
5 A. G. Dickens, *Lollards and Protestants in the Diocese of York* (Oxford, 1959), p. 251. For analogous statements in 1941 and 1957 see my *Reformation Studies* (London, 1982), pp. 156–7, 182; *The English Reformation* (London, 1964), pp. 308, 318, 336–7.

6 R. B. Manning, *Religion and Society in Elizabethan Sussex* (Leicester, 1969), ch. 3; E. T. Stoneham, *Sussex Martyrs of the Reformation*, 3rd edn (Burgess Hill, 1967), shows that, with two or three exceptions, they were manual workers from sixteen places in East Sussex.

7 Foxe's main passages on Suffolk are in *Acts and Monuments*, ed. S. R. Cattley (London, 1837–41), VIII, pp. 145–8, 424–7. He has also much on Lollardy there: ibid, III, pp. 584–600. The most important record-sources are treated by R. A. Houlbrooke: 'Persecution of Heresy and Protestantism in the Diocese of Norwich under Henry VIII', *Norfolk Archaeology*, 35, (1973), and in his *Church Courts and the People during the English Reformation* (Oxford, 1979), ch. 8, especially pp. 222–42. Compare Foxe's own statement: 'Many other, yea a great multitude were persuected in Suffolke also, whych for that I lack their names, I omyt at this time.' This passage was removed from the editions of the *Acts and Monuments* after that of 1563, but restored in J. Pratt's edition of 1877, vol. VIII, App. vi (unpaginated). On Sussex see M. J. Kitch, 'The Reformation in Sussex', *Studies in Sussex Church History*, ed. M. J. Kitch (London, 1981), pp. 77–98; G. J. Mayhew, in 'The Progress of the Reformation in East Sussex 1530–1559: The Evidence from Wills', *Southern History*, 5 (1983), pp. 38–67. On Norfolk see R. A. Houlbrooke: 'Persecution of Heresy' and Elaine Sheppard, 'The Reformation and the Citizens of Norwich', *Norfolk Archaeology*, 38 (1983), pp. 44–58. Gloucestershire is more fully treated in this present article: see notes 20–2 below.

8 J. E. Oxley, *The Reformation in Essex* (Manchester, 1965), chs ix, x, describes the main personalities and martyrs, but does not bring out the volume of early Protestantism in that county. Dr Fines's *Register* names 304 early Essex Protestants, including some thirty-nine martyrs. On other local features see D. M. Loades: 'The Essex Inquisitions of 1556', *Bulletin of the Institute of Historical Research*, 35 (1962), pp. 87–97.

9 C. Haigh, 'Puritan Evangelism in the Reign of Elizbaeth I', *EHR*, 92 (1977), pp. 30–58.

10 Dr Haigh has warned against this tendency: *Reformation and Resistance in Tudor Lancashire* (Cambridge, 1975), pp. 76–7; 'Recent Historiography' pp. 1002–3.

11 For statistics on the Marian martyrs, see e.g., J. H. Blunt, *The Reformation of the Church of England* (London, 1896), II, pp. 220–4; H. E. Malden, 'Notes on the Local Progress of Protestantism in England', *TRHS*, NS 2 (1885), pp. 61–76. Blunt, *Reformation*, pp. 275–8, comments on belief in deliverance from pain.

12 Foxe, *Acts and Monuments*, VIII, p. 407.

13 Moralist attacks on alehouses by e.g., Fisher, Cranmer, Crowley and Christopherson preceded those by Elizabethan Puritans. See also P. Clark, 'The Alehouse and the Alternative Society', D. Pennington and K. Thomas, eds, *Puritans and Revolutionaries* (Oxford, 1978), pp. 61–7. Bishop Bonner forbade his flock to visit alehouses, go hawking or hide at home in service-time (Gina Alexander, 'Bonner and the Marian Persecution', *History*, 60 (1975), p. 387). Compare

the licensing statutes, 5 & 6 Edward VI, cap. 25 and 2 & 3 Philip and Mary, cap. 9. Towns also could prohibit drinking in service-time, e.g. in 1555 at Coventry, *The Coventry Leet Book*, pt 3, *Early English Text Society*, original series, 138 (1909), p. 812.

14 J. Strype, *Ecclesiastical Memorials* (Oxford, 1822), III (pt 2), p. 434. In 1556 Clement also wrote a long confession of faith (ibid., pp. 446–67) and died in the King's Bench prison (Foxe, *Acts and Monuments*, VIII p. 151).

15 M. Claire Cross, the two articles cited in note 34, below; D. M. Palliser, *The Reformation in York* (Borthwick Institute, York, 1971), p. 32.

16 R. Howell, *Newcastle upon Tyne and the Puritan Revolutuion* (Oxford, 1967), pp. 63–82 *VCH, Warwickshire*, II (1908), pp. 33–8, gives the main references for the Marian persecution at Coventry; on its striking earlier Tudor Lollardy, see Foxe, *Acts and Monuments*, IV, 133–5, 557–8, together with the recent discoveries by J. Fines, 'Heresy Trials in the Diocese of Coventry and Lichfield', *Journal of Ecclesiastical History*, 15 (1963), pp. 160–74; G. R. Elton, *Policy and Police* (Cambridge, 1972), pp. 133–5. On John Rough in northern England, see A. G. Dickens, *Lollards and Protestants* pp. 197–9.

17 Foxe, *Acts and Monuments* VI, pp. 676–8.

18 D. M. Palliser, 'Popular Reactions to the Reformation during the Years of Uncertainty', in Felicity Heal and Rosemary O'Day, eds, *Church and Society in England. Henry VIII to James I* (London, 1977), pp. 35–56.

19 *State Papers of Henry VIII*, I (London, 1830), p. 463.

20 Dr Fines's *Register* has only 64 named early Protestants in Gloucestershire. Of these about 40 are distributed across 20 parishes, the rest being in Gloucester and Bristol, which latter obviously contained numerous Protestants outside these lists.

21 Richard Webb was reported to More (as Lord Chancellor) for scattering 'pestilent' books in the streets and leaving them on doorsteps. See T. More, *The Confutation of Tyndale's Answer*, Complete works, Yale edition, VIII, pt 2, pp. 813–15. Webb was later one of Foxe's informants; see K. G. Powell, 'The Beginnings of Protestantism in Gloucestershire', *Transactions, Bristol and Gloucestershire Archaeological Society*, 90 (1971) p. 143.

22 F. D. Price, 'Gloucester Diocese under Bishop Hooper', *Transactions of the Bristol and Gloucestershire Archaeological Society*, 60 (1939), p. 147.

23 I. T. Shield, 'The Reformation in the Diocese of Salibsury 1547–1562' (University of Oxford B. Litt. thesis 1960) pp. 211–24. On Newbury, see C. G. Durston, 'Wild as Colts Untamed: Radicalism in the Newbury Area,' *Southern History*, 6 (1984), pp. 36–52.

24 *VCH, Warwickshire*, III (1908), pp. 33–4 gives main references.

25 H. Robinson, ed., *The Zurich Letters* (Parker Society, 1842), pp. 86–7.

26 This survey was made by a research student some years ago; it has not yet been checked or printed.

27 For this region see Imogen Luxton, 'The Reformation and Popular

Culture', in Heal and O'Day, eds, *Church and Society in England*, pp. 57–77.

28 The best background account is in P. Heath, 'Staffordshire Towns and the Reformation', *North Staffordshire Journal of Field Studies*, 19 (1979), pp. 1–21.

29 The subsequent passage is based upon Foxe, *Acts and Monuments* VIII, pp 255–6, 401–5, 429. Compare British Library, Harleian MS 421, fos 69, 73, 78. Joyce Lewis, Robert Glover, Laurence Saunders, Anthony Draycot, Augustine Bernher and Bishop Baines are all in the *Dictionary of National Biography*. The detail on the Glover family is mainly in Foxe, *Acts and Monuments*, VII, pp. 384–402. Baines and Draycot were active in the case of the blind martyr of Derby, Joan Waste (Foxe, *Acts and Monuments*, VIII, pp. 247–50).

30 J. Fines, 'An Incident of the Reformation in Shropshire', *Transactions of the Shropshire Archaeological Society*, 57 (1961–4), pp. 166–8; C. Haigh, *Reformation and Resistance*, pp. 76–9, gives further references on heresy in the diocese of Lichfield.

31 C. Haigh, *Reformation and Resistance*: for Bradford and Marsh see chs 10–12, *passim*; for Hurst, pp. 85, 172–3, 187–92, 208; for Holland pp. 46, 50, 161, 190, 193. On reputed immorality, index s.v., and on traditional piety, chs. 5, 11, 12.

32 The modern religious history of the county is well summarized by W. A. Shaw in *VCH, Lancashire*, II, pp. 68–96.

33 A. G. Dickens, *Lollards and Protestants* pp. 1–7.

34 Ibid., index s.v. Halifax, Hull, Leeds, Beverley; M. Claire Cross, 'The Development of Protestantism in Leeds and Hull, 1520–1640. The Evidence from Wills', *Northern History*, 18 (1982), pp. 230–8; ibid., 'Parochial Structure and the Dissemination of Protestantism ... A Tale of Two Cities', in D. Baker, ed., *Studies in Church History*, XVI (London, 1979), pp. 269–78.

35 R. Whiting, 'The Reformation in the South-West of England' (University of Exeter Ph. D. thesis, 1977). Note especially pp. 293–8, 'The Impact of the Reformation'. *The Western Rebellion of 1549* (London, 1913) nevertheless remains a mine of information. A. L . Rowse based upon it an excellent account in *Tudor Cornwall* (London, 1941), ch. 11.

36 F. E. Halliday, ed., *Richard Carew of Antony. The Survey of Cornwall* (London, 1953), pp. 196–7. Carew first published the work in 1602.

37 R.A. Houlbrooke, *Church Courts*, has much information on the conservative diocese of Winchester, see also *VCH, Hampshire*, II, pp. 66–75. On the stubborn citizens of Winchester, note Bishop Horne's letter of January 1562 in *State Papers, Domestic, Elizabeth*, XXI, no. 7. The main Protestant hero is Archdeacon John Philpot (Foxe, *Acts and Monuments* VI, pp. 396ff; VII, pp. 605–714, VIII, pp. 171–3), and the horror story that of Thomas Bembridge (*Acts and Monuments* VIII, pp. 490–2; *Acts of the Privy Council*, VII, p. 361).

38 The arguments for a strong continuous Catholic survival are well put by C. Haigh, 'The Continuity of Catholicism in the English Reformation', *Past and Present*, no. 93 (1981), pp. 37–69. The view is

supported by J. J. Scarisbrick, *Reformation*, ch. 7. On spontaneous revival under Mary, see D. M. Loades, *The Reign of Mary Tudor* (London, 1979), pp. 351–2.

39 *Calendar of State Papers, Venice*, v, p. 346.
40 I refer to More's declaration at his trial (R.W. Chambers, *Thomas More* (Peregrine edn, 1963), pp. 325–6).
41 P. Clark, *English Provincial Society from the Reformation to the Revolution. Religion, Politics and Society in Kent, 1500–1640* (Hassocks, 1977), pp. 41, 58–60, 76–7, 100, 102, 152, 420 (notes 73–3); Mayhew, 'Progress of the Reformation', pp. 38–67; A. G. Dickens, *Lollards and Protestants* pp. 171–2, 215–18, 220–1; D. Wilson, *A Tudor Tapestry* (London, 1972), p. 260; W.J. Sheils, *The Puritans in the Diocese of Peterborough* (Northamptonshire Record Society, 30 1979), pp. 15–18; D.M. Palliser, *The Reformation in York*, p. 32; M. Claire Cross, 'Parochial Structure', *passim*; 'The Development of Protestantism in Leeds and Hull, *passim*; Sheppard, 'The Reformation and the Citizens of Norwich,' pp. 44–58. In addition note the smaller groups of wills cited by Margaret Spufford, *Contrasting Communities*, and by C. Haigh, *Reformation and Resistance*, pp. 68–71, 82, 194, 220–1, 227; these latter concern the numerous Lancashire wills printed by the Chetham Society and elsewhere. It should finally be noted that Dr Susan Brigden in her Cambridge Ph. D. thesis (1977) 'The Early Reformation in London', pp. 333–48, also finds wills important as an index to religious change in London.
42 There was certainly an upsurge of Protestant wills, with a full-blown non-Catholic preamble and absence of traditional religious legacies, in London from the mid-1530s (Scarisbrook, *Reformation*, p. 6). On methodology see M. L. Zell, 'The Use of Religious Preambles as a Measure of Religious Belief in the Sixteenth Century', *BIHR*, 1 (1977), pp. 246–9.
43 C. Haigh, 'Recent Historiography', and elsewhere.

10

CALVINISM AND THE ENGLISH CHURCH 1570–1635

Peter Lake

Like Collinson, Peter Lake has found a good deal of consensus between puritans and non-puritans in the Elizabethan Church. Like Tyacke, he finds agreement on a Calvinist view of grace as the theological basis for this consensus. And like both, he finds the Arminian and Laudian threats after the accession of Charles to have been calamitous for the unity of the Church. A close look at his work, though, reveals that he has not thereby abandoned either puritanism or the high road. He adds to the usual array of religious issues – anti-popery, predestination, preaching – a more fundamental question dividing the Church of England from its very foundation: How can an inclusive, national church be established on a theology that assumes a distinction between the elect and the reprobate? Puritans, who perceived themselves to be elect and attempted to act out their election with pious and disciplined behaviour ('practical divinity'), were committed to further reforming the state church from within, not separating themselves from it. But the tension implicit in their understanding of the true church as the community of the godly necessarily surfaced as they combated enemies of reform within the visible church – especially when those enemies denied predestinarian theology.

Lake is among the first historians to focus explicitly on moderate puritans, rather than on their more extreme colleagues, without simply amalgamating them into middle-of-the-road protestantism, as Collinson and others have. In order to draw the line between moderate puritans and the non-puritan Calvinists whom he also examines, he follows R. T. Kendall[a] in distinguishing two kinds of predestinarianism within English Calvinism: 'experimental predestinarians' were those committed to acting out their election with godly behaviour and pious activity; they were inclined to define the true church as those whose behaviour gave visible testimony to their doctrine. Theirs was the problem of how an inclusive national church, many of whose formal members were not particularly godly in action, could nevertheless be a true church. 'Credal predestinarians', by contrast, affirmed the doctrines of predestination, election and assurance, but did not insist on a behavioural distinction between the godly and ungodly within the national church. They preferred to assume and encourage the unity and comprehensiveness of the visible Christian community. It will be useful to keep this distinction in mind as you read the following chapter.

* * *

In a recent number of *Past and Present*, that reading of the political history of the early seventeenth century which has come to be known as revisionism was subjected to critical review from a variety of different perspectives.[1] This critical assault was both widened and continued by Peter White's article[2] on the rise of English Arminianism.[b] White's article raises issues which no historian of late sixteenth- and early seventeenth-century English religious and political history can ignore. The idea of a Calvinist consensus has been used to deny the existence of any nexus of distinctively puritan interests or concerns in the Jacobean Church. As Patrick Collinson has observed, 'Calvinism can be regarded as the theological cement of the Jacobean Church ... a common and ameliorating bond uniting conformists and moderate puritans.'[3] Building on that insight, other historians, like Conrad Russell, have presented Puritans as but the most self-consciously godly elements within a Calvinist consensus. Puritanism is now defined largely in personal and pietistic terms and is denied any direct political significance until the rise of an aggressive Arminianism created a politically assertive Puritanism where there had been none before. Since Calvinists – Puritans included – were the dominant force in the Jacobean Church, their aims can be presented as essentially conservative, founded on memories of a golden age of Elizabethan Protestant purity and unity. It was the sudden rise to power of Arminianism in the reign of Charles I that represented the truly destabilizing, even revolutionary, event in the history of the early Stuart Church.[4]

In arraying his arguments against this 'revisionist' case, White has addressed both theological and political issues. In his view, predestination becomes again a 'Puritan' issue and the major religious conflict of the period becomes once more that waged between a radical predestinarian Puritanism and a moderate Anglican mainstream. The polarization between the revisionist view and that put forward by Peter White does not, however, exhaust the possibilities. It is quite possible to take issue with many of White's assertions without simply underwriting the views he is attacking. In short, one can argue for both the heterogeneity of 'Puritanism' and the revolutionary implications of the impact of Arminianism.

In the first place, it must be emphasized that the notion of a Calvinist consensus does not necessarily imply that all the English who regarded themselves as Protestant in the period before 1625 were explicitly Calvinist or that the only serious religious or theological divide in that period was that involving the theology of grace between Calvinists and anti-Calvinists. We are dealing here with the culture of educated, literate Protestants. We are concerned with the opinions of an educated élite. Moreover it is not necessary, in order to argue for the dominance of Calvinist orthodoxy within that élite, to maintain that all of its members were indeed convinced Calvinists. Examples of individuals who were not will not clinch the argument. The question is one of degree: which opinions predominated and at whose expense.

The basic point, therefore, concerns Calvinist hegemony. But hegemony is not monopoly. Despite Calvinist predominance, there were anti-Calvinists in the Elizabethan and Jacobean Church. Indeed one can easily accept the claims of men like Humphrey Leech and Benjamin Carier that their open expressions of dissent represented but the tip of an iceberg of discontent and unease.[5] The existence of such people and their silence represent powerful evidence of the extent to which Calvinism had established itself in control of the crucial cultural media of the day and was thus able to suppress overt criticism.[6] On this view it is not even necessary to argue that anti-Calvinists were systematically excluded from preferment. Clearly they were not. However, the path to preferment did not lie through the open expression of such sentiments.

I

In 1571, in a sermon against the papists delivered at St Paul's Cross, a preacher addressed himself to the text that 'God so loved the world that he gave his only begotten son that all that believe on him should not perish but have eternal life.' According to that preacher, the text contained

> all the causes of our salvation even the ground work and principles of Christianity, the lock and key of our religion, which being opened all controversies at this day in question between us and our adversaries (as depending hereon) are apparent and soon decided.

To justify what might seem an extravagant claim, the text was subjected to a full-scale Calvinist gloss. 'The world' which God so loved that he gave his only son to save it was equated with the elect. The opposite opinion, that God wanted and Christ died to save all men, was explicitly denounced as a Pelagian and popish error:

> To say therefore it is God's will that all men should be saved is a false principle. But thus say the papists and wrest the words of God to deny his eternal purpose of election and reprobation, the papists, therefore, make an evident liar of God. For if God would, who could resist the will of God?

The preacher was adamant that neither man's works nor God's foreknowledge of them had anything to do with this process, whereby the elect were saved. To suggest that they did was a popish opinion.[7]

Again in the 1570s another divine cited a long passage from Beza,[c] describing the four types of members of the visible church. Of these, the first were those 'whom we call by the word of God reprobate and vessels of anger appointed to destruction'. Admittedly, some such might in 'appearance, that is in outward profession, yea and a certain semblance of faith' resemble the truly godly and come to be 'reckoned among the members of the church'. Yet they would not persist in such godly ways, prompting the judgement of John: 'if they had been of us they would have tarried with us.' The second category of church members comprised those 'chosen in Christ by eternal election' who had yet to come to a proper outward profession of true belief. Such had been Paul when 'he was a long time the member of Satan persecuting Christ', and it was to people of this type that the apostle had been referring when he wrote that 'God loved us when we were his enemies'. The third type of church member consisted of those 'that both by election and indeed are the sons of God'. The fourth category was made up of such members of the elect who had been called and actually engrafted into Christ but who, 'having fallen in something', had been 'excommunicated or delivered to Satan not that they should perish (for it is not possible that they should perish which are the members of Christ) but that godly sorrowfulness may cause repentance', and to avoid 'offence to the other members'.[8]

Theological opinion, of course, does not lend itself to quantification. The citation of example and counter-example in itself proves nothing. However, on White's argument it would be reasonable to expect the authors of these two extreme predestinarian outbursts to have been precisian radicals of some sort. Not so. The first was John Bridges, a prebendary of Winchester in 1571 and a future bishop of Oxford. He was also the author of perhaps the longest and probably the most boring conformist[d] defence of the English Church against presbyterianism. In that book he had countered Puritan claims that the sixteenth of the Thirty-nine Articles allowed that even the elect could fall from grace, with an explicitly Calvinist gloss on the relevant passages.[9] Indeed it was a crucial part of Bridges's case against the Puritans that there were no points of doctrine at stake in the debate with the presbyterians. For Bridges it was an argument about the details of discipline. The Puritans were much to be blamed for breaking the peace of the Church over such inessential issues when unity prevailed over those central questions of doctrine upon which salvation depended and which united all English Protestants against the papists.[10] The second of the two authors quoted above was none other than John Whitgift, writing against Thomas Cartwright[e] in the Admonition Controversy. In that controversy Whitgift repeatedly made Bridges's point about the true doctrine of the English Church, and Cartwright at no point demurred.[11] This surely implies the existence of a formal consensus on the theology of grace, uniting leading apologists of the English Church with the leading proponents of presbyterianism.

What, however, did this Calvinist consensus on the issue of predestination involve? Did it imply a similar uniformity of religious world-view uniting Puritans and conformists? On some readings Nicholas Tyacke's work could be taken to suggest that it did. But this is neither a necessary implication of Tyacke's work nor of the argument advanced here. To return to Whitgift's citation of the passage from Beza, he quoted Beza in the course of a long discussion of the relationship between the visible and invisible church. That was a discussion prompted by Cartwright's attempt to limit membership of the visible church to those Christians who, on his definition, had attained to a proper visible godliness. Whitgift, asserting the impossibility of a final division between the elect and reprobate in this life, used Beza to underwrite his own much more broad-bottomed view of the Christian community, enshrined in the membership of the visible church.

This disagreement about the visible godliness of the visible church or, stated differently, over the extent and nature of the Christian community, was arguably the crucial divide in English Protestant opinion during this period. While it would be an overstatement to claim that the debate about the government of the Church was *really* about two rival views of the Christian community and its relations to the visible church, and only tangentially about what Scripture had to say on the polity[f] of the church, it remains true that different views of the Christian community lay very close to the centre of the presbyterian/conformist debate.[g]

Both Puritan and conformist positions on these issues could be buttressed by tenets taken from the heart of Calvinist orthodoxy. To see how this worked, we need to have recourse to a distinction first formulated by R. T. Kendall. It is the distinction between credal and experimental predestinarianism. Experimental predestinarians wanted to place their view of predestination, election and assurance at the centre of their practical divinity, to erect a style of piety on the foundations provided by a Calvinist doctrine of predestination, and to define the godly community (and in some cases the visible church) in terms of those who both understood those doctrines and acted upon them.[12] The links between such a style of piety and a view of the visible church which sought to restrict active membership to the visibly godly and to use an aggressive spiritual discipline to effect the necessary division between the godly and the ungodly are clear enough. Though clear, however, those links were contingent rather than necessary. Not all exponents of an experimental predestinarian style of divinity felt compelled or chose to follow the presbyterian or semi-separatist logic of their position. Given the legal and political consequences of doing so (certainly in the period after 1590), there were inducements enough to retard such a process. However, it may be no accident that many of Kendall's leading experimental predestinarians (and here one thinks of William Bradshaw, William Ames, John Cotton, Paul Baynes, Thomas Hooker), at one point or another in their careers, ended up on the semi-separatist left. The efforts of their more moderate or politic contemporaries to restrict the divisive, radical implications of experimental predestinarianism led to subtle but important changes in the nature of Calvinist orthodoxy itself. Certainly, it was an experimentalism severely limited to the individual rather than the collective level which was the dominant strain of theological opinion among the 'Calvinist episcopalians' (to borrow Tyacke's phrase) who presided over the Jacobean Church.

Credal Calvinists, while they might agree whole-heartedly with the formal content of Calvinist predestinarianism, had no impulse to take the doctrine into the popular pulpit or to derive a view of the Christian community from it. Indeed, to a greater or lesser extent, they tended to be alarmed by the antinomian and subversive consequences of such an experimental style of divinity. This can be seen clearly in Whitgift's contribution to the Admonition Controversy. There he used a Calvinist view of the doctrine of predestination to shift much of Cartwright's rhetoric about the glory and purity of the church from the visible to the invisible church. By doing so, he was able to clear the way for that Erastian dominance of the Church by the magistrate for which his work is famous, and to challenge the significance of a practical division between the godly and the ungodly as the crucial act in the creation of a true church.

* * *

The author at this juncture in his essay points out an alternative both to Whitgift's credal predestinarianism and to the puritans' experimental predestinarianism. The Elizabethan apologist Richard Hooker, author of The Laws of Ecclesiastical Polity, *provided a very different apologetic for an inclusive national church, one not dependent on a Calvinist view of election.*

* * *

Richard Hooker belongs to the opposite pole of conformist thought to that occupied by Whitgift. Starting from an even more generous definition of the Christian community than Whitgift, Hooker did not resort to any sort of developed predestinarian argument to justify his position.[13] Still less did he start quoting Beza. Rather he adopted a more Christocentric approach, implying that since Christ died for all men, all men were actually or potentially part of Christ's body, the church. Moreover, Hooker tried to impart a positive religious content to that membership by playing down the role of preaching in the church and placing far more emphasis on 'public worship', prayer and the sacraments than had earlier conformist apologists. In particular, it was through his vision of the sacrament really offering Christ's body and blood to all who received it in good faith that Hooker broke down the barrier between the visible and the invisible church. It was through his vision of the sacrament that he was able to apply to the former an intensely Christocentric rhetoric (centred on the incorporation of the believer into Christ's mystical body) which properly belonged, as he himself admitted, only to the latter. The resulting view of true religion, and of the church, sat rather uneasily next to what passed for Calvinist orthodoxy. But while there are some explicitly anti-experimental predestinarian remarks in the *Polity*, there are no such attacks on formal Calvinist doctrine.

With Hooker we are close to the ideological origins of English Arminianism. They lie in the need to legitimate and infuse with a positively religious content that view of the Christian community to which all conformist divines were committed by the logic of their polemical situation. As the century drew to a close, the issue of church polity[h] faded into relative obscurity, leaving these two visions of what the Christian community could and should be like to continue in implicit and often unstated opposition to one another, within the mainstream of the Jacobean Church.

There were, of course, a number of issues other than those concerning predestination around which public discussion of this basic division could be organized. Here perhaps the most obvious example is the debate about the visibility and continuity of the church, which burst into life in the 1620s. The second obvious issue around which such differences might crystallize was the role and nature of 'worship' in the life of the church. This involved the whole question of the relative importance of preaching compared to that of set prayer and the sacraments. Again, by implication, the issue of the nature and extent of the Christian community was raised. Was membership of that community best defined by the proper internalization of right doctrine and consequent godly conversation of true believers, or through the observance of the hierarchically transmitted and defined practices of the national church? Of course the two approaches were not mutually exclusive, any more than an emphasis on preaching was imcompatible with reverence for the sacrament. Indeed there is no reason to suppose that many ministers, moderate Puritans as well as conformists, did not manage to combine the demands of order and edification, sacrament and sermon, in some sort of balanced synthesis. However, the balance struck between those two elements could clearly vary, and by emphasizing the demands of one element in the synthesis at the expense of the other, it was possible to produce radically different visions of the minister's role and of true religion. The start of that process can be seen in the 1590s when both John Howson and Richard Hooker, reacting against what they saw as the Puritans' almost idolatrous overvaluation of the sermon, attempted to produce a style of piety and view of the ministry centred far more on public prayer and the sacraments than on the pulpit.[14] Such opinions, which were rather novel, at least in the context of Elizabethan Protestanism, attracted considerable criticism from evangelical Calvinists.

The exact nature of the division of opinion on this issue in the early Stuart Church awaits further study, but it is clear that divisions did exist. It can also be argued that those divisions raised issues of relevance to the debate over predestination, if only because of the role of that doctrine in the experimental predestinarian style of preaching and piety. Only when the purposes to which such preachers and their lay followers and patrons put the doctrine of election had been suppressed could the opponents of that style of divinity be said to have won control of the church. Predestination had another significance; it was the one issue on which even the most moderate and careerist of traditional Protestants found it hard to compromise. For those wishing to purge the English Church of evangelical Calvinism, it represented an ideal shibboleth with which to expose and discomfort their adversaries. But precisely because it was such a contentious issue, predestination could only be used in that way by anti-Calvinists when their cause was really, perhaps definitively, in the ascendant. Even then, as we shall see, it had to be treated with caution, but until then anti-Calvinists had to content themselves with other issues. Perhaps significantly, the two under discussion here – the visibility and continuity of the church and the nature and role of worship – were both first raised in a coherently anti-Puritan and indeed anti-experimental predestinarian context by Richard Hooker. Again, it seems, all paths lead back to the Elizabethan debate about the government of the church and, in particular, to Hooker's contribution to that debate.

What, then, are we left with? We have evidence of a formal Calvinist consensus linking Whitgift and Bridges with Puritans (both moderate and presbyterian) like Cartwright, Fulke, William Whitaker and Laurence Chaderton. But we have within that consensus considerable differences of tone and emphasis, which were indicative of deep yet largely unstated disagreements about what true religion was and what the practical consequences of right doctrine were. Finally, we have some evidence that the internal contradictions within Calvinist conformity were prompting a new style of divinity[i] which was not based on Calvinist views of predestination and, indeed, was capable of generating a critique of tenets central to contemporary Calvinist orthodoxy.

This situation, and particularly the tensions within Calvinism itself, explains a great deal about Whitgift's attitude to the Lambeth Articles. I have argued elsewhere that those Articles, even after Whitgift's emendations, were Calvinist in tone; they can be taken to represent Whitgift's continuing allegiance to Calvinist orthodoxy. However, the differences between Whitgift and the heads of the Cambridge colleges, albeit not ones of formal doctrine, were serious enough for all that. For Whitgift predestination was a subject of difficulty, even of danger in the wrong hands. It might be the subject of dispute among scholars, but not in the popular pulpit. Most significantly for the present argument, the point about which Whitgift had most difficulty in 1595–6 and during the Admonition Controversy was assurance. Whitgift surely found it difficult on both occasions because it was assurance, seen as a doctrine and an experience, which underwrote that Puritan tendency to insist on visible godliness as a qualification for membership of both the church and the Christian community, the divisive and subversive implications of which Whitgift so abhorred.[15] Yet in the last analysis, doctrinal and experimental predestinarians agreed on formal doctrine and that formal agreement was enshrined in the Lambeth Articles.

II

The Lambeth Articles failed, definitively, to carry the day as a test for doctrinal orthodoxy. They failed because of the personal intervention of the queen, not because of any backsliding or second thoughts on Whitgift's part.[16] Where did that leave the doctrinal position of the English Church? It left it ambiguous. The failure of the Lambeth Articles to achieve official sanction, and Whitgift's embarrassment at that failure, had exposed the dubious nature of Calvinist claims to represent official ortho-doxy. The Thirty-nine Articles were left exposed to glosses other than those produced by orthodox Calvinists. Once token assent to the Lambeth Articles had been extracted, there was little that even Whitgift could do. But from the débâcle of the Lambeth Articles onwards, there were two sides, the members of which knew who each other were and disliked each other heartily.

As White points out, members of both these groups were to be found inside the Jacobean establishment. It is necessary at this point to deal with the 'myth' of James's Calvinism. Again the distinction between a credal and an experimental predesti-narianism is of crucial importance. For the exchange at Hampton Court between John Rainolds, Overall and the king (described by White) fits this schema perfectly. James emerges from that episode as a credal but not an experimental predestinarian. Prepared to suggest minor changes in the Articles of Religion to move them closer to the Calvinist position, James also wished that the doctrine of predestination might be very tenderly handled and with great discretion, lest on the one side God's omnipotency might be called in question by impeaching the doctrine of his eternal predestination or on the other a desperate presumption might be arreared by inferring the necessary certainty of standing and persisting in grace.

When such questions arise among scholars the quietest proceeding were to determine them in the universities and not to stuff the book with all conclusions theological. . . . The better course would be to punish the broachers of false doctrine as occasion should be offered.[17]

In 1610 James told a visiting group of Dutch representatives that he had studied the doctrine of predestination long and hard; he had come to realize that not all men had agreed with his present position. Obviously he felt that his own opinion was the right one, but it was not a point upon which he thought that his salvation depended. In the United Provinces, where the issue was causing open dispute and controversy, a judicious silence seemed to be the best policy.[18]

In England, as White observes, silence was often the price of preferment. Some, however, were more silent than others; or rather the issues on which silence was advisable varied according to a man's position on the spectrum of religious opinion. Evangelical Protestants and Calvinists had to keep quiet about conformity and the polity of the Church. If they wanted preferment, they had to accept the *iure divino* case for episcopacy and defend the king's status as a ruler by divine right against the assaults of the papists and the presbyterians. Anti-Calvinists found neither of those tasks a strain. They, however, had to keep quiet about their anti-Calvinism.

Throughout James's reign there is evidence to show that Calvinists and anti-Calvinists knew who each other were and tried, as circumstances allowed, to do one another down. For instance, the early career of William Laud was blighted by the hostile attentions of both Robert and George Abbot. In 1611, when Laud was the leading candidate for the mastership of St John's College, Oxford, George Abbot denounced him to the Chancellor of the University as 'a papist or, at least, very popishly inclined'. In 1614 he was denounced from the pulpit by Robert Abbot as a papist 'in points of free will, justification, concupiscence being a sin after baptism, inherent righteousness and certainty of salvation'. Abbot's influence at Court was used consistently to block his path and he was forced to rely entirely on the support of Bishop Neile.[19]

In 1617 Archbishop Abbot described the extent of Arminian penetration in England. Apart from 'one Dr Baro a Frenchman', only Samuel Harsnet and John Overall had voiced such opinions. Harsnet had been rebuked by the High Commission and had since mended his ways. Overall, however, was another matter:

> he did infect as many as he could till by sharp rebuke and reproofs he was beaten from the public avowing these fancies. But certainly to this day, being now in an higher place he doth retain that leaven [and] underhand doth smother those conceits among us but is contented to send beyond the sea all the encouragement he can. And he maketh no bones as I fear to deliver doubtful things for true and feigned things for certain.[20]

If Overall's position faithfully represented that of the English Church, as White claims, it would appear that no one had told the Archbishop of Canterbury.

What was the king's attitude to all this? James was prepared to give favour and preferment to anti-Calvinists and to allow a range of theological opinion within the establishment of the Church. But he did not want open theological debate or dispute, and in order to avoid it he imposed silence on the anti-Calvinists, while at the same time distancing himself from the excesses of hyper-Calvinism. That, of course, was precisely the sort of policy which he urged on the United Provinces.

III

It is this which explains the 'irenic' instructions given to the delegation sent to Dort. James had no desire to sponsor an extreme Calvinist heresy hunt. The delegates were not to sell the pass to the hyper-Calvinism of a Gomarus,[k] nor to accept any formulary of faith which made unity among the reformed churches more difficult than was absolutely necessary. Nor were they to agree to anything which might reflect badly on the ecclesiastical status quo in England.[21] Ideally Dort was to end in amicable agreement and unity. But whatever happened, it was to end in unity. As C. Grayson has pointed out, the linchpin of James's policy towards the religious disputes in the Low Countries had been the maintenance of the unity of the United Provinces. Originally that aim had seemed attainable through a degree of latitudinarian tolerance, accompanied by silence on the controverted issues. By 1617 that was no longer an option. Religious and political tension had grown so great that unity could only be achieved through the imposition of silence by one side on the other.[22] The only alternative was a formal toleration, which James and his advisers regarded as tantamount to anarchy.

It is clear from the correspondence between Archbishop Abbot and Dudley Carleton, English ambassador to the Low Countries, that James had come to blame this situation on the Arminians; they were the potential schismatics, it was their errors that were threatening the unity and purity of the reformed faith, and it was consequently their opinions that would have to be suppressed.[23] That Dort was called at all represented the result of a crushing political defeat for the Remonstrants[1] at the hands of Prince Maurice. The synod was the means by which the victors sought to condemn and outlaw the opinions of their defeated opponents.[24] James was well aware of that fact, and by lending his support to the synod at all he sanctioned that process. The delegates chosen were all Calvinists, albeit moderate ones. Had James wanted to send a genuinely impartial or even pro-Remonstrant delegation he could have done so. As White has pointed out, he had men of Arminian sympathies available to him within the inner circle of ecclesiastical power. The Remonstrants, at least, knew who their friends were; they wanted Buckeridge, Neile and Overall.[25]

When, after the synod, James had dinner with the newly preferred Bishop Carleton and denounced the Remonstrants as simply Pelagians and heretics, before an unprotesting Lancelot Andrewes, none of those present can have harboured any doubts that James both knew who had won and who had lost at Dort, and thoroughly approved of the outcome.[26] It is simply not credible to claim that the most theologically sophisticated of English monarchs had just made a mistake. For political as well as religious reasons, James wanted an end to the religious disputes in the Low Countries. Ideally that should be brought about by argument and agreement among fellow Protestants. In practice it meant the condemnation of the Remonstrants. The English delegates were sent to Dort to do that, but to do it without giving too many hyper-Calvinist hostages to fortune. There can be no doubt that James's chosen representatives shared his moderate Calvinist outlook. Hall's opening address stressed the need for moderation and unity.[27] Samuel Ward consulted Bishop Lake of Bath and Wells on how best to conduct himself and most fairly frame the Calvinist position. Like Hall, Lake emphasized the difference between doctrine fit for the schools and that fit for the popular pulpit. The stress of the English delegation was always pastoral and edificational. They played up those aspects of the Calvinist case which left room for an element of human responsibility and effort and which avoided the possibility of fatalism and desperation in the laity. It was this aim which prompted the most serious modification of the Calvinist case proposed at Dort by Ward and Davenant – their hypothetical universalism. Christ, they argued, had indeed died for all men. Thus the evangelical promises embodied in Christ's sacrifice could be offered to the generality of mankind, with no hidden limitations or reservations. The means to salvation were offered in Christ (and the word and sacraments) to all men. Such a view had the advantage of fitting more easily with certain well-known passages of Scripture (not to mention the logic of an inclusive, national church) than the existing Calvinist position. It was also entirely in accord, on Ward's view, with crucial passages in Augustine and other patristic anti-Pelagian writers who had never condemned the idea that Christ died for all men as a Pelagian opinion. They had merely distinguished between the elect, who believed and were given the gift of perseverance, and the rest, who although they might believe for a time, in the end fell away into sin and unbelief. These, because of their unbelief, were justly condemned.

* * *

In a section of his article omitted here, the author describes other modifications of Calvinist doctrine that the British delegates to Dort urged for pastoral reasons: in addition to rejecting discussion of obscure theological points and metaphysical speculation, they argued for moderate language in the canons lest people be put off by too 'cold and abstract' an expression of Calvinism. While affirming assurance of salvation, they also declined to insist that individual believers must achieve a high level of personal certainty of their election, lest failing that, they fall into despair. Finally, the delegates wished to encourage good works by omitting 'effort' from the list of things unnecessary to salvation. The potential exists, they said, for even the elect to fall from grace, although divine grace will inevitably thwart that potential for the elect.

* * *

In thus modifying both the presentation and the content of English Calvinism, Ward and Davenant were drawing on at least three elements within the English Protestant experience. Of these, the first was that strain of evangelical Calvinism or practical divinity which, while predicated on a Calvinist doctrinal position, set out to inculcate an active piety in the laity. This was the style of divinity termed by Kendall experimental predestinarianism. In the modified or moderated Calvinism produced by Ward and Davenant at Dort, this experimental tradition can be seen operating on and subtly changing the doctrinal core of credal Calvinism. Second, the logic of an inclusive, national church can be discerned imposing itself on a style of divinity which, at times, came uncomfortably close to providing a rationale for semi-separatism. The changes involving the extent of the atonement and the soft-pedalling of assurance can all be presented in this light. Third, it seems likely that in changing their stance at Dort, Ward and Davenant were drawing on the experience of the 1595–6 theological disputes in the University of Cambridge. It is certainly possible to see Ward's modifications of the Calvinist position as an attempt to incorporate or defuse the main objections raised against it in 1595–6, within a position which yet retained its essentially Calvinist (that is, in the context of Dort, anti-Remonstrant) orientation. The resulting position also had the supreme advantage of according very closely with the king's own preferences and polemical needs of the moment.

Comparing Ward's position with that of Bridges shows just how far English Calvinism had come in the intervening fifty years. It is all the more striking, therefore, that Ward should still have reacted so strongly against the opinions of both the Remonstrants and Richard Montagu.[m] For Ward had no doubt of the orthodoxy of his own position or of its reliability as a basis from which to attack the Remonstrants. They held that Christ died for all men and that the efficacy of that sacrifice depended on the existence and exercise of human free will, not on the gift of God's free grace. Thus Ward could argue that the distinction between the *impetratio* and *applicatio* of Christ's sacrifice, while not inherently Pelagian, became so when it was used to take away the effects of the application of Christ's sacrifice from the special gift of grace and to attribute it to man's free will and God's foreknowledge of man's faith. The whole point about hypothetical universalism was that it was hypothetical. Hence, in a diagrammatic exposition of the differences between the Remonstrant and Contra-Remonstrant positions, Ward juxtaposed his own view of the atonement with that of the Remonstrants. Ward held that

> Christ died for all men sufficiently but God accepted not the price of redemption but only for the elect. Remission, redemption, reconciliation etc. no way belong to the reprobate for if the benefit of these belong to all then should the gospel be preached to all and Christ intercede for all, both which are false.

The Remonstrants, on the other hand, taught that 'Christ died for all, obtained remission for all, yet only believers have the benefit'.[28]

At first, men like Hall and Ward no doubt hoped that the Remonstrants would come round. Bishop Lake certainly retained hopes that if

> the orthodox propositions were fairly offered and their distasteful accessories ... judiciously removed they would be brought to think better of them than they have written and happily perceive that the distance is not great between them and those whom they oppose.[29]

From the outset, then, the division had been between 'orthodoxy' and its opponents. The sorts of changes and modifications suggested by Lake and Ward were no doubt designed to render the Calvinist position as acceptable as possible to the Remonstrants. But still the Remonstrants would not settle.

Moderation and irenical intent had become, had to an extent always been, a means to take away all excuse from the enemies of orthodoxy. Anyway, the upshot of all this was that the English delegation, and through them James I, accepted the clear-cut Calvinist repudiation of the Remonstrant position that was enshrined in the final Canons. Ward was quite clear that even his own modified and moderate theological position represented both an explicit rejection of the opinions of the Arminians (whose position was simply Pelagian) and an accurate reflection of the doctrinal position of the English Church. Judging from the very favourable response both his and the other delegates' efforts received from the king, these were opinions which James himself endorsed.

IV

White seeks to cast doubts on all this. In doing so he transfers arguments from one level of historical discourse or analysis to another. We are told that Arminianism, as a theological position, developed out of Calvinist or reformed traditions of thought. As a statement drawn from the intellectual history of Arminian theology (particularly in Holland and, indeed, France) that is unexceptionable enough. It cannot, however, be simply transferred to the evaluation of the theological politics of England during the 1620s. Both the disputes of 1595–6 and, more obviously, the Synod of Dort had ensured that there were two sides. If contemporaries perceived two sides, their perceptions have to be integrated into our account. As Stuart Clark has recently pointed out, early modern English people tended to see the world in terms of binary oppositions and inversions.[30] Political and religious polemic was conducted by assimilating the position of one's opponent to that occupied by an individual or group of unimpeachable unsoundness and corruption. This was the role played in much contemporary polemic by the images of popery and Puritanism. The point at which amicable debate and disagreement became open conflict arrived when one or both sides started that process of assimilation and name-calling. Ward, despite his 'moderate' Calvinism, did it with a will to the Remonstrants, whose opinions he routinely assimilated to those of the Pelagians.[31] His colleague at Dort, George Carleton, did the same to Richard Montagu in print, as did Abbot's chaplain

Daniel Featley in his appositely titled pamphlet, *Pelagius redivivus: or, Pelagius Raked out of the Ashes by Arminius and his Scholars*.[32] The other prime exponent of this tactic was, of course, White's irenic Anglican, Richard Montagu, who both in print and in his private letters to John Cosin tried to turn the term 'Calvinist' into an insult by assimilating it to an already established rhetoric of anti-Puritanism.[33]

This is odd behaviour if there were really no points of importance at stake. If there was nothing especially Calvinist about Whitgift's Lambeth Articles or indeed about the Canons of Dort to which White's irenical Anglicans assented readily enough, and if the likes of Montagu, Laud and Buckeridge formed part of an undifferentiated spectrum of 'Anglican' theological opinion, why did Laud, Buckeridge and Montagu object so strongly to the Lambeth Articles and the Dort Canons? For object they did. In a letter to Buckingham, Buckeridge, Howson and Laud described the doctrines approved at Lambeth and Dort as 'fatal opinions' contrary to all 'civil government in the commonwealth [and to] preaching and external ministry in the church'. They went on to extol the doctrines broached by Montagu as 'the doctrine of the church of England or agreeable thereunto'.[34]

To judge from their correspondence, Ward and Davenant regarded Montagu as both a theological opponent and a thoroughly unpleasant man. Ward and the other delegates took exception to Montagu's quite unjustified assertion that at Dort they had connived at the condemnation of the discipline of the Church of England. Their sense of grievance was not limited to such issues. They construed Montagu's outburst in print as a direct attack both on their own theological position and that of the English Church. As Davenant wrote to Ward,

> your vindicating of those that were at the synod of Dort from the rash and false imputation laid on us by Mr Montagu was laudable and necessary work. I could wish for his own good that he had a more modest conceit of himself and a less base opinion of all others who jump not with him in his mongrel opinions.

'His opinion concerning predestination and total falling from grace is undoubtedly contrary to the common tenet of the English Church ever since we were born'.[35] Here, then, is clear and unequivocal evidence that theologically sophisticated contemporaries from the centre of the ecclesiastical establishment regarded Montagu's statements in print as an attack on both their own opinions and what they took to be the doctrinal position of the English Church since the beginning of Elizabeth's reign. It is simply not possible to write off the measured judgement of such well-informed and moderate men as the product either of Puritan extremism or anti-papal war fever.

Nor can there be any doubt that from 1628 onwards the likes of Davenant and Ward thought of themselves as having lost the battle for influence at the centre of ecclesiastical affairs to an emergent 'Arminian faction': Davenant himself had first-hand experience of this. Preaching at Court in 1629, Davenant had delivered what he claimed was 'the received doctrine of our Church established in the 17th article'. Immediately after the sermon he was told that 'his majesty was much displeased that I had stirred this question which he had forbidden to be meddled withal'. Davenant replied that he assumed that the king's declaration did not and could not forbid the handling of core doctrines established by the Thirty-nine Articles, but had only been intended to prevent the 'raising of new questions or adding of new sense thereunto, which I had not done nor ever should'. For his pains Davenant was denounced in front of the Privy Council by Samuel Harsnet and forced to accept that the royal proclamation did indeed mean that he could not handle such topics again in the pulpit.

White makes great play with the fact that when Davenant saw the king, Charles had neither condemned nor commended the bishop's theological position, but merely insisted that 'he would not have this high point meddled withal or debated either the one way or the other because it was too high for the people's understanding'. Three years before, Davenant had feared that the king's earlier proclamation would be used by 'those of Durham house' to silence their theological opponents under the guise of suppressing new opinions.[36] Perhaps Davenant's court sermon was intended as a test case to see how far such a partisan interpretation had won official acceptance. If it was, the outcome can have left little doubt in Davenant's mind, and by 1631 he can be found complaining to Ward about the overtly partisan way in which the king's declaration was being applied.[37]

Ward's other correspondents confirm this picture. Writing in 1631, Thomas Gataker told Ward that 'for the points of Arminianism publicly preached it is commonly bruited that few come up either at court or cross but that touch upon them'.[38] Four years earlier, Ward had congratulated Archbishop Ussher on a court sermon 'touching the repressing of the Arminian faction. God's blessing be upon you for this good service so opportunely performed. I pray God his majesty may have a true apprehension of the ensuring danger.'[39] In 1630 Gataker was forced to inform Ward that the king had undergone no such change of heart. 'That faction seem to carry all with a high hand and to have great backers above.'[40] Such complaints continued throughout the 1630s.

Nor can there be any doubt that under this assault a new sense of 'sides' and solidarity emerged among Ward and his friends. The cause was God's and opponents of that cause constitute a faction; their actions were partisan and divisive. Equally zealous pursuit of God's cause represented merely a necessary and inherently moderate response to the threat of heresy and division. Nevertheless, the actions prompted or legitimated by such rhetoric as often as not led to division and conflict. This should not surprise us, since precisely the same language and the assumptions which underlay it can be found in the printed works and private letters of Richard Montagu. In Montagu's view, most of the opinions which he was concerned to denounce were simply 'Puritan'. His opponents were, in the main, 'those classical Puritans who were wont to pass all their strange determinations, sabbatarian paradoxes and apocalyptical frenzies under the name and cover of the true professors of protestant doctrine'.[41] He referred to them as a 'faction' or sometimes even as 'the faction'.[42] His own cause, however, he described simply as that of 'the Church' or, less often, that 'of God'.[43]

It simply will not do to pass off Montagu as some moderate, irenical figure, surprised by the extremity of response which his works had stirred up. It would be difficult to find a more bitterly polarized view of contemporary theological opinion than that presented by Montagu in his letters, with his talk of 'Puritan bishops' and would-be bishops, his very developed sense of both who was on which side and of the need to gain access to and leverage on the centres of power at court.[44] While Montagu clearly felt that his own position represented a faithful reflection of the doctrinal position of the English Church as enshrined in the Prayer Book, the Articles of Religion and the Homilies, he was also quite aware that the Church was dominated by men who did not share that view. If the theological issues were allowed to go to Convocation, he feared he would lose.[45] He could count only five of the contemporary bench of bishops as favourable to him and he worried constantly about the courage under fire of some of them.[46] Anyone who wants contemporary evidence for the *de facto* Calvinist dominance of the upper reaches of the Jacobean Church need look no further than the letters of Richard Montagu. Montagu's position represented only one possible gloss on the Thirty-nine Articles and one which, in the context of contemporary theological opinion, constituted a highly partisan and polemically aggressive act, undertaken against the school of opinion dominant in the Church.

V

Both sides, then, were addicted, on the one hand, to the language of moderation and consensus, and, on the other, to that of divisive faction. This should not surprise us. As Mark Kishlansky has shown, in the arena of secular politics, seventeenth-century English people found the fact of political conflict very hard to accept and still harder to explain. In the face of it they resorted to the rhetoric of faction and consensus. Frequent invocation of such a rhetoric cannot be taken as an index of either moderation or agreement. Rather its use by two parties to a dispute was an indication of deep and irreconcilable differences and bitter party feelings.[47] It is this which explains both Montagu's willingness to assimilate the position of his adversaries to that of the Puritans, and their eagerness to assimilate his position to that of the Arminians, the Pelagians and the papists.

Whatever else this means, it should prevent the historian from accepting such claims at face value. This, surely, is what White tends to do in his treatment of Montagu. He is far too willing simply to accept Montagu's assertion of his own 'Anglican' moderation and the Puritan radicalism of his opponents. Yet just before he characterizes the reaction against Montagu as yet another failed Puritan attempt to hijack the Church of England for extreme predestinarianism, White cites as his best example of such Puritan extremism Bishop Morton's conduct at the York House Conference.[48] That should at least give us pause for thought; as should the central involvement in the campaign against Montagu of establishment figures like Daniel Featley and Thomas Goad, who were both chaplains to Archbishop Abbot, or even more centrally placed figures like Ward and Davenant. While it is impossible to deny the links between the style of churchmanship espoused by men like Morton and late Elizabethan moderate Puritan divinity, it remains true that Morton and his ilk had had to work their passage into the establishment through an open repudiation of Puritan opinions about conformity or church government.

Morton brings us back to a central theme in the ecclesiastical history of James's reign – the detachment of Calvinism, both credal and experimental, from the issues of church polity and conformity and hence, on the predominant view, from Puritanism. By his conduct before, during and after the Hampton Court Conference, James had offered favour and preferment to erstwhile moderate Puritans (and that, of course, meant predestinarians, even of a robustly experimental hue) in return for their abnegation of whatever scruples they might once have felt about either ritual conformity or episcopal government. The result was that the incipient links between anti-Calvinism and anti-Puritanism which the Calvinist heresy hunts of the 1580s and 1590s had started to engender were stillborn. Those enemies of Calvinism who detested experimental predestinarianism were left devoid of a public rhetoric of denunciation with which to attack the godly and in terms of which they could effectively denounce them to authority.[49]

What altered this situation? Here White's insistence on the importance of the war with Spain is of considerable significance. The Spanish match and the drive towards war with Spain served to overturn the careful balance of the mid-Jacobean period. It served to politicize once again differences of religious opinion by giving them a direct relevance to policy options now of crucial interest to the king. The public agitation against the Spanish match, which involved men of erstwhile impeccable Calvinist and conformist respectability broaching intimate questions of royal policy before the people, served to reawaken in James his latent fear of a populist Puritanism.[50]

The argument has been made elsewhere that the differences

between those two views of the Christian community outlined in the first half of this chapter were expressed in two similarly different views of the nature of the popish threat. Anti-popery was never a Puritan monopoly, but certain attitudes towards Rome were linked to a 'Puritan' view of the community of the godly. Sensitivity on that issue meant, of course, opposition to the Spanish match and support for war. James was impaled upon the anti-papal rhetoric which had often been used to legitimate his regime and which he had often enough employed himself.[51] We know enough about James's hatred of war and his dislike of the policy to which Charles and Buckingham were trying to commit him to know that he would have relished any excuse to ignore such advice. We also know that he had intermittently entertained rather unrealistic ecumenical hopes of a reunion of Christendom, to be accomplished by a general council, presided over by Christian princes and to be based upon a core of truly catholic doctrines.[52] The need to negotiate a match with Spain would have only re-emphasized the political and diplomatic utility of a view of popery more moderate than that held by Archbishop Abbot and his Calvinist colleagues on the episcopal bench. Thus Richard Montagu's two books are perhaps best seen as an exercise in the polemical manipulation of the king's religious and political susceptibilities. As such, they were designed to emphasize points of agreement with Rome and to challenge the pope's identity as Antichrist in an effort to bolster James's opposition to the religious war he so feared. Second, they were designed to reactivate his fear of Puritanism, this time organized around not the issue of presbyterianism but of key Calvinist doctrines, which, broached before the people, were alleged to be subversive and thus to constitute the first step on a road that led inexorably to a presbyterian populism. This would serve to encourage James's existing tendency to dismiss as Puritans those people clamouring for war and denouncing the Spanish match in pulpit and Parliament.

Earlier in the reign, similar attempts had been made to gain the king's favourable attention for an explicitly anti-Calvinist reading of the position of the English Church. In the course of those efforts Calvinism had been isolated and condemned as an openly schismatic form of Protestantism, different both from the opinion of moderate English Protestants and from the official doctrinal position of the Church, not to mention those of moderate and well-affected papists. As such, it represented the great obstacle to a *rapprochement* with Rome, and could be equated with a redefined and refurbished image of Puritan subversion. The existence of these earlier attempts represents good evidence of the presence of anti-Calvinist opinions within the English Church and the recognition that such a 'pitch' constituted the best hope of winning over James I. Both of these earlier attempts failed – an index of their failure can be gained from the fact that they were produced by two men about to defect to Rome.[53] Why, then, did Montagu succeed where Carier and de Dominis failed? The answer lies in the political circumstances in which the attempt was launched, with the furore over the Spanish match and Protestant war fever pushing James towards a confessional conflict which he abhorred.

EDITOR'S NOTES

World Copyright: The Past and Present Society, 175 Banbury Road, Oxford, England. Reprinted in abridged form with the permission of the Society and the author from *Past and Present: A Journal of Historical Studies*, no. 114 (February 1987), pp. 32–76.

a *Calvin and English Calvinism to 1649* (Oxford, 1979).

b It is interesting to note that White's work was initially a counter to the political revisionism (represented in this volume by Conrad Russell) which in White's view depended too heavily on Tyacke's substitution of Arminianism for puritanism as the spark igniting civil war. In the present volume, White is categorized (along with Sharpe) as himself a revisionist on the grounds that his work has revised the earlier (pre-Tyacke) version of a radically polarized Elizabethan and Jacobean church as drastically as Tyacke himself had. White and Sharpe represent an alternative revisionism.

c Calvin's successor in Geneva.

d Episcopalian and anti-puritan.

e Presbyterian reformer in the reign of Elizabeth.

f Governing and judicial structure.

g Presbyterian polity was aimed in part at weeding the ungodly from the visible church by means of church discipline carried out by lay elders along with ministers. Those experimental predestinarians who questioned whether even presbyterian discipline could properly sort things out in the English Church took the more extreme course of separating themselves from the corrupted state church, either by forming a subgroup of the godly within the parish (semi-separatism) or by renouncing the national church altogether (separatism). The latter course was a punishable offence in this era, when national churches were presumed necessary to the unity of the realm.

h Episcopal or presbyterian.

i Focused more on the sacraments and public prayer than on preaching.

j Ordered by God's law.

k Francis Gomar, professor of theology at Leiden 1594–1611, was known for his extreme predestinarianism, including his defence of 'double predestination' (of reprobation to Hell as well as election to salvation). He taught and published against Arminius (also a professor at Leiden) and resigned his position when Arminius was succeeded by another anti-Calvinist, Conrad Vorstius.

l Dutch Arminians, condemned at the Synod of Dort (see chapters 3 and 5, above) in large part for political reasons, since the synod's sponsor, Count Maurice of Nassau, found his support among the majority Calvinist party in his power struggle against Oldenbarnevelt, Advocate of Holland, who championed the Arminians.

m See chapter 3, above.

n Obtaining and [effective] application. The difference is between the *potential* of Christ's death for all men and the *actual* justification of only the elect by grace. For Ward and other English Calvinists, human free will had no place in this equation.

NOTES

1 'Revisionism Revised: Two Perspectives on Early Stuart Parliamentary History', *Past and Present*, no. 92 (Aug. 1981): T. K. Rabb, 'The Role of the Commons', pp. 55–78; and D. Hirst, 'The Place of Principle', pp. 79–99; also see C. Hill, 'Parliament and People in Seventeenth-Century England'; pp. 100–24.

2 P. White, 'The Rise of Arminianism Reconsidered', *Past and Present*, no. 101 (Nov. 1983), pp. 34–54.

3 P. Collinson, *The Religion of Protestants* (Oxford, 1983), p. 81. Collinson is there quoting N. R. N. Tyacke, 'Puritanism, Arminianism and Counter-Revolution', in C. Russell, ed., *The Origins of the English War* (London, 1973), pp. 119–34.

4 C. Russell, *Parliaments and English Politics* (Oxford, 1972), pp. 26–32.

5 Humphrey Leech, *A Triumph of Truth* (Douai, 1609), dedicatory epistle; B. Carier quoted in G. Hakewill, *An Answer to a Treatise Written by Dr Carier by Way of a Letter to His Majesty* (London, 1616), p. 283.

6 So the existence of anti-Puritan and anti-Calvinist feelings in St John's College, Cambridge, in the 1580s and 1590s should not surprise us, but neither should the failure of those feelings to gain expression in a coherent or articulated ideological or theological platform. See P. G. Lake, *Moderate Puritans and the Elizabethan Church* (Cambridge, 1982), ch. 8.

7 John Bridges, *A Sermon Preached at Paul's Cross on the Monday in Whitsun Week 1571* (London, 1573), pp. 1–2, 15–16, 22–3, 25, 28–9.

8 *The Works of John Whitgift*, ed. J. Ayre, 3 vols (Parker Society, Cambridge, 1858), III, pp. 142–3.

9 John Bridges, *A Defence of the Government Established in the Church of England* (London, 1587) pp. 1309–12.

10 Ibid., 'The Preface to the Christian Reader', and pp. 49–50.

11 *Works of John Whitgift*, III, pp. 7–8, 314; II, p. 243.

12 R. T. Kendall, *Calvin and English Calvinism to 1649* (Oxford, 1979). For the basic distinction between credal and experimental predestinarians, see pp. 1–13.

13 For Hooker's very broad-bottomed definition of church membership, see *Works of the Learned and Judicious Divine Mr Richard Hooker*, ed. Keble, II, pp. 368–80.

14 For Howson, see C. M. Dent, *Protestant Reformers in Elizabethan Oxford* (Oxford, 1983), pp. 208–20; for Hooker, see *Works*, II, pp. 86, 88, 93, 121, 128, 524.

15 I am summarizing here the conclusion of ch. 9 of my *Moderate Puritans and the Elizabethan Church*.

16 Ibid., pp. 228, 232–3.

17 E. Cardwell, *A History of Conferences and Other Proceedings Connected with the Book of Common Prayer, 1558–1690* (Oxford, 1840) pp. 181, 185.

18 Cited in F. J. Shriver, 'Orthodoxy and Diplomacy: James I and the Vorstius Affair', *EHR*, 85 (1970), p. 453.

19 P. Heylyn, *Cyprianus Anglicus* (London, 1669), pp. 53–68.

20 PRO, SP 105/95, fo. 9^v.

21 For James's instructions, see T. Fuller, *The Church History of Great Britain*, ed. J. S. Brewer, 6 vols (Oxford, 1845), V, pp. 462–3.

22 C. Grayson, 'James I and the Religious Crisis in the United Provinces, 1613–19', in D. Baker, ed., *Studies in Church History: Subsidia 2* (Oxford, 1979), pp. 195–219.

23 For this, see the correspondence contained in a letter-book of Dudley Carleton's in SP 105/95. I should like to thank Simon Adams for drawing this document to my attention.

24 Ibid., fos 34^v–6^r, Carleton to Abbot, 8 Apr. 1618.

25 Tyacke, 'Arminianism and English Culture', in A. C. Duke and C. A. Tamse, eds, *Britain and the Netherlands*, VII (The Hague, 1981), p. 98.

26 PRO, SP 14/109/60, George Carleton to Dudley Carleton, 30 May 1619; see also SP 14/109/144, George Carleton to Dudley Carleton, 20 July 1619.

27 *The Works of Joseph Hall*, ed. P. Wynter, 10 vols (Oxford, 1863), X, pp. 253–61.

28 A diagrammatic exposition of the difference between the Remonstrant and Contra-Remonstrant positions in a theological notebook, headed 'Dr Ward, Synod of Dort', in the Ward MSS, Sidney Sussex College.

29 Bodd., Tanner MS, vol. 74, fos 174^{r-v}, Lake to Ward 12 Feb. 1619.

30 Stuart Clark, 'Inversion, Misrule and the Meaning of Witchcraft', *Past and Present*, no. 87 (May 1980), pp. 98–127.

31 See the long paper headed 'An Remonstrantium sententia longe absit a Pelagiana', in the Ward MSS, Sidney Sussex College.

32 G. Carleton, *An Examination of Those Things wherein the Author of the Late Appeal Holdeth the Doctrines of the Pelagians and Arminians to be the Doctrines of the Church of England* (London 1626).

33 See, for instance, Montagu, *Appello Caesarem*, p. 4. Montagu's habitual assimilation of his theological opponents to 'Puritanism' can be seen throughout his correspondence with John Cosin, *Correspondence of John Cosin*.

34 *The Works of William Laud*, ed. W. Scott and J. Bliss, 7 vols (Oxford, 1847–60), VI, pp. 244–6. Laud, John Howson, John Buckeridge to Buckingham, 2 Aug 1625; see also p. 249, Montaigne, Neile, Andrewes, Buckeridge and Laud to Buckingham, 16 Jan. 1626.

35 Bodl., Tanner MS vol. 290, fo 81^r, Davenant to Ward, 10 Oct. 1625; vol. 72, fo. 6^r, Davenant to Ward, 8 Dec. 1625.

36 Ibid., vol. 290, fo. 86^v, Davenant to Ward, 16 Mar. 1629; vol. 72, fo. 13^r, Davenant to Ward, 22 June 1626.

37 Ibid., vol. 71, fo. 10^r, Davenant to Ward, 12 Oct. 1631.

38 Bodl., Tanner MS, vol. 71, fo 68^r, Gataker to Ward, 17 Feb. 1631.

39 *Whole Works of the Most Reverend James Ussher*, xv, p, 347, Ward to Ussher, 5 July 1626.

40 Bodl., Tanner MS vol 71, fo. 102^v, Gataker to Ward, 2 Sept. 1631.

41 Montagu, *Appello Caesarem*, sig. a2^v.

42 Ibid., sig. a2^r; p. 3; *Correspondence of John Cosin*, I, p. 34, for a reference to 'the faction'; see also ibid., p. 47.

43 *Correspondence of John Cosin*, I, pp. 21, 22, 24, 26, 48.

44 Ibid. p. 22.

45 Ibid., p. 42, 'I fear nothing in the convocation except they obtrude the synod of Dort.'

46 A point made by Patrick Collinson in his *Religion of Protestants*, p. 80. For Montagu's doubts about Laud's steadfastness see *Correspondence of John Cosin*, I, p. 24.

47 M. Kishlansky, 'The Emergence of Adversary Politics in the Long Parliament', *JMH*, 49 (1977), pp. 617–40.

48 White, 'Rise of Arminianism Reconsidered', pp. 49–50.

49 For those links, see Lake, *Moderate Puritans and the Elizabethan Church*, pp. 240–1; Dent, *Protestant Reformers in Elizabethan Oxford*, p. 235; Harsnet's sermon of 1584 is cited above.

50 For an expansion of these remarks, see K. C. Fincham and P. Lake, 'The Ecclesiastical Policy of James I', *JBS*, 24 (1985), pp. 169–207, and recently expanded to the reign of Charles I in *The Early Stuart Church*, ed. Kenneth Fincham (London, 1993).

51 See P. G. Lake, 'The Significance of the Elizabethan Identification of the Pope as Antichrist', *JEH*, 31 (1980), pp. 161–78; also P. G. Lake, 'Constitutional Consensus and Puritan Opposition in the 1620s: Thomas Scott and the Spanish Match', *HJ*, 25 (1982), pp. 805–25.

52 W. B. Patterson, 'King James I's Call for an Ecumenical Council', in

G. J. Cuming and D. Baker, eds., *Studies in Church History*, vii (Cambridge, 1971), pp. 267–75; W. B. Patterson, 'King James I and the Protestant Cause in the Crisis of 1618–22', in S. Mews, ed., *Studies in Church History*, xviii (Oxford, 1982), pp. 319–34.

53 The first such attempt was made by Benjamin Carier in his *A Treatise Written by Mr Dr Carier* (Liège, 1614). The second was launched by Marc Antonio de Dominis: see his *M. Antonio de Dominis Declares the Cause of His Return out of England* (St Omer, 1623); R. Neile, *M. Ant. de Dominus, Archbishop of Spalato, II His Shiftings in Religion* (London, 1624). See also W. B. Patterson, 'The Peregrinations of Marc Antonio de Dominis', in D. Baker, ed. *Studies in Church History*, xv (Oxford, 1978), pp. 241–57.

11

POPULAR POLITICS BEFORE
THE CIVIL WAR

David Underdown

The Marxist view of the Civil War as a social conflict (in its crudest form, the first bourgeois revolution) has been generally rejected in the face of contrary evidence: popular conservatism now appears to have been significant, a self-conscious middle class was non-existent, and Parliament clearly numbered gentlemen and peers alike among its adherents. Not all historians, however, have abandoned efforts to set wartime allegiance in a socio-economic context. David Underdown's work on Wiltshire, Dorset and Somerset approaches the problem by looking at regional patterns of allegiance and correlating them to cultural development. He finds that the Civil War can be traced to the earlier emergence of two opposing cultures. One was traditional, paternalistic, hierarchical and deferential, committed to the preservation of customary religious and communal rituals and festivities. The other was a culture of reform and discipline, intent on repressing popular festivities in the interests of godliness and order. The two cultures were regionalized, but not as the old version had it, with North and West conservative, South and East progressive. Underdown's more complex pattern identifies traditional culture in arable regions of England, and the culture of discipline in cloth-making and wood-pasture regions, where economic change had been most pronounced in the sixteenth century and the parishes were most socio-economically polarized. He finds that the culture of discipline drew mostly from the gentry and middling sort, concerned with order in the face of economic dislocation. He thus reinstates a 'high road' interpretation, albeit in much revised form, and sees the war as a fundamentally cultural conflict.

* * *

On a Sunday in April 1632, there was a riot outside the church at Newland in the Forest of Dean, when two forest officers were attacked by a hostile crowd. The officers were much hated figures in the neighbourhood, having recently arrested a certain John Williams, a miner who under the nickname 'Skimmington' had led a series of popular risings in the area. At least one of the assailants was armed with a stoolball staff.[1] By itself the incident is a trivial one. But the conjuncture of a riot, a forest community, 'Skimmington' and stoolball neatly encapsulates a whole complex of social and political forces, and provides a vividly symbolic illustration of how cultural attitudes were translated into politics.

Before we proceed further, though, we might pause to ask what 'politics' actually meant for the English common people in the early seventeenth century. Politics involves those matters pertaining to the *polis*, the community. There was a politics of the kingdom, a politics of the shire, a politics of the town or village, all in various ways related to each other. People were engaged with these several levels of politics in different ways according to their place in society. The marginal landholders, cottagers and labourers were involved primarily in the third kind, and then only as subjects or victims of policies devised and implemented by others, except on the rare occasions when they combined in riotous protests serious enough to require the attention of the county governors, or even of King and Council. The better-off 'persons of credit', on the other hand, participated actively in village politics at parish meeting or at manor court, and were at least intermittently involved in the remoter politics of shire or kingdom as taxpayers, jurymen and (occasionally) voters. They were also more likely to be literate and to have formed opinions on matters of national concern, especially during times of crisis.

Popular politics thus encompassed a wide range of attitudes and types of behaviour. Yet people of all social levels shared similar ideas about how their families and communities ought to be ordered: with due respect for legitimate authority, but also with the expectation of appropriate behaviour by their governors, which in turn meant due respect for law, natural justice and customary rights. These ideas formed the basis for their political attitudes, whether towards the matters that most immediately affected them – town governance, common rights, food supplies – or the more distant affairs of the kingdom. At the lowest level the most universal outlook was a conservative localism: a stubborn reliance on ancient custom, and a tendency to view national issues through the prism of town or village life. This did not mean blind submission to authority, for when authority fell short of the expected standard of good rule resistance was easily provoked. There were, then, some common values. They were expressed, however, in different ways in different regions. Political behaviour is an expression of culture, and like culture it often took distinctively regional forms.

The circumstances most likely to provoke popular political action, and in which the behaviour of different regions can best be compared, were ones involving an immediate threat to subsistence, such as the encroachment on common rights by enclosing landlords, or the failure of magistrates to enforce protective market regulations. In all kinds of community the first resort when customary rights were threatened was legal action: a petition to the justices, or a lawsuit with costs financed out of a common fund. If this failed there might be a gradual escalation of violence – verbal or written warnings, sporadic damage to property. When a resentful inhabitant of Ramsbury, Wiltshire, was being escorted to the House of Correction he burst out 'that he hoped to see Ramsbury so in fire upon some of the best of the parish there'. If enough people were convinced that there was no justice in the courts, a chain of small-scale, isolated incidents might become sufficiently serious to merit the name of riot.[2]

Enclosure riots occurred occasionally in all types of regions. But there are some striking differences between those of the arable and those of the wood-pasture areas, which reflect underlying cultural contrasts. The political distinctiveness of the wood-pasture districts is clearly evident in the disorders which began in the western counties in 1626. The riots were provoked by the Crown's sale of royal forests to courtiers and entrepreneurs who hoped to profit by enclosing and 'improving' hitherto underutilized forest land. Although these were not, as sometimes pictured, totally arbitrary enclosures – agreement was reached with neighbouring manorial lords, and propertied farmers were compensated with leases from the new proprietors – the landless artisans and cottagers who swarmed in these woodland areas lost their rights of common almost completely.[3]

The result was a serious breakdown of law and order. Gillingham Forest erupted in 1626, and sporadic rioting there reached a climax two years later when the sheriff of Dorset had to retreat after finding the rioters too numerous and well armed to be dispersed.[4] There were less violent disorders in Neroche Forest, in south-west Somerset, in 1629, and in the spring of 1631 more serious ones in the Forest of Dean, soon followed by others in the Wiltshire forests of Braydon, Chippenham and Melksham and by at least one outbreak in Selwood. The arrest of John Williams did not end the troubles in Dean. Enclosures were still being thrown down in July 1633, and after an interlude of uneasy peace there was more violence by coalminers in 1637.[5]

In all these riots villagers of middle and lower rank were combining to protest violations of their traditional rights by outsiders. The 'class' nature of the forest risings should not be exaggerated.[6] The targets were not local gentlemen and farmers, but the clique of courtiers and Londoners intent on disrupting the forest community in the name of improvement and private profit. Apart from the labourers caught up in it, the only local people to suffer were collaborators like the servant of Sir John Hungerford who turned informer and had his house burned down in retaliation. The commoners' enemies were not the local gentry.[7]

Many of the rioters were, to be sure, people of little wealth or status. Gentlemen and yeomen had access to the courts if they were dissatisfied with their compensation, and were naturally reluctant to combine in riot with the disorderly poor, about whose 'lewd lives and conversations' they had been complaining for years. One respectable Dean householder kept his doors locked to prevent his servants joining the rioters. Yet even propertied farmers suffered from the enclosures. They received secure title to their now enclosed lands, but they also lost common grazing rights and were likely to be paying heavier poor rates to support their dispossessed neighbours.[8] They were unlikely to shed many tears over losses suffered by the outsiders who were the chief beneficiaries of disafforestation. Some felt strongly enough, or were under sufficient local pressure, to join the rioters. Of the seventy-four people convicted in the Gillingham outbreaks twenty-one were yeomen or husbandmen, an impressive number in proportion to the social composition of a forest community.

The ambivalence of propertied opinion is clearly shown by the half-hearted measures taken by the local authorities to restore order. Repeated Council instructions to JPs and deputy-lieutenants to 'take better care for the peace of the country' produced only foot-dragging and excuses. The militia and the *posse comitatus*, composed of local men reluctant to fire on their poorer neighbours, were clearly unreliable. The attitude of the local justices emerges well from the Gloucestershire JPs' report on the affray at Newland. They agreed that popular resentment against Skimmington's captors was behind the riot, but excused it as unpremeditated and as a response to the two forest officers' provocations.[9] The western gentry regretted violence and riot, but they were distinctly unhappy about having to do the Council's dirty work.

Although the Skimmington rioters were for the most part cottagers and poor artisans, they were inspired more by localism than by class antagonism. 'Here were we born and here we will die', the Gillingham men declared when the sheriff came against them. There were long traditions behind the foresters' forcible defence of common rights: in Dean the name 'Robin Hoods' had been applied to participants in a 1612 outbreak. But the Dean men had a strong sense of legitimacy, and when they burned timber that the Earl of Pembroke had unjustly cut, they did so to shouts of 'God Save the King!'[10]

This combination of conservatism and rebelliousness is perhaps easier to understand if we consider the riots' 'skimmington'[a] associations. The word served in north Wiltshire as a symbol for other kinds of threats to the well-being of a community besides those presented by assertive women. In 1625, when the men of Wilton invaded the neighbouring parish of Burbage 'with a jest to bring skimmington there', it was invoked as a pretext for a festive inter-village brawl, analogous to a football match.[11] A skimmington in this sense was something undesirable brought into the village by outsiders, and which, like an unruly woman, must be dealt with by communal action. The application of the term to the riots is logical enough. The disafforesting courtiers' antisocial behaviour is inspired by the spirit of 'skimmington', and is resisted by appropriately ritualized actions. At Mailescott in Dean in March 1631 the 'burying of Skimmington' was proclaimed. A procession of rioters broke down hedges and filled in ore pits sunk by the hated Mompesson, whose effigy was then ceremonially buried in one of the pits. The agent of another projector was warned that the rioters would return on May Day 'to do him the like service'.[12]

But 'skimmington' has other meanings. It also denoted a ritual action against the chosen target: to 'ride skimmington' was to take part in a demonstration against the skimmington in the pejorative sense. And the riots were headed by leaders who adopted the name' Skimmington' in the case of Williams, 'Lady Skimmington' in the case of the trio of leaders in Braydon. Skimmington briefly becomes a folk hero, similar to Robin Hood or to 'Captain Cobbler' and 'Captain Pouch' in earlier peasant uprisings, regarded as able to redress all sorts of popular grievances.[13] These then were skimmingtons (demonstrations) led by Skimmington (Williams and his counterparts) against Skimmington (Mompesson and company). We here encounter a rich complex of associations. A skimmington is something undesirable: the leaders defiantly assume the name, as if to restore the subverted moral order by inverting it yet again. In Braydon, where Skimmington was also a lady, we recognize the further element of gender inversion. The three Braydon leaders dressed themselves in women's clothes, and were eventually punished by having to stand in the pillory so attired.[14]

Rituals of inversion were common in other parts of England. The customary world has been turned upside-down by enclosers; the protesters symbolically turn it upside-down again (dressing as women, parodying the titles and offices of their social superiors) in order to turn it right side up. The prominence of women in enclosure and grain riots is well known and is one more sign of rejection of the submissive ideal. Female rioters were often joined by men disguised in women's clothes. The practice had protective purposes, but it also involved elements of ritual inversion, and appropriately ritualized punishments were sometimes inflicted.[15] But although inversion rituals were known in other parts of England, nowhere were they as prominent a feature of the local culture as in these western wood-pasture regions. The greater sense of individual identity expressed in the 'domestic' skimmington ritual, the tension between individual and community reflected in stoolball,[b] both helped to mould the character of the Skimmington riots. That one of the Newland rioters carried a stoolball staff is thus almost poetically appropriate. Many other features of the riots – the assaults on Council messengers, the burning of warrants, the rescue of prisoners, the reprisals against collaborators, the sheltering of suspects, the silent as well as the open resistance – further illuminate the culture of a region in which individuals could unite over wide areas when their rights were challenged. There was less collusion between the three main centres than has sometimes been supposed – the 'colonel' of the Gillingham group failed when he tried to get the Braydon rioters to join forces with him – but the foresters certainly knew what was happening in the other places, and had some sense of common purpose.[16]

The disorders had no explicit connection with other kinds of political or religious discontent. Still, in Braydon at least there were plenty of Puritans, and there is a possibly significant number of 'Puritan' first names in the list of rioters there. As for Dean, people at Newland were thought to have been stirred up by the curate, Peter Simon, who preached that 'setting the King's place and quality aside, we were all equal in respect of manhood unto him', though he denied any seditious intent. There is a hint of awareness of national politics in a Gillingham appeal to the Somerset JP Arthur Pyne, son of a man notorious for indiscreet speeches against the Court, to intercede with the justices of assize on behalf on the victims of disafforestation. It seems unlikely that a JP from outside Dorset would have been approached for any other reason than his family's reputation of support for popular causes.[17]

The evidence for direct political associations is slender. Indirectly, however, the western riots had important political consequences. Disafforestation was one among several of Charles I's policies which upset the delicate balance between national and local institutions, between 'Court' and 'Country'. The West Country gentry and yeomen had no objection to improvement and enclosure, as long as they were the beneficiaries. When these things were done, however, for the profit of outsiders, and when in consequence they had to defend law and order against their aroused inferiors, it was a different matter. Disafforestation left the areas affected with a worse problem of poverty than ever, with a population less inclined to see the king as their benevolent protector or the Court as anything but an oppressive, alien force, and with well-developed habits of collective action. When in 1642 the gentry and middling sort turned against the Crown, they were to find willing support from the lower orders in these regions.

The forests were not the only sites of resistance to agricultural improvement. The eastern fens and their smaller Somerset counterparts offered similar opportunities for profit and provoked similar protests. Royal grants to entrepreneurial aristocrats and courtiers – the same sort of people as those behind the disafforestation projects – led to a series of ambitious drainage schemes and aroused determined opposition by the poorer commoners. There were complicated lawsuits in which the inhabitants tried to protect their rights of common, but also intermittent rioting, which by 1637 had intensified and spread from Lincolnshire into other eastern counties. Events that year in Huntingdonshire show the familiar combination of popular action and connivance by members of the local élite. One of the fenlanders' gentry sympathizers was a hitherto obscure local squire named Oliver Cromwell.[18]

Riots provoked by food shortages or high prices reveal similarly conservative popular attitudes. They tended, naturally, to occur in clusters after especially bad harvests, as in the 1590s, and in times of depression and unemployment like the 1620s. As the cloth industry was largely situated in regions that were not self-sufficient in food production, it naturally followed that the clothing districts were usually the worst affected. North-east Somerset, the JPs of the neighbourhood reported in 1623, 'a great part of it being forest and woodlands, and the rest very barren for corn', was particularly vulnerable.[19] So were the adjoining parts of Wiltshire. The aims and methods of food rioters and the reaction of the authorities to them exemplify many of the same characteristics of popular protest that we have observed in the enclosure outbreaks.

The typical grain riot was directed against people, usually outsiders, transporting grain to markets outside the area affected.[20] The intention was usually to compel authority to maintain a traditional order, rather than to overturn it. Religious teachings and government pronouncements alike contributed to the prevailing belief that shortages were the result of individual greed and sin rather than of a system of market relations or the pursuit of class interests.[21] Food rioters and petitioners were inspired by the values of a vaguely sensed 'moral economy', in contrast to the values of the market economy now being adopted by increasing numbers of the middling sort. It is true that there are few known cases of *taxation populaire*, in which corn was sold off at the 'just' rather than the market price. But there are some.[22] Just as intimidation rather than actual physical violence was the hallmark of most of the riots, so too was the careful respect for legitimate procedures and even for property rights. The carts should not pass, a Kent rioter declared in 1596, but he added that he and his fellows could not 'touch the corn'; all they could do was halt its shipment 'in her Majesty's name'. In the same county in 1631 the cry 'One half . . . for the King, the other for them' was heard, in effect a claim to the reward promised in royal proclamations to those who uncovered violations of export regulations. The same concern for legality was evident in Wiltshire in 1614 and Somerset in 1629, when rioters asked local officials to take charge of allegedly illegal shipments they had intercepted.[23] Grain riots, like protests against enclosure, demonstrate the intense legalism of popular politics, as well as the readiness of the inhabitants of towns and villages, particularly in the wood-pasture and clothing districts, to take direct action to defend their rights.

In their resistance to disafforestation and fen drainage, in their demands for the enforcement of traditional market regulations, the common people of England were expressing a set of values deeply rooted in their culture, which also had important political implications. Behind the regional differences we have been discussing, there was a political culture shared by people in all areas, a culture whose elements included assumptions about the permanent validity of ancient laws and customary rights, and about the existence of appropriate modes of government in church and state. Popular political horizons were necessarily largely bounded by the limits of town and village, shire and region. To what extent, though, it is natural to ask, could commoners look beyond the parish pump to the wider politics of the kingdom? And to the degree that they did so, what was the nature of their involvement in that broader national politics?

There is in fact plentiful evidence that in the early seventeenth century ordinary Englishmen had opinions on national issues that reflected their underlying concern for law, custom and 'good rule'. They tended, naturally enough, to view these issues primarily in terms of their impact on their local communities. A man at Lyneham, Wiltshire, got so carried away during a Sunday morning argument in the churchyard in 1618 that he disturbed the congregation by talking 'somewhat loud . . . about the composition money for the King'.[24] As the national political temperature rose, more and more of the clergy and gentry were moved to remind their inferiors of the relevance of the kingdom's grievances to their own affairs. Edmond Peacham, rector of Hinton St George, was tortured and died in prison in 1616 when his draft of a sermon on Court misgovernment was construed as treasonable. The bells and bonfires which greeted Charles I's reluctant acceptance of the Petition of Right, and the ballads and seditious verses which celebrated the subsequent assassination of Buckingham, all confirm the impression that political matters had by now assumed a large place in the popular consciousness.[25]

But if the common people were becoming more politically aware it might still be argued that they were not autonomous, that they were in fact the pawns and agents of their superiors. Certainly the hierarchical structure of this society, with its patriarchal ideology, ensured that the gentry could expect, and draw on, a deep fund of deference.[26] The limits of deference, however, are apparent in electoral as well as in county politics. The assumption that tenant votes could routinely be delivered by their landlords was common enough – it was made, for example, in the 1614 Somerset election. But the early seventeenth-century electorate was both more numerous and less easily controlled by the élite than historians used to suppose, and middling-sort voters had to be wooed, not commanded. As one of the Somerset candidates in 1614 lamented, 'we have to do with a wavering multitude which are apt to alter in the instant that I have done'.

So Englishmen of the middling sort were becoming more involved in national policies in the early seventeenth century than ever before. Then, as in later periods, they were often preoccupied with matters that may seem unrelated to the broader themes of national debate. Yet disputes over the appointment of a parish clerk at Blandford, over the authority of a bailiff at Thornbury, over the extent of ecclesiastical jurisdiction in cathedral cities, continually sharpened already deep-rooted habits of participation and self-government.

But there were, after all, wider issues. It has become a familiar commonplace that in the early seventeenth century provincial Englishmen generally viewed national politics through the prism of localism. This does not mean, however, that they were totally detached from the broad questions of constitutional debate, for what was national politics but the resultant of countless forces arising from the interaction between Westminster and the localities? The Ship Money controversy is an obvious example of these interactions. At one level it appears to involve the principled opposition of men like John Hampden,ᶜ at another to be simply a confusion of local disputes over ratings and assessments. But the two levels are inextricably connected. It was natural for yeomen and husbandmen to limit their protests to technical matters such as ratings rather than to stick their necks out and challenge the legality of the tax – that sort of thing was for the gentry. When by 1636 it became clear that Ship Money was not to be an occasional emergency levy, but a permanent annual tax, rating disputes proliferated in a way that reveals increasing popular discontent.

The point is that Ship Money, like so many other aspects of Charles I's policy of centralization, was *new*, and thus an affront to popular as well as élite notions of law and good rule. In 1638 the Somerset grand jury complained of 'the great and heavy taxations by new invented ways upon the county', of which Ship Money was of course the most burdensome.[27] The defence of local rights and interests was only one aspect of a general defence of ancient custom. Complaints about assessments in Somerset often focused on alleged departures from the 'Hinton rate', the system adopted in 1569, which had by now acquired an almost mystical authority.[28] That Ship Money was in many ways a more rational, equitable tax was irrelevant, for as Sir Henry Slingsby reflected, 'The common people judges not with things as they are with reason or against; but long usage with them is instead of all'.[29] Long usage; custom; traditional rights: the common people had their own version of that 'ancient constitution' to which their superiors in Parliament were so constantly appealing. The connection between local and national liberties was becoming all too clear. The clique of courtiers who had ridden roughshod over the rights of the western foresters, was the same clique that was advising Charles I to violate the country's liberties in such matters as the Forced Loan, arbitrary imprisonment, and Ship Money. Whether it was local or national liberties that were in question, the instinctive reaction was the same: the appeal to ancient law. When the king was trying to revive the forest laws in his favour in 1634, a member of an Essex grand jury empanelled for that purpose promptly demanded to see a copy of King John's charter.[30]

There was, then, a right and proper way of doing things, and there was a wrong, and hence tyrannical, way. On this gentry and middling-sort voters agreed, for they shared important elements of a common political culture, and their resistance to perceived illegalities thus reinforced each other's. How far down the social scale this rough consensus went is less clear. But the behaviour of the poor and oppressed in grain and enclosure riots suggests that such people did indeed have their own notions of political right and wrong. These notions were often expressed in nostalgic yearnings for a vanished past, as in the opinion of other Essex labourer in Elizabeth's reign that 'it was a merry England when there was better government': that was how the popular mind worked.[31] The rhetoric of MPs about legal rights and liberties was bound to have most impact on the literate, tax-paying middling sort, but even at the lowest level of society there were standards by which government could be judged.

And by those standards many aspects of early Stuart government were found wanting. The cultural stereotypes of 'Court' (corrupt, effeminate, popish, tyrannical) and 'country' (virtuous, patriotic, Protestant, liberty-loving) were steadily gaining ground during James I's reign.[32] The very word 'courtier' was becoming a term of abuse.

All this was common to the whole kingdom, and makes it easier to understand the virtually unanimous demand for reformation of both church and state – articulated by the gentry in Parliament but shared by their inferiors in the provinces – of 1640. The unanimity, however, while conspicuous in political matters, was less profound in matters of religion. There were marked regional variations in the intensity of Puritan feeling, variations which help to explain the subsequent division of the nation into two sides capable of fighting a civil war. Opposition to Laudianism was fiercest in the wood-pasture areas, and especially in the clothing districts. In these parishes it was strongest among the middling sort, the parish oligarchies of yeomen and clothiers who had for so long been struggling to impose their notions of godly discipline upon the disorderly poor, and who now took the lead, as at Mells and Beckington, in resisting Laud's altar policy. But it was not confined to the middling sort, for there were many lesser folk in the clothing parishes who went gadding to sermons, attended conventicles and flocked to hear itinerant preachers.[33] Even where there was no overt resistance to the altar policy, resentment at the overturning of hallowed parish custom must have been fanned by the expense of making the change, which often included costs for attendance at the ecclesiastical court.[34]

So when the political atmosphere was transformed by the meeting of Parliament in 1640 there was a surface unity among all sorts and conditions of Englishmen, but the seeds of division had long since been sown. The unity was on political matters like Ship Money, centralization and the threat to ancient liberties: on these the Long Parliament spoke for a nation in which high and low, town and country, arable and pasture regions were, in so far as they understood the issues, of one mind. But religious and cultural differences of long standing ensured that the potential for future strife still existed. Richard Baxter recalled that before 1640 anyone who took religion seriously enough to go gadding to sermons 'was made the derision of the vulgar rabble, under the odious name of a Puritan'; his own father was so labelled 'only for reading Scripture when the rest were dancing on the Lord's day, and for praying . . . in his house, and for reproving drunkards and swearers, and for talking sometimes a few words of Scripture and the life to come'.[35] The conflict, it must again be stressed, was partly rooted in social divisions. But it was also rooted in regional and cultural ones.

The unity of 1640 was fleeting, but for a time it was real enough. The meeting of the Long Parliament in November awakened universal expectation that church and state could be reformed, good governance restored, through the co-operation of King, Parliament and 'Country'. 'We dream now of nothing more than of a golden age', wrote the Devon squire John Bampfield, in a typical expression of the prevailing optimism.[36] Eventually the menacing outbursts of popular violence which erupted as the political temperature became more feverish and the hand of authority weaker – by London mobs shouting against Strafford and the bishops, rural mobs destroying fences and drainage works – divided the propertied nation into a 'party of change' and a 'party of order'.[37] But in 1640 the underlying social, religious and cultural divisions were hidden behind the façade of outward political unity.

The divisions which led to civil war were sharpened by the intrusion of the popular element into national politics. Comfortable assumptions that the lower orders shared the gentry's preference for moderate reform were soon put to the test. Some had been sceptical from the start. Mob violence after the dissolution of the Short Parliament caused the scholar James Howell to worry about the threat of popular insurrection: 'strange principles' had been infused into the common people.[38] There soon appeared many impressive indications of the intensity of popular feeling – the joyful crowds which greeted the released Star Chamber victims, the uglier ones which demonstrated against the hated Strafford and gave vent to 'universal rejoicing' at his execution. The revolutionary street politics of 1641 in London are sufficiently well known not to need recapitulation.[39] They provide, however, the essential background to the process of division which led to civil war. Few Parliament men had any desire to enlist the common people as anything but law-abiding voters or petitioners. Yet in executing Strafford, destroying Star Chamber and other prerogative institutions, and discussing farreaching reforms of the Church, they were themselves striking at the whole frame of authority. The common people, Sir Henry Slingsby lamented, were bound to think themselves 'loose and absolved from all government, when they should see that which they so much venerated so easily subverted'.[40]

'Loose and absolved from all government': the spectre of popular upheaval loomed in much else besides the violence against Strafford and the bishops. The fens and forests again erupted at this time, and by 1642 parts of the eastern counties were in a state of virtual rebellion. Like those in the western forests ten years earlier, the fen riots were directed mainly against courtiers, peers and projectors – outsiders destroying the customary economy in the name of profit and 'improvement'. They naturally took on an anti-Court colouring, and the fenmen again received a good deal of sympathy and support from Commons' leaders like Oliver Cromwell. Lincolnshire rioters who defied the authority of the Lords conceded that 'if it had been an order of the House of Commons' they would have desisted.[41]

The arousal of public feeling was most dramatic in matters

of religion. Middling-sort Puritans might content themselves with implementing orders to remove altar rails and superstitious monuments, with reviving lectureships and with religious exercises preparing them for further reformation. 'All our business', it was reported from Devonshire in October 1641, 'is to pray and pay, and our chiefest farmers ... begin to bristle up for a lay eldership.'[42] But in many places popular hostility to Laudian ritual was too intense for people to be content with quiet methods of reform. Incidents involving the violent destruction of altar rails, 'popish' monuments and stained glass occurred in all parts of the country, and were particularly common in London and the home counties. Sometimes they provoked a good deal of festive rejoicing, which may have attracted people who were far from Puritan. At Latton, Essex, a bonfire of altar rails was combined with a beer party in the church porch; at Chelmsford the smashing of stained glass occurred in the aftermath of Gunpowder Treason celebrations.[43]

Suspicion of Catholics was one of the most basic common denominators of popular politics, easily ignited in times of crisis. A steady drumbeat of accusation and innuendo, assiduously encouraged by John Pym and other leaders in Parliament, aroused widespread fears of a vaguely defined yet profoundly threatening popish conspiracy by courtiers, army officers and Laudian bishops against the liberties of Protestant England. The riots that erupted in London after the dissolution of the Short Parliament were directed against the queen's household, the Catholic peers, the papal agent – and Archbishop Laud. The 'great fear' of Catholic conspiracy, fed by rumours of Army plots fomented by the queen to put an end to Parliament altogether, steadily intensified during the following year. Earlier local panics were dwarfed by the ones that followed the Irish Rebellion in the autumn of 1641. Papists everywhere were believed to be collecting arms, plotting to burn towns. Sir Robert Harley's warnings to his family caused panic in Herefordshire and the adjoining counties; in every village people were 'up in arms, with watch all night in very great fear'. Rumours that Irish rebels were coming, inspired by nothing worse than the arrival of a few Protestant refugees, swept through the West Riding clothing districts.[44]

However slender their foundation, such fears were easily turned to political account. In early 1642 petitions from the

localities had one recurrent theme: all the troubles of the kingdom – religious, political, economic – were the fault of the
'popish Lords and bishops'. The depression of the cloth trade,
the inhabitants of Tavistock complained, was caused by 'dread
of the Turks at sea, and of popish plots at home'. The fishing
industry, a Plymouth petition declared, had been disrupted by
Irish rebels encouraged 'by certain popish and ill-affected lords
and bishops'. County petitions from Dorset, Somerset and
Wiltshire, and from many other places, had the same refrain:
the papists were on the march and could only be frustrated
by the exclusion of the bishops from the House of Lords.[45]

Beliefs of this kind blended with more explicitly political
elements to form the popular stereotype of the 'Cavalier' whose
emergence, along with the corresponding stereotype of the
'Roundhead' on the other side, both reflected and heightened
the division of the kingdom.[d] Stereotypes – cultural construc-
tions that express in a form of public shorthand the negative
characteristics of opponents – are the inevitable product of deep-
seated political divisions. When they acquire an aura of total
moral exclusiveness, providing symbolic expression of fundamentally opposed ideologies and moral codes, they intensify
pre-existing divisions and solidify group identities. They are of
course of particular value when complicated political issues
have to be articulated in forms readily accessible to large, imper-
fectly informed populations. Such was the case in England in
1642.

The 'Cavalier' stereotype combined other components with
the Catholic one. A crucial element was the 'swordsman' figure,
derived from the impression that Charles I was surrounded by
irresponsible, swaggering soldiers, intent on destroying English
liberties and taking bloody aristocratic revenge for the plebeian
slights heaped upon the king, queen and Court. Political,
religious, cultural and social prejudices all converged in the
formation of the rival stereotypes. Puritan perceptions of the
Herefordshire JP Wallop Brabazon, a leading enemy of the Harleys,[e] provide a good example. He had been 'very forward' in
urging payment of Ship Money, had violated common rights,
entertained papists in his house, licensed a tenant to keep an
alehouse where bowling on the sabbath was permitted, and as
churchwarden had introduced Laudian innovations and forced
the parish to employ an organist who also taught music to

Brabazon's children. Only the military element is missing, and that was added when Brabazon became a Commissioner of Array and brought soldiers into the neighbourhood. Brabazon was not himself a papist, but his connections and his Laudian views made it easy for him to be loosely identified as one. By 1642 'papist', 'malignant', and 'Cavalier' were virtually interchangeable synonyms, all three conjuring up the figure of a menacing, armed enemy of Protestantism and English liberties.[46]

The corresponding 'Roundhead' stereotype, like its Cavalier equivalent, contained a kernel of truth, sharpened, exaggerated and caricatured to create a composite symbol. The notion that opposition to Charles I was confined to a handful of ill-disposed Puritans, shattering the old harmony of English society by their divisive individualism and sanctimonious rejection of popular amusements, was a convenient fiction for royalists. Not all Puritans were kill-joys, and not all parliamentarians were Puritans, but the ones who were offered an easy target for abuse and ridicule. Like 'Cavalier', the label 'Roundhead' evoked a combination of responses. It was a term charged with social meaning, expressing the contempt felt by officers and gentlemen for people of inferior rank; Pym and his allies were self-interested upstarts turning the world upside-down, 'to make subjects princes and princes slaves', an East Anglian jingle put it.[47] At another level it encoded a set of religious and cultural assumptions: Roundheads were Puritans who wore their hair short and were against maypoles and honest recreations. No matter that many parliamentarians were not Puritan in anything but the loosest sense of that term. The cavalier mob who assaulted a group of inoffensive Lincolnshire gentlemen as Roundheads after a coronation-day celebration at York in March 1642 showed how deeply the notion had taken root. Throughout the spring and summer the stereotypes regularly surfaced in outbreaks of mutual invective as communities divided throughout the length and breadth of England.[48]

We are again reminded that the divisions of 1642 were as much cultural as religious or political. The war, Baxter reflected, 'was begun in our streets before king or parliament had any armies'.[49] Its origins lay, in other words, in that same cultural conflict that had for so long ranged Puritan minorities against their neighbours. Baxter knew this from his own experience. When he went to Kidderminster as lecturer in 1641 he encountered a typically divided wood-pasture parish: 'an ignorant, rude and revelling people for the greater part', but also 'a small company of converts, who were humble, godly, and of good conversations'. The former – mostly poor journeymen and servants – still had their revel feast, where they 'brought forth the painted forms of giants and suchlike foolery', and they rioted when the godly churchwardens tried to remove the churchyard cross and the 'popish' images. The familiar socio-cultural polarization was soon solidified in the popular stereotypes. 'If a stranger passed, in many places, that had short hair and a civil habit', Baxter tells us, 'the rabble presently cried, "Down with the Roundheads"; and some they knocked down in the open street.' Baxter was driven from Kidderminster and took refuge at Puritan Gloucester.[50] The stage was set for civil war.

The political unity of 1640 foundered in the renewal of religious and cultural conflict. The immediate precipitant of civil war – the constitutional dispute over the militia power – concealed more fundamental antagonisms that went beyond matters of government to differences about the very nature of society. These divisions existed in every community, every region. Yet some regional patterns are unmistakable. In some areas the dominant outlook was shaped by those of the gentry and middling sort who pressed unwaveringly for 'godly reformation' and regarded Cavaliers as agents of 'popery and profaneness'.[51] In others the public mood was set by those who saw in the traditional order and its communal rituals the only guarantee of social harmony, and feared the disruptive consequences of Puritanism more than the mythical popish conspiracy.

Most people, understandably, were appalled at the prospect of civil war and tried to stay out of it as far as possible. A preference for neutrality, however, did not necessarily mean indifference to the outcome. And even the more partisan shared elements of a large common stock of ideas about society and government, shaped by long collective experience in the ordering of their communities. The handful of zealots, particularly on the side of Parliament, who rejected these traditional values have a historical importance out of all proportion to their numbers. But their failure to establish the New Jerusalem they yearned for was in the end the result of the tenacious attachment of most of their countrymen to ancient laws and customs.

In 1641 the common system of values was skilfully translated into political language. A national oath of loyalty, the Protestation, was enacted by the Commons during the great fear of a counter-stroke against Parliament by Charles I. Initially the oath was taken only by MPs and by voluntary subscription in a few parishes, but in January 1642 it was sent down into the countryside and the clergy ordered to administer it to all adult males.[52] Its subscribers swore to maintain 'his Majesty's royal person and estate': the patriarchal, monarchical core of the social and political order. They swore to defend 'the power and privilege of Parliaments, the lawful rights and liberties of the subjects': the ancient constitution and laws from which stemmed the rights of individuals and of the kingdom's component communities. And they swore to preserve 'the true reformed Protestant religion expressed in the doctrine of the Church of England, against all Popery and popish innovation': the religion which united, rather than divided them. Patriarchy; law; liberty; the Protestantism of Queen Elizabeth's days: the Protestation expressed a set of simple, unifying ideas which were to surface again repeatedly in popular politics during and after the Civil War.

The Protestation was originally designed to cement public opinion behind Parliament, and to isolate Catholics and other 'malignants'. In the hectic early months of 1642 it became a powerful parliamentarian symbol, carried on pikes and swords by Londoners demonstrating their support of the Five Members, worn in the hats of Buckinghamshire gentlemen accompanying their county petition to Westminster.[53] It could be used, in other words, for highly partisan purposes. But it was also available as a statement of basic principles that transcended the disputes now dividing the kingdom. The reading of the Protestation after morning service, and the solemn ceremony of subscription, must have been unforgettable experiences for many humble villagers as they publicly affirmed the unity of the nation. The fracturing of that unity by civil war did not eradicate the appeal of the Protestation's simple, obvious statement of consensus ideas. Like their predecessors in the forest and fen riots with whom this chapter opened, the subscribers to the Protestation had their own ill-defined, yet deeply felt version of the ancient constitution.

EDITOR'S NOTES

Reprinted in abridged form from chapter 5 of David Underdown, *Revel, Riot and Rebellion: Popular Politics and Culture in England 1603–1660* (Oxford, 1987), with permission of Oxford University Press.

a Generally, a highly ritualized communal demonstration directed against unacceptable behaviour by a member of the community – a cuckold or a scold, for instance.

b A ball-and-bat game popular in wood-pasture regions. Underdown construes it as reflecting the more individualistic elements in the culture of these regions. The individual confrontation between batsman and bowler contrasts with the more purely team sports (like football) popular in the arable downlands.

c Hampden, a substantial Buckinghamshire gentleman and leader of the Commons' opposition to extraparliamentary taxation in the Long Parliament, had refused to pay his Ship Money levy in 1637. He was arrested and convicted, but by a vote of seven to five, suggesting that even the king's own judges saw legal problems with Ship Money. Hampden was killed fighting for Parliament in 1643.

d Royalists were popularly called 'Cavaliers' and identified with the frivolity and self-indulgence of Court life as well as with the reputed brutality of the Spanish Caballeros. Those who fought for the parliamentarian and Puritan cause were called 'Roundheads', a term of opprobrium associated initially with the shorn heads of London apprentices and later with the close haircuts of parliamentary soldiers.

e Zealous Puritans and prominent members of the Herefordshire gentry. Sir Robert was an outspoken leader of the Commons' opposition to Arminianism, ceremonies and eventually even episcopacy, both in the 1620s parliaments and in the Short and Long Parliaments. Lady Brilliana is known for her defence of their county base, Brampton Bryan, under royalist siege in 1643.

NOTES

1 *CSPD, 1631–3*, p. 312.

2 *Records of Wilts.*, pp. 115–16. For the escalation of protest see, for example, Anthony Fletcher, *Tudor Rebellions* (London, 1980), p. 69.

3 The most complete account of the western riots is by Buchanan Sharp, *In Contempt of All Authority: Rural Artisans and Riot in the West of England, 1586–1660* (Berkeley and Los Angeles, 1980). For the point discussed here see esp. pp. 134–55.

4 The ringleaders were subsequently punished in Star Chamber and a precarious order restored: Sharp, *In Contempt*, pp. 86–9, 98.

5 Ibid., pp. 87–96, 121, 208–18. See also F. Kerridge, 'The Revolts in Wiltshire against Charles I', *Wiltshire Archaeological Magazine*, 57 (1958–60), pp. 67–9; T. G. Barnes, *Somerset 1625–1640* (Cambridge,

Mass., 1961), pp. 157–8; J. H. Bettey, 'Revolts over the Enclosure of the Royal Forest at Gillingham 1626–1630', *Dorset Natural History and Archaeological Society Proceedings*, 97 (1975), pp. 21–4; W. B. Willcox, *Gloucestershire* (New Haven, 1940), pp. 194–202. For earlier disorders in Dean see Sharp, *In Contempt*, pp. 191–2; and Willcox, pp. 193–4, 280.

6 For reasons that will become clear, I do not accept Sharp's argument (*In Contempt*, esp. ch. 5) that only the poorest foresters were involved in the riots.

7 Sharp, *In Contempt*, pp.84–96, 101–2, 207. Barnes, *Somerset*, p. 157.

8 Willcox, *Gloucestershire*, pp. 156–7, 196. E. Kerridge, 'Agriculture *c.* 1500–*c.* 1793', *VCH, Wiltshire*, iv, pp. 43–64.

9 *CSPD, 1631–3*, p. 312. A local jury refused to convict the assailants: Sharp, *In Contempt*, p. 102.

10 Willcox, *Gloucestershire*, pp. 193–4, 279–80. Sharp, *In Contempt*, p. 191.

11 WRO Dean's Peculiar, Presentments 1625, no. 19; D/AB28 (Act Book, 1622–7), fos 180–1. See also M. Ingram, 'Le Charivari dans l'Angleterre du XVIe et du XVIIe siècle', in *Le Charivari*, ed. J. le Goff and Jean-Claud Schmitt (Paris, 1981), pp. 251–64. See esp. p. 255.

12 Sharp, *In Contempt*, pp. 95–6, 129.

13 As at Frampton-on-Severn: Sharp, *In Contempt*, pp. 105–6. For Capt. Cobbler see Fletcher, *Tudor Rebellions*, pp. 21–2; for Capt. Pouch, Edwin F. Gay, 'The Midland Revolt and the Inquisitions of Depopulation of 1607', *TRHS* NS, 18 (1904), p. 217n.

14 Sharp, *In Contempt*, pp. 100, 104–5, 108, 129.

15 After enclosure riots at Datchet, Bucks., in 1598 the women convicted were sentenced to the cucking-stool, the men to stand in the pillory in women's clothes: John Hawarde, *Les Reportes del Cases in Camera Stellata 1593 to 1609*, ed. W. P. Baildon (London, 1894), p. 104; and PRO STAC 5/K5/23, 5/K6/24 (*Kedermister v. Hales*, 1598). For women in riots see John Walter, 'Grain Riots and Popular Attitudes to the Law: Maldon and the Crisis of 1629', in *An Ungovernable People*, ed. J. Brewer and J. Styles (London, 1980), pp. 62–3.

16 Sharp disposes of earlier suggestions that Williams operated outside Dean: *In Contempt*, pp. 97–104.

17 Kerridge, 'Revolts', p. 69. Sharp, *In Contempt*, pp. 110–11, 132–3. Barnes, *Somerset*, pp. 34, 70, 163, 262.

18 H. C. Darby, *The Draining of the Fens*, 2nd edn (Cambridge, 1956), ch. 2; Joan Thirsk, *English Peasant Farming* (London, 1957), ch. 5; Clive Holmes, *Seventeenth Century Lincolnshire* (Lincoln, 1980), pp. 124–30; Antonia Fraser, *Cromwell the Lord Protector* (London, 1973), pp. 52–5; Keith Lindley, *Fenland Riots and the English Revolution* (New York, 1982), ch. 2.

19 Quoted in David Underdown, *Somerset in the Civil War and Interregnum* p. 18. For harvests see W. G. Hoskins, 'Harvest Fluctuations and English Economic History 1480–1619', in W. C. Minchinton (ed.), *Essays in Agrarian History* (Newton Abbott, 1968), I, pp. 93–116; and 'Harvet Fluctuations ... 1620–1759', *Agricultural Hist. Rev.* 16

(1968) pp. 15–31. J. Walter and K. Wrightson ('Dearth and the Social Order in Early Modern England', *Past and Present*, no. 71 (1976), pp. 22–42) p. 27, argue that most grain riots occured in grain-producing areas when supplies were being exported. It will be seen that in the western counties, however, they tended to occur in wood-pasture regions on the fringes of the producing areas.

20 John Walter's 'Grain Riots and Popular Attitudes to the Law: Maldon and the Crisis of 1629', in *An Ungovernable People*, pp. 47–84, is an excellent case-study.

21 Peter Clark, 'Popular Protest and Disturbance in Kent, 1558–1640', *Economic and History Review*, 2nd series, 29 (1976), pp. 370, 378–9. Walter and Wrightson, 'Dearth and the Social Order', pp. 28–9, 31, 34.

22 There are instances in Kent and at Southwark in 1595: Clark, 'Popular Protest', p. 368. But cf. Walter and Wrightson, 'Dearth and the Social Order', p. 33; and Sharp, *In Contempt*, pp. 33–4.

23 Clark, 'Popular Protest', pp. 374–5. Walter and Wrightson, 'Dearth and the Social Order', p. 33.

24 WRO AW/ABO 5 (Act Book, 1616–22), fo. 30.

25 Bonfires were reported in some places, following false rumours that Buckingham was to be sent to the Tower: *The Court and Times of Charles I*, ed. Thomas Birch and [R. F. Williams] (London, 1848) I, p. 362.

26 Which explains why historians have usually confined their investigations of early Stuart politics to the aristocracy and gentry.

27 *Somerset Assize Orders, 1629–40*, p.60.

28 Barnes, *Somerset*, pp. 213–14, 217.

29 *Diary of Sir Henry Slingsby*, ed. Daniel Parsons (1836) p. 68.

30 *Journal of Sir Simonds D'Ewes*, p. 150.

31 J. Samaha, 'Gleanings from Criminal-Court Records: Sedition amongst the "Inarticulate" in Elizabethan Essex', *Journal of Social History*, 8 (1975), pp. 61–79, esp. p. 69 Cf. the comment of the Essex preacher, George Gifford, quoted in W. A. Hunt, *The Puritan Moment*, (Cambridge, Mass., 1983) p. 148.

32 For the stereotypes see Perez Zagorin, *The Court and the Country: The Beginning of the English Revolution* (London, 1969), pp. 33–9; and L. Stone, *The Causes of the English Revolution, 1529–1642* (London, 1972), pp. 105–7.

33 Margaret Stieg, *Laud's Laboratory* (Lewisburg, Penn., 1982), pp. 287–90, 297–301.

34 Charges arising from moving the communion table are recorded, for example, in Gloucestershire churchwardens' accounts: GRO P 34, CW/2/1 (Barnsley, 1609–55), 1636; P 107, CW/2/1 (Daglingworth, 1624–1803), 1637; P 328, CW/2/1 (Stroud, 1623–1716), p. 29.

35 *Reliquiae Baxterianae*, ed. M. Sylvester (London, 1696), pp. 2–3.

36 HMC, *Fifteenth Report*, VII (Seymour MSS), p. 64. For other examples of the mood of expectancy see Stone, *Causes of the English Revolution*, pp. 51–3; and David Underdown, *Pride's Purge: Politics in the Puritan Revolution* (Oxford, 1971), p. 14.

37 See B. Manning, *The English People and the English Revolution*, (London, 1976), ch. 3.

38 *Epistolae Ho-Elianae*, ed. Joseph Jacobs (London, 1892), I 352.

39 Manning, *English People*, pp. 2–3, 10–18. A. Fletcher, *The Outbreak of the English Civil War* (London, 1981), pp. 6, 15–16.

40 *Diary of Sir Henry Slingsby*, p. 68.

41 Manning, *English People*, pp. 124–37. Thirsk, *Peasant Farming*, pp. 125–6. Holmes, *Lincolnshire*, pp. 139–40, 153–7. Fletcher, *Outbreak*, pp. 312, 377. Lindley, *Fenland Riots*, ch. 3.

42 *CSPD, 1641–3*, pp. 144. Among lectureships founded or revived in 1642 were ones at Martock, Shepton Mallet and Bridport: *CJ*, II, pp. 610, 692; HMC, *Fifth Report* (House of Lords MSS), pp. 28, 37.

43 *English History from Essex Sources*, pp. 76–7. Hunt, *The Puritan Moment*, pp. 292–3. For similar events in other Essex parishes see J. A. Sharpe, 'Crime and Delinquency in an Essex Parish' in *Crime in England 1550–1800*, ed. J. S. Cockburn (Princeton, 1977) p. 105; and Philip L. Ralph, *Sir Humphrey Mildmay: Royalist Gentlemen* (New Brunswick, N.J., 1947), p. 167. See also Fletcher, *Outbreak*, pp. 109–10; and Manning, *English People*, pp. 33–6.

44 Robin Clifton, 'The Popular Fear of Catholics during the English Revolution', *Past and Present*, no. 52 (Aug. 1971), pp. 23–55. Manning, *English People*, pp. 22–30, esp. pp. 27–8. Fletcher, *Outbreak*, pp. 59–61, 136–40, 200–7.

45 Andriette, *Devon and Exeter*, pp. 44–6. Underdown, *Somerset*, pp. 28–9. Fletcher, *Outbreak*, pp. 200–14.

46 HMC, *Portland*, III, p. 76. BL Loan 29/50 (Misc. Harley papers), Leominster petition [1642?]. See also Fletcher, 'Factionalism in Town and Countryside: The Significance of Puritanism and Arminianism', in D. Baker, ed., *Studies in Church History XVI* (Oxford, 1979), pp. 291–300, esp. p. 296; and *Outbreak*, pp. 302–6, 410–11.

47 Fletcher, *Outbreak*, p. 294.

48 Fletcher provides many examples: for example, *Outbreak*, pp. 280–1, 370. There were cries of 'Roundhead' during the disputes at Leominster: BL Loan 29/121 (Harley Papers), J. Tombes to Sir R. Harley, 31 July 1642. The term was already in common use in Herefordshire: *Letters of the Lady Brilliana Harley*, ed. T. T. Lewis (Camden 1st ser. 1854, LVIII, pp. 170–2.

49 Quoted in Fletcher, *Outbreak*, p. 409. It will be seen that my reading of Baxter's meaning differs from Fletcher's.

50 *Reliquiae Baxterianae*, pp. 20, 24, 40–1. Many similar comments could be cited: for example, those of John Tombes on the 'ignorant and superstitious' common people at Leominster: HMC, *Portland*, III, p. 76. Fletcher notes the presence of sabbatarian, anti-festive elements in some of the 1642 petitions: *Outbreak*, p. 219.

51 William Hinde, *Faithfull Remonstrance* (London, 1641), p. 6.

52 Text in *Constitutional Documents of the Puritan Revolution*, ed. S. R. Gardiner, 3rd edn (Oxford, 1906), pp. 155–6. The returns are calendared in HMC, *Fifth Report* (House of Lords MSS), pp. 120–34. For

the circumstances surrounding the Protestation see Fletcher, *Outbreak*, pp. 15–16, 77–9, 209–10.
53 Fletcher, *Outbreak*, pp. 185, 196, 209.

12

NEWS AND POLITICS IN EARLY SEVENTEENTH-CENTURY ENGLAND

Richard Cust

Revisionists have identified the division of the 1640s in terms of a 'functional breakdown' of the centre under the stress of war and fiscal constraint, with relatively little interest or willing involvement in the counties. A new examination of the role of the press and the reception of news and propaganda in the countryside suggests that the conflict was actually more principled in nature and that its development can be traced in the provinces in the decades before 1642. Intellectual historians like Johann Sommerville[a] describe an ongoing intellectual debate about the constitution in the early seventeenth century; here Richard Cust finds that debate conducted at the local and popular level. Contemporary rhetoric about consensus, order and obedience must be set against his compelling evidence of popular criticism, complaint and confrontation. The distinction frequently made between high and low politics, between court élite and country people, must also be amended in light of apparent popular interest in public affairs and principle. The revisionist notion of popular disinterest in central policy even in the 1640s looks increasingly suspect in the face of these data.

* * *

One of the more problematic issues currently being discussed by early seventeenth-century historians relates to the impact of news. Although few attempts have been made to address this directly, it is central to an understanding of political attitudes, particularly in the localities. It has implications for debates about the awareness and independence of electors and the role of the 'county community'; and at a more refined level it affects our

232

judgement of the place of principle in politics and the extent to which its processes were perceived as adversarial.[1] News is of considerable importance, and yet historians have been unable to agree about its impact.

Most would accept that the volume of political news was increasing during the early seventeenth century; but the consequences of this are uncertain. Those writing within the Whig tradition have argued for a relatively direct connection between this increase and a heightening of political conflict. Hence Zagorin has linked interest in current affairs and the appearance of the first newspapers to division between 'Court' and 'Country'; and Stone has cited the Earl of Newcastle's advice to Charles II, that to avoid the unrest of his father's reign he should suppress newsletter-writers.[2] These views have, however, been treated with scepticism by a more recent generation of historians, whose research into local archives has revealed only limited evidence of such influences at work. Hirst, after examining numerous elections and detailing the methods by which parliamentary events were published in the shires, has stressed none the less that 'nowhere prior to the 1630s was there a consistent record of political arousal on the part of the electorate'. Morrill has emphasized that, although there was plenty of material in circulation, much of it 'treated great affairs of state in a surprisingly trivial manner', leaving the reader confused rather than enlightened, 'knowing a good deal that was distasteful and unpleasant about the Court, but knowing and understanding less about the real constitutional issues'. And, drawing on this work, Russell has argued that the pressures exerted by constituents on their MPs related mainly to local concerns such as taxation.[3] These conclusions have, however, been challenged in turn: Holmes and Hughes, on the basis of their local research, suggest links between the gentry's receipt of news and their understanding of broad issues of principle; Hill has pointed to ways in which the general awareness of constituents created pressures for MPs; and Hirst himself has shown that voters were often able to differentiate candidates for election in terms of broad political alignments.[4] Moreover, in a detailed account of the outbreak of civil war, Fletcher has continually highlighted the effects of the news. Not only did it keep the localities informed about national events and encourage widespread discussion, it also gave rise to a series of petitioning campaigns which revealed both the sophistication of local élites and their concern to influence politics at the centre.[5]

Fletcher's work, in particular, invites a reassessment of the role of news, and this is the main purpose of this chapter. It will first of all look at how news circulated to the shires, in order to assess its volume and likely audience; then investigate its content, and the ways in which it was prepared and perceived; and finally suggest some of its effects for the formation of political attitudes and ideas. The discussion will draw mainly on evidence of domestic politics during the 1620s; but it will be argued that the conclusions apply more widely, to reflect a series of general developments in the period before 1640.

Prior to the 1640s the printing of domestic news was tightly controlled by the Privy Council. The corantoes which appeared at this time – and which have attracted considerable attention as the forerunners of the newspaper – dealt only with foreign affairs, and were generally careful to avoid controversial topics lest they forfeit their licences.[6] In spite of this, however, a good deal of sensitive material still came into circulation. Some of it was printed abroad – usually in the United Provinces or Germany – and then imported; but most was written in England and circulated in manuscript, either as newsletters or what were known as 'separates'. These took the form of transcripts or detailed reports of proceedings in Parliament, state trials, advice to the Crown, diplomatic negotiations, military campaigns and so on. Together with newsletters they generally avoided conciliar restrictions, and from the 1580s onwards these two sources provided the basis for an expanding network of news.[7]

Originally the newsletter had been largely unformalized, consisting simply of news items sandwiched between personal and business correspondence in letters to friends or relations. This sort of communication continued – and probably remained the most common method for conveying written news – but alongside it there developed the 'pure newsletter', given over wholly to news, both domestic and foreign. These 'pure newsletters' were the forerunners of the internal news-sheets of the 1640s and were in many cases being produced by an emerging class of semi-professional journalists who ranged from well-connected men of affairs, such as John Chamberlain, to the sort of anonymous hack caricatured in Ben Jonson's play, *News from the New World*:

a factor of news for all the shires of England, I do write my thousand letters a week ordinary, sometimes twelve hundred, and maintain the business at some charge both to hold up my reputation with mine own ministers in town, and my friends of correspondence in the country. I have friends of all ranks and of all religions, for which I keep an answering catalogue of dispatch, wherein I have my puritan news, my protestant news and my pontifical news.[8]

It is possible to learn a good deal about some of the more prominent members of this group, and their networks of correspondence reveal much about the way provincial readers were kept in touch with public affairs. Sir John Scudamore in Herefordshire, for example, paid £20 a year for the services of John Pory, who was at various times a geographer, overseas adventurer and MP, and who numbered among his contacts Archbishop Abbot, Sir Dudley Carleton, the Earl of Warwick and two leading Warwickshire gentlemen, Sir Thomas Lucy and Sir Thomas Puckering.[9] Another acquaintance of Pory's – Joseph Mead, the Cambridge theologian – provided a comparable service for the Suffolk gentleman, Sir Martin Stuteville, keeping him up to date by sending as many as four letters a week, collected from various London correspondents.[10]

As the newsletter developed and altered its form so too did the 'separate'. From providing an occasional account of a really notable public event in the late sixteenth century, it had been extended to cover almost anything which attracted the public interest; in particular, it provided the means for circulating the first public account of events in parliament, the proceedings and debates for 1628.[11] Moreover, unlike the newsletter, which was by nature ephemeral and frequently open to correction, the 'separate' was regarded as an authoritative record, and as such was copied into commonplace books and preserved in library collections.

As the market expanded, techniques of production evolved rapidly. A seller of 'separates', like the antiquarian, Ralph Starkey, could employ a whole team of scriveners and copyists and produce detailed accounts of newsworthy occurrences within a few days. This sort of organization helped to keep prices down, and for much of the period they were running at levels comparable to printed works: in 1628, for example, items relating to the Parliament were selling for between 6*d*. and 2*s*.; and in 1637 Sir Richard Grosvenor was buying 'separates' for between 2*s*. and 3*s*., while paying 2*s*. and 2*s*. 6*d*. for printed sermons. There was also competition to reproduce material as cheaply as possible, with London scriveners undercutting each other in selling transcripts of Justice Croke's Ship Money judgement.[12] This all ensured a very considerable volume of production. The numbers of copies made of popular items must have run into hundreds, if not thousands.

In spite of this rapid expansion of written material, however, it seems that the commonest method of passing on news remained word of mouth. This was in keeping with the habits of a society which was still only partially literate and in which the opportunities for oral exchange were growing with the development of internal trade and increasing resort to London. It also avoided some of the hazards attached to writing down news which was controversial. By its very nature, of course, much of the evidence for this has been lost to the historian; none the less, what was said can still sometimes be traced. Mead recorded conversations which he had had with travellers passing through Cambridge, and Pory referred to gossip and hearsay as the basis for his reports. The most revealing source, however, is a 'news-diary' kept by John Rous, a Suffolk clergyman who spent most of his life in his immediate locality.[13] On one occasion he mentions journeying to London, and on another going abroad to Geneva, but apart from this he rarely seems to have travelled beyond East Anglia. His social contacts were similarly restricted. There is no mention of direct contact with his eminent cousins, the Rouses of Henham, or with other leading gentry of the area, and he appears to have passed most of his time in the company of fellow clergymen, minor gentry and literate yeomen.[14] His diary, therefore, can be taken to indicate the news available to a well-informed, but essentially provincial, observer.

Most of this came in the form of gossip. Rous mentions receiving the odd newsletter and coranto from London, and journeying to Thetford to read proclamations pinned to the corner-post of the Bell inn; but the source he most frequently indicates is local talk, variously described as 'some say', 'it is commonly said', 'great talk', 'it was tould us', 'a rumour there was', 'country intelligence' and, most often, simply as 'ut dicitur'. Occasionally he was more specific and elaborated on the sources of news: on one occasion it was a conversation with a shop-keeper on the way to Wickham market; on another, a visit to the minister at Feltwell in Norfolk; and on a third, the report given out by Sir Roger Townsend returning home during a recess of Parliament. In spite of this diversity, however, the content of the material was very similar to the reports in newsletters or 'separates'. Thus 'country intelligence' in June 1626 was speculation about the causes of dissolving Parliament; the 'news held currant' in February 1627 was of national resistance to the forced loan; and Townsend's report was of Parliament's determination to proceed against the Duke of Buckingham in 1628.[15] In fact much of this oral news has the appearance of being derived from written sources, as well as vice versa.

This overlap is again apparent in the last of the principal agencies of news, the verses and ballads recited in alehouses and other places where people met to socialize. Of all the media considered, this is the most problematic, since it is very hard to discover the origin of these verses or their intended audience. There is some evidence indicating that they were performed in public: for example, a Star Chamber trial in 1627 involving two Middlesex fiddlers arrested for performing a libellous ballad about Buckingham; or the comment made about Thomas Cotton of Colchester in the 1630s, that he was accustomed to reading out the latest news on market-day with locals flocking around him 'as people use where ballads are sung'. There are also occasional references by Rous and others which suggest that the verses they recorded originated with the 'vulgar multitude' and reflected their opinions.[16] However, it is hard to know whether all popular verses fell into this category or whether some were perhaps intended for a more educated audience. What, for example, would a gentleman-collector such William Davenport have made of the verses which he recorded on the Parliament of 1621?

> The[y] saye Sejanus doth bestowe
> What ever office doth befalle
> But tis well knowen it is not soe
> For he is soundlye paide for all. . . .

When Charles hath gott the Spanishe gyrle
The Purytans will scowle and brawle
Then Digebye shall be made an Earle
And the Spanishe gould shall paye for all. . . .

When the Banquettine howse is finisht quite
Then James Sir Kingoe wee will calle
And poet Ben brave maskes shall wryte
And the subsidie shall pay for all. . . .

Sir Giles is much displeased with the Kinge
That he a Parliament did calle
But my hoste and hostyces both doe singe
The daye is come to paye for all. . . .

When Yelverton shalbe released
And Buckinghame begin to falle
Then will the Commons be well pleased
Which daye hath lounge beene wishte of all.[17]

The references to Sejanus and to Digby, Jonson and Yelverton suggest that these were intended for a relatively knowledgeable and sophisticated audience. On the other hand, the generally derisory tone of all the references, from the king across the board to opponents of his Spanish policy, seems to preclude any serious political purpose. Probably Davenport would have looked on them as akin to the early political cartoons which appeared at this time, an amusing and graphic way of presenting political commonplaces.[18]

Perhaps the most satisfactory conclusion one can offer is that verses of this sort often appear to have operated on at least two levels. They served to entertain and interest the literate contemporaries who collected them; but at the same time they provided a means of disseminating news and opinion to the illiterate and semi-literate, employing a familiar form derived from the ballad traditions of popular culture.[19] This dual function was illustrated in a set of verses produced late in 1627 after the Duke of Buckingham's return from the disastrous expedition to the Ile de Rhé.[b] Rous recorded these with some distaste as an example of the depths of vulgar muck-raking, but, at the same time, they indicate the more subtle side of popular news:

238

And arte returnde againe with all they faultes
Thou greate commander of the All goe naughts?
And lefte the Isle behinde thee: what's the matter?
Did winter make thy chappes beginne to chatter? . . .
Or diste thou sodenly remove thy station
For jealous fear of Holland's supplantation?
Or wast for want of wenches? or didst feare
The King thou absent durst wrong'd Bristoll heare? . . .
Or didst thou hasten headlong to prevent
A fruitlesse hope of needfull parliament?
All these, no question, with a restles motion
Vexte thy besotted soule as that blacke potion
Tortured the noble Scotte, whoses manes will tell
Thy swolne ambition made his carcase swell. . . .
Could not thy mother's masses nor her crosses
Nor sorceries prevent those fatal losses? . . .
Could not thy zealous Cambridge pupill's prayers
Composed of Brownist and Arminian ayres
Confound thy foes? . . . [20]

The imagery employed here bordered on the scatological and pornographic, and there was a tendency for such material to fit political figures into popular stereotypes, such as the good lord or evil counsellor.[21] None the less, these verses do still present a view of politics which was relatively sophisticated, both in its frame of reference and in its underlying assumptions. The allusions to Buckingham's chancellorship of Cambridge and the activities of his Arminian clients, to his supposed complicity in the murder of King James and the Duke of Hamilton and to his persecution of the Earl of Bristol all reflected complaints made against him during the 1626 Parliament; and the mention of the Earl of Holland and the Countess of Buckingham's reputation for popery implied a knowledge of events at court.[22] Whether the inclusion of these references means that the alehouse audience was entirely familiar with national politics, however, must remain an open question. These verses had a whole series of different aspects and operated according to the perceptions of those who heard them or wrote them down. The political allusions would probably have been picked up first and foremost by the educated connoisseur, while the less refined imagery may have had a greater impact in a public performance.

None the less, we should beware of drawing too clear a distinction. In this context, it is significant that such material was being presented at all, and this suggests that the separation often made between popular and élite culture was in practice sometimes non-existent. Here, at least, the literate and the illiterate shared the same medium.

This is important when it comes to assessing the impact of news. The implication is that this was not confined exclusively to the educated, but also had the potential to shape attitudes among the lower orders. The means by which news was transmitted varied considerably and that which was available at a popular level was generally less accurate and less refined; however, in terms of content and direction the different sorts of news were broadly similar. Developments in its circulation, then, were coming to affect a broad social spectrum.

This was particularly the case after 1620, from which date there is a marked increase in the survival of newsletters and 'separates', reflecting public interest in the Thirty Years War, negotiations for the Spanish match and renewed meetings of Parliament.[23] As a result those with access to written news came to be presented with an increasingly detailed insight into current affairs, much of it provided by semi-professional journalists with a reputation for accurate reporting. At the same time those who relied primarily on oral sources were being offered a broader and richer range of material, often supplemented from the written news. Inevitably all of this had important consequences for politics, and it is possible to explore some of these by looking more closely at the content.

One of the more obvious effects of the news was that it helped to further a sense of the integration of local and national. This was, of course, a complex process, related to a wide variety of cultural, social and institutional influences; but it was one in which news appears to have played a significant part. Its impact was enhanced by the way in which newsgathering centred on St Paul's Walk and the Exchange in London. The news from London was, however, not simply London news. Rather the city tended to serve as a melting-pot for information from all parts of the country. Whenever there was a significant occurrence in the shires, news of it was likely to reach the capital. This material was then worked together and retransmitted to the shires as part of a connected sequence of events, generally set alongside what was happening at the centre. It was this process which encouraged contemporaries to view local events in a wider perspective, and something of this can be seen in the 'news-diary' of Walter Yonge. Yonge lived at Colyton in Devon and, although a JP and linked with John White's Dorchester Company, during the 1620s he rarely travelled beyond his immediate locality. His diary was therefore basically a record of local events, but it was one spiced and given perspective by the letters and reports which he frequently received from friends in London. These helped Yonge to bring out the national significance of what was happening in his shire: for example, when describing the efforts to train the militia in 1626 he was able to record first of all that the scheme had been adopted nationally, and then the details of the sergeant sent to Colyton; when he talked of his county's refusal to pay Ship Money in February 1628 he did so in the context of a postponement of Parliament; and when discussing the forced loan he first described its launching nationally, then the response within his county, and finally the sufferings of his neighbour and friend, Sir Walter Earle, involved in the Five Knights Case.[c, 24] These examples, and others, demonstrate the sort of mental link which Yonge was accustomed to making, and in this he appears to have been typical of his contemporaries. In a similar vein, Rous related billeting within his shire to preparations for the Ile de Rhé expedition; while both Joseph Mead and the Earl of Clare, another prolific writer of newsletters, described local parliamentary elections in 1628 in terms which suggested that they were part of a concerted protest against the Court.[25] Centralized newsgathering, then, helped to shape the attitudes of the recipients of news. In a different way it also had a considerable impact on those involved in making the news.

One of the consequences of the growth in the volume of material was to make the activities of national politicians highly visible to a wide public. The implications of this for Parliament have been explored by Hirst and Russell. They have shown how the growing practice of reporting back to constituents and providing 'separates' of parliamentary proceedings led MPs to become more accountable and at the same time enabled them to shape local opinion. This brought credit for individuals whose actions were favourably reported and also enhanced the reputation of Parliament as a whole;[26] however, such processes were not confined exclusively to Parliament. Events outside were coming to be treated in almost as much detail with reports of Council meetings, diplomatic negotiations, Court intrigue and almost anything else which captured public attention. This exposed politicians to what must often have been an uncomfortable scrutiny; at the same time, however, it presented them with opportunities which they were quick to recognize and exploit.

Something of this can be seen from the way in which Privy Councillors were ready to 'leak' information in what appears to have been a quite calculated fashion. It was surely no accident that between 1626 and 1628, during discussions over the Forced Loan and the resummoning of Parliament, particular names appeared in the news again and again. The Council was split down the middle over these issues and for some members there was considerable advantage to be gained from making their views known more widely. As a result, by the 1620s, if not before, the circulation of news had become an integral part of the political process, something which politicians had to make allowance for, and which they appreciated could substantially affect public attitudes.

Perhaps the most significant consequence of all this, however, lay not in the degree of exposure which it gave to national politicians, but rather in the effects it had on perceptions of their actions. These were intimately related to the fact that newsletters, 'separates' and oral reports tended to present an image of politics which was at considerable variance with contemporary rhetoric. Naturally enough, they focused on the events which made the headlines and treated their readers to a succession of dramatic incidents: Court scandals, state trials, disputes in Parliament, attacks on the duke and almost anything else of unusual interest. In the process, evidence of everyday agreement and co-operation tended to be ignored. Hence the papists got into newsletters not when they were being submissive or loyal to the Crown, but when they seemed to threaten national security. Similarly, the billeting of soldiers was ignored during the three years in which it proceeded comparatively peaceably, and reached the newsletters only when it became a matter of political controversy, early in 1628. Then it was the subject of a series of grossly exaggerated reports suggesting, among other things, that soldiers had set fire to Banbury and massacred local inhabitants in Witham.[27] All this was, perhaps, much as one would expect; however, it is worth considering its effect on political attitudes.

Recent historiography has tended to stress that these were dominated by the continual drive towards consensus. Kishlansky has argued that the debates and procedure of Parliament were designed to secure agreement between Crown and subject; and Russell and Judson have shown that the predominant emphasis of parliamentary rhetoric was on unity. The same appears to have been true locally. Addresses made at quarter sessions, assizes or meetings of subsidy assessors repeatedly harped on the need for co-operation.[28] This was understandable, and to some extent necessary, given the ambiguities and scope for disagreement inherent in the political ideas of the period. Nevertheless, it should be recognized that this was not the only view of politics presented to the political nation. There was also the image of the news, with its characteristic stress on conflict.

This would seem to have operated at several levels. On the most general, it helped to erode the impression of harmony and consensus conveyed in the rhetoric. One does not have to look very far in the news material to appreciate the extent to which this focused on the dramatic constitutional clashes rather than the mundane evidence of agreement. Just as parliamentary diarists, according to Russell, omitted much of the consensual rhetoric, so newsletters' reports tended to concentrate on the conflict: in 1621 it was the misdeeds of monopolists and the imprisonment of MPs; in 1625 arguments over supply and the treatment of recusants; in 1626 the proceedings against Buckingham;[d] and in 1628 the grievances of the subject and the struggle for the Petition of Right.[e, 29] Similarly, one can frequently find evidence of the king himself being implicated in such conflicts, rather than being raised above them as tended to be assumed in the rhetoric. Hence in May 1626 Mead was recording that Charles had taken all Buckingham's charges on his own head and informed the Commons that 'he would make them know he was their King'; as a result it was generally thought 'that the last parliament of King Charles his reign will end within this week'. A few months later he was describing the king as 'utterly disliking' the idea of a parliament, declaring to the Council that he did 'abominate that name'.[30] Such unflattering references to the king were by no means untypical, and the widespread dissemination of a portrait so much at odds with the contemporary ideal inevitably undermined the prestige of the Crown and confidence in the status quo.[31]

This process was advanced a stage further by a second aspect of much of this news, the way in which it presented politics as a process involving division, struggle and the need to oppose disruptive influences. A good deal of this material was slanted against the Court and tended to support a 'country' or 'oppositionist' line, that the source of political problems lay with those close to the king; however, not all of it was of this type. A small amount, at least, could be taken to imply that the cause of difficulties lay elsewhere, among elements such as the Puritans or the 'popular multitude'. The precise implications of the news could vary a good deal, according to the origins of a report or the nature of events being described. None the less, what the majority of this material had in common was a continuing stress on conflict which counterbalanced the emphasis on consensus to be found in much of the rhetoric.

Perhaps the most effective way of investigating the impact of news is to look in detail at compilations of news items made by contemporaries. Through examining their processes of selection and comment it should be possible to see something of how they reacted to the material which they received. These compilations are generally of two sorts: either collections of 'separates' and newsletters, such as that made by Davenport; or what can best be described as 'news-diaries', of the sort kept by Rous and Yonge. The 'separate' collections generally contain full transcriptions of particular documents with little or no comment; the diaries, on the other hand, show extensive evidence of their authors' involvement, with summaries and abbreviations of news often accompanied by remarks as to its implications and significance.

The perspective of diarists varied considerably: Yonge was evidently a committed Protestant, concerned particularly with recording the struggles of the godly; Rous attempted to remain more detached and compile an impartial account of contemporary events; while Simonds D'Ewes, in a cipher diary which he kept as law student in London, described his aim as to 'set downe each particular day's passages of my owne life which were most memorable'.[32] These variations, however, had little effect on the basic subject-matter. All three diarists appear to have derived the major part of their information from a common stock of London news, similar to that contained in less selective collections such as Mead's letters to Stuteville. This is significant because it allows us to observe the effects of similar material on individuals of different viewpoints.

In some cases the impact would appear to have been relatively straightforward. A good example is provided by a 'news-diary' covering the period from 1625 to 1627. The identity of the author has remained a mystery, beyond the fact that he was sympathetic to the godly, strongly critical of the Crown, and had obvious connections with Cambridge University and the neighbouring counties of Cambridgeshire and Northamptonshire.[33] Nevertheless, his comments clearly indicate the way in which regular news of national events could confirm an individual in an 'oppositionist' viewpoint. The stories he recorded were invariably of the more dramatic and sensational sort, ranging from rumours of Catholic plots and omens of catastrophe to a lengthy account of Parliament's attempts to impeach Buckingham and reports of the various revenges which the duke exacted on his enemies. Amid all this, there was little space for the gentler procedures evolved for securing consensus, and this was reflected in the diarist's comments. For example, in 1625 Mr Glanville's criticisms of Buckingham were described as 'speaking for the country against the King'; while in 1626 bishops and peers were categorized according to whether or not they appeared to side with the duke, with those opposing him being described as 'courageous' or 'of the best'. Politics was generally presented as process involving conflict, and this was nowhere more apparent than in the references to the king. Once again, what is striking is the way in which Charles was brought into the analysis and assumed to be personally responsible for many of the actions hostile to the subject. Thus he was depicted as protecting the crypto-Catholic Bishop Goodman from his own convocation, dispatching loan ships to help the Catholic king of France against the Huguenots, persecuting members of the nobility who defied the Court and above all, continually defending the interests of Buckingham, to which end he was instrumental in dissolving the 1626 Parliament 'to the grief of all good subjects'. These critical comments culminated in a particularly robust condemnation of the Forced Loan: 'The King now sets afoot his royall subsidy which, if it be yielded to, it wilbe the greatest conquest since William the Conqueror.'[34] Remarks like this were very much at odds with the presumption of the king's virtue which normally dominated the rhetoric. None the less, they represented a reasonable reflection on the record of events set down by the diarist. At work here there was, of course, a very complex interaction between the nature of the events themselves, the ways of presenting them defined by the medium and the diarist's own preconceptions; and the precise weight of each is difficult to determine. However, the end result was clear enough, and this was to present the 'Court' as the most disruptive element within the political order, and conflict as the logical consequence of the need to provide a remedy.

A similar impression is to be gained from the rather different sort of diary kept by John Rous. Rous's approach to politics was altogether more conservative, and in many respects he stood in the middle ground of contemporary opinion. He claimed that 'I would alwaies speake the best of that our Kinge and State did, and thinke the best too, till I had good groundes'; and in keeping with this he laid stress on material which demonstrated the hoped-for unity between king and subject, such as the king's confirmation of the subject's liberties in his answer to the Petition of Right or the loyal celebrations which greeted the birth of his heir in 1630.[35] Notwithstanding all this, however, there are unmistakable signs that Rous's thoughts were moving more and more in the direction suggested by the bulk of his news, towards accepting a 'Country' analysis of the problems of the day.

The first indications of this are visible in the late 1620s. Rous's reports describe in considerable detail the apprehension among his neighbours as the king appeared to be embarking on a policy of prerogative government in partnership with Buckingham and a group of Arminian clerics. In 1627 he described the reaction to the Rhé expedition among local villagers, one of them, a Mr Paine, speaking 'distastefully of the voyage and then of the warre with France which he would make our King the cause of for not establishing the queene in her joynture'; and another, Mr Howlett, reciting 'ould discontents for the parliament being crossed, expenses, hazard of ships, etc.' He himself was not immune to such doubts. These came to a head at the time of the 1628 Parliament. The apparent success of the Petition of Right was seen by many at the time as a vindication of the basic unity between king and subject; but Rous was more pessimistic, and worried particularly about the influence of those around the king. Eventually it was this which seems to have prompted him to make a long and revealing confession:

> I have all this while . . . laboured to make the best construc-
> tion of all, that the subjecte might be satisfyed, least discon-
> tents should burst out to our adversarie's rejoicing; yea I
> have yeelded reasons for carriage of state business . . . for
> the necessityes of greate supplies to the King, for the great
> affayres on foote. I knowe the error of the vulgar which is
> to judge of all things by the event and therefore to speake
> according to our harde successe . . . but when I heare any
> alledging that the whole parliament feareth some miscarry-
> ing by trechery . . . then is my mouth stopped which other-
> wise hath beene free to speake my reach on the King's
> behalfe.[36]

From a different perspective, then, his diary confirms what has already been argued, that the publicity given to clashes at the centre, and the way these were presented in the news, contributed to undermining faith in the established order.

This article has argued, in line with the Whig view, that news contributed to a process of political polarization in the early seventeenth century. In particular, it has been emphasized that the image of politics presented in the news was very different from that contained in contemporary rhetoric: it suggested that conflict and struggle were as much a feature of the process as the deference and willingness to compromise implied in clichés about unity.

Another notable development was the increase in the distri-
bution of national news to the 'middling sort' and the lower orders. The effects of this are difficult to measure, but it is at least clear – from the descriptions given by Rous and others – that the literate yeomen, who comprised the bulk of county freeholders, were now capable of discussing national politics with considerable sophistication. Moreover they often appear to have done so in terms which omitted the consensual phras-
eology and polite restraint of their social superiors. This helps to explain a tendency which has been noted elsewhere, for the lower orders to view politics in terms of radical and clear-cut distinctions.[37]

As this last example indicates, the precise effects of news are

often barely discernible or recoverable amid the various influences shaping political opinion. None the less, on the evidence
presented here it is reasonable to conclude that news did contribute to a process of polarization. And it is finally worth noting
that in this, as in many other aspects of the period, the instincts
and judgements of S. R. Gardiner remain a reliable guide. One
of the sources to which he attached most weight in assessing
the development of public opinion was the printed collection of
Mead's newsletters.[38] This article suggests that he was right to
do so.

EDITOR'S NOTES

World copyright: The Past and Present Society, 175 Banbury Road,
Oxford, England. This article is reprinted in abridged form with the
permission of the Society, from *Past and Present: A Journal of Historical
Studies*, no. 112 (1986), pp. 60–90.

a *Ideology and Politics* (London, 1986).
b Abortive attempt by Buckingham to aid the Huguenots of La
  Rochelle.
c 1627 suit for habeas corpus designed to challenge the king's arbitrary
  arrest of opponents of the Forced Loan. Charles refused to have the
  loan's legality tested in court, and the justices upheld the Crown's
  emergency power of arrest.
d The 1626 Parliament attempted to impeach the Duke of Buckingham
  for corruption.
e Parliamentary petition to the king to affirm the traditional liberties
  of subjects, including habeas corpus, taxation by parliamentary consent, and freedom from arbitrary imprisonment.

NOTES

1 D. Hirst, *The Representative of the People?* (Cambridge, 1975),
  pp. 132–88; C. Hill, 'Parliament and People in Seventeenth-Century
  England', *Past and Present*, no. 92 (Aug. 1981), pp. 100–24; A. Fletcher
  and C. Hill, 'Debate: Parliament and People in Seventeenth-Century
  England', *Past and Present*, no. 98 (Feb. 1983), pp. 151–8; J. S. Morrill,
  The Revolt of the Provinces (London, 1976), pp. 13–31; C. Holmes,
  'The County Community in Stuart Historiography', *JBS*, 19 (1980),
  pp. 54–73; D. Hirst, 'Revisionism Revised: Two Perspectives on Early
  Stuart Parliamentary History: The Place of Principle', *Past and Present*, no. 92 (Aug. 1981), pp. 79–99; J. H. Hexter, 'Power Struggle,
  Parliament and Liberty in Early Stuart England', *JMH*, 1 (1978),
  pp. 24–30.
2 P. Zagorin, *The Court and the Country* (London, 1969), pp. 106–8; L.

Stone, *The Causes of the English Revolution, 1529–1642* (London, 1972), p. 91.

3 Hirst, *Representative of the People?*, p. 145; Morrill, *Revolt of the Provinces*, pp. 22–3; C. S. R. Russell, *Parliaments and English Politics, 1621–1629* (Oxford, 1979), pp. 78–9, 164–84, 233–4, 249–51.

4 Holmes, 'County Community in Stuart Historiography', pp. 61, 65–7; A. I. Hughes, 'Warwickshire on the Eve of the Civil War: "A County Community"?', *Midland History*, 7 (1982), pp. 56–9; Hill, 'Parliament and People in Seventeenth-Century England', pp. 115–18; D. Hirst, 'Court, Country and Politics before 1629', in K. Sharpe, ed., *Faction and Parliament* (Oxford, 1978), pp. 134–7.

5 A. Fletcher, *The Outbreak of the English Civil War* (London, 1981), pp. xxv–xxx, 191–227.

6 J. Frank, *The Beginnings of the English Newspaper, 1620–1660* (Cambridge, Mass., 1961), pp. 5–7, 14.

7 S. L. Adams, 'Captain Thomas Gainsford, the *Vox Spiritus* and the *Vox Populi*', *BIHR*, 49 (1976), pp. 141–4; *Commons Debates for 1629*, ed. W. Notestein and F. H. Relf (Minneapolis, 1921), pp. xx–xli; F. J. Levy, 'How Information Spread among the Gentry, 1550–1640', *JBS*, 21 (1982), pp. 20–4.

8 Holmes, 'County Community in Stuart Historiography', p. 61; G. Cranfield, *The Press and Society* (London, 1978), pp. 5–10; W. Notestein, *Four Worthies* (London, 1956), pp. 29–119; *The Works of Ben Jonson*, ed. F. Cunningham and W. Gifford, 9 vols (London, 1875), VII, p. 336.

9 W. S. Powell, *John Pory, 1572–1636* (Chapel Hill, 1977), pp. 55–8.

10 BL, Harleian MSS 389, 390.

11 *Commons Debates, 1628*, ed. R. C. Johnson, M. F. Keeler, M. J. Cole and W. B. Bidwell, 4 vols (New Haven and London, 1977–8), I, pp. 4–20; Russell, *Parliaments and English Politics*, p. 389.

12 PRO, C. 115/N. 4; *Companion to Arber*, ed. W. W. Greg (Oxford, 1967), pp. 176–8; *Commons Debates for 1629*, pp. xxxiii–xxxiv; Eaton Hall, Cheshire, Grosvenor MS, no. 45, pp. 143–50; A. L. Hughes, 'Politics, War and Society in Warwickshire, c. 1620–1650' University of Liverpool Ph.D. thesis, 1980), pp. 153–5.

13 *The Court and Times of Charles I*, ed. T. Birch, 2 vols (London, 1848), I, pp. 164, 190, 207; Powell, *John Pory*, pp. 56–7; *The Diary of John Rous*, ed. M. A. Everett Green (Camden Soc., 1st ser., 66, London, 1856).

14 *Diary of John Rous*, pp. v–x, 10–12, 31, 44–5.

15 Ibid., pp. 2–3, 5, 8, 10–11, 14–18, 31–3, 47; BL, Add. MS 28640, fo. 102 (this is a commonplace book belonging to Rous).

16 BL, Add. MS 48057, fo. 54; W. A. Hunt, *The Puritan Moment* (Cambridge, Mass., 1983), pp. 261–2; *Diary of John Rous*, pp. 18–22; *Poems and Songs Relating to George Villiers, Duke of Buckingham*, ed. F. W. Fairholt (Percy Society, XXIX, London, 1850), p. 6. The libellous ballad about Buckingham had the refrain 'The cleane, contrary way' (ibid., pp. 10–13).

17 Chester CRO, CR 63/2/19, fos 26^v–27^r.

18 See, for example, BL, Satirical Prints, no. 91 (1621), 'The Description of Giles Mompesson Late Knight, Censured by Parliament'.

19 P. Burke, *Popular Culture in Early Modern Europe* (London, 1978), pp. 91–148; M. E. James, *Family, Lineage and Civil Society* (Oxford, 1974), pp. 78–80.

20 *Diary of John Rous*, pp. 18–22; *Poems and Songs Relating to George Villiers, Duke of Buckingham*, pp. 19–24.

21 Burke, *Popular Culture in Early Modern Europe*, pp. 150–5.

22 S. R. Gardiner, *History of England, 1603–1642*, 10 vols (London, 1883–4), vi, pp. 59–121; Russell, *Parliaments and English Politics*, pp. 260–322.

23 Levy, 'How Information Spread', p. 23; Clark, *English Provincial Society from the Reformation to the Revolution*, p. 219. For further examples, see the letter collections of Sir John Wynn of Gwydir or the Leighs of Lyme Park, which indicate the regular receipt of news from 1620 onwards but not before: National Library of Wales, Aberystwyth, Wynn of Gwydir MSS, *passim*; John Rylands Library, Leigh of Lyme MSS, *passim*.

24 *Diary of Walter Younge*, ed. G. Roberts (Camden Society, 1st ser., xli, London, 1848), pp. 90, 98–100, 109–11.

25 *Diary of John Rous*, p. 14; BL, Harleian MS 390, fo. 356ᵛ; *Letters of John Holles*, ii, pp. 376–7; Nottingham Univ Lib, Ne.C. 15404, p. 210.

26 Hirst, *Representative of the People?*, pp. 178–81; Russell, *Parliaments and English Politics*, pp. 19–22, 388–9.

27 *Court and Times of Charles I*, i, pp. 56, 58, 251, 328, 331; G. E. Aylmer, 'St. Patrick's Day, 1628, in Witham, Essex', *Past and Present*, no. 61 (Nov. 1973), pp. 139–48.

28 M. Kishlansky, 'The Emergence of Adversary Politics in the Long Parliament', *JMH*, 49 (1977), pp. 619–21; Russell, *Parliaments and English Politics*, pp. 53–4; M. Judson, *The Crisis of the Constitution* (New Brunswick, 1949), pp. 1–107; R. P. Cust and P. G. Lake, 'Sir Richard Grosvenor and the Rhetoric of Magistracy', *BIHR*, 54 (1981), pp. 46–8; *Wentworth Papers*, pp. 152–5.

29 Russell, *Parliaments and English Politics*, p. xix; *The Court and Times of James I*, ed. T. Birch, 2 vols (London, 1848), ii, pp. 234–84; *Court and Times of Charles I*, i, pp. 40, 86–104, 346–64. Newsletters sometimes included dramatic detail which was omitted from the diaries: Hill, 'Parliament and People in Seventeenth-Century England', p. 111.

30 *Court and Times of Charles I*, i, p. 104; BL, Harleian MS, 390, fo. 132.

31 *Diary of John Rous*, pp. 2–3; Trinity Coll. Lib., Cambridge (hereafter TCLC), MS 0.7.3, f. 4ᵛ (I am grateful to Maija Cole for this reference).

32 *Diary of Walter Yonge, passim*; *Diary of John Rous*, pp. x–xi, 109 (see also his comments on Scott's *Vox populi*; BL, Add. MS 28640, fo. 100); *The Diary of Sir Simonds D'Ewes, 1622–1624*, ed. E. Bourcier (Publications de la Sorbonne, v, Paris, 1974), p. 38.

33 TCLC, MS 0.7.3, fos 3–10.

34 Ibid., fos 3–4, 5ʳ 7ᵛ, 8ᵛ.

35 *Diary of John Rous*, pp. 4–6, 12, 19, 36–9, 40–1, 43.

36 Ibid., pp. 2–19, 49–50, 123–5, 131; Fletcher, *Outbreak*, pp. 42–90, 125–57.
37 D. Hirst, 'Unanimity in the Commons, Aristocratic Intrigues, and the Origins of the English Civil War', *JMH*, 1 (1978), pp. 59–60; Hill, 'Parliament and People in Seventeenth-Century England', pp. 115–18.
38 Gardiner, *History of England*, vi, pp. 131, 150, 154–8.

13

LOCAL HISTORY AND THE ORIGINS OF THE CIVIL WAR

Ann Hughes

Continuing the theme of local interest and principled involvement in central policy are recent family studies like Jacqueline Eales's of the Harleys of Herefordshire, and local studies like Ann Hughes's of the county of Warwickshire. Both reject the revisionist picture of localism and neutralism determining county response to troubles at the centre. In the article below, Hughes grants that many English people preferred to avoid armed conflict in 1642; however, she argues that this need not imply neutral opinions. The political and judicial experience of local gentlemen, and the information available to them and their constituents, produced polarities in county opinion and commitment long before the outbreak of war. She finds 'sharp ideological divisions' in nearly all counties, as well as alignments that reflected fears arising from the social restructuring of the previous century, now aggravated by political and religious division. She rejects both the notion of a monolithic county response and class-based allegiance. Her own study of Warwickshire and Lord Brooke's parliamentarian leadership there, together with her summary of other local studies, draws a much more complex picture. Informed political ideology and religious commitment emerge as central, and the Civil War as far from 'accidental'.

* * *

In the introduction to his *Parliaments and English Politics*, Conrad Russell wrote: 'The object of this book is to reconstruct the Parliamentary history of the 1620s using a set of analytical tools which owe more to local studies than to previous Parliamentary Studies.'[1]

A particular approach to local studies, especially county studies, has made a major contribution to the ways of understanding the Civil War which have, perhaps unfairly, come to be comprehended under the label of revisionism. This chapter seeks to unravel some of the connections between local approaches to early seventeenth-century English history and interpretations of the Civil War. Its first sections are critical and rather negative but I later argue that local history can help to create a more satisfying general account of the origins of the war than has hitherto been provided. The focus is mainly on county history but a broader range of local studies is also considered.

The most obvious and important thrust of county studies has been to discredit general theories explaining the origins of the Civil War. The idea of the war as a social conflict has been undermined by two rather different kinds of county studies. Some works are in part attempts to use the county as a laboratory in which the various theories put forward by the 'gentry controversy' could be tested. Studies of the gentry in Yorkshire, Lancashire and other countries gave little support to any of the attempts to link social and economic change with political conflict and civil war allegiance.[2] A rather different approach was pioneered by Alan Everitt in his study of Kent. Here the county is not simply a means by which a convenient sample and a set of sources can be generated, it is a 'community' – a social reality for seventeenth-century men and women and a crucial theoretical concept for historians. Everitt's work undermines any notion of the Civil War as a social conflict simply because, in seventeenth-century Kent as he described it, social conflict hardly occurs. The gentry of Kent, long established in the shire and bound together by elaborate kinship ties, formed one harmonious society. They were 'one great cousinage', 'unusually deeply rooted in their native soil, temperamentally conservative and excessively inbred'. There was little tension between the gentry and the 'lower orders' who were instead united by vertical social links forged by local loyalties. A benevolent patriarchal rule made the gentry's 'organic conception of their community, as a single united family' into a reality.[3]

Whereas Blackwood and Cliffe found a clear ideological division (based on religion) between royalist and parliamentarian gentry, Everitt's account eliminated ideological as well as social explanations. Everitt wrote that local and national awareness were both increasing in this period but this point has not really been developed: his main emphasis is on the cleavage between local and central concerns, and the gentry's ignorance of the antipathy towards national politics: 'for most of the people, most of the time, political matters scarcely existed'. The provincial gentry's non-political suspicious and obstructionist resentment of central interference underlies the major developments in mid-seventeenth-century England. It was this stubborn localism that paralysed Charles I by 1640 but also defeated the attempts of successive parliamentarian regimes to establish an alternative system. The cleavage of 1642 cannot be, and is not, explained in the same way and indeed, on the Everitt approach, the Civil War is irrational, inexplicable.

Everitt's view of 1642 as an unnatural division is echoed by Ronald Hutton, who writes of 'an artificial insemination of violence into the local community', while John Morrill in *The Revolt of the Provinces* regards provincial gentry as 'sub-political' – they 'responded to the effects of royal politics rather than to their origins or purpose which remained concealed'.[4] Morrill distinguishes between the backwoodsmen who made up the 'pure country' opposition to Charles and the 'official country' of Bedford, Warwick, Saye, Pym and Hampden. The former simply wanted to stop central government interference or pressure whilst the latter wanted to reform or change the direction of that government and formed 'an alternative court, a shadow cabinet'. Morrill also shares with Everitt the view that the war was created by a minority of extremists who, particularly on the Parliament's side, are now usually seen as motivated by an irrational religious impulse.

The county history inspired by Everitt has had some salutary effects on Civil War studies. We are now well aware that politics or ideological commitment were not all-important in the lives of the gentry and others, and it is no longer possible to believe (if anyone ever did) that the English divided neatly and easily into royalists and parliamentarians in 1642. The hesitation and anguish with which people approached civil war are now appreciated. The study of local activities and loyalties and the recognition of England's regional diversity and complexity are crucial to a full understanding of the war. However, we are left with a fundamentally unsatisfactory account of the Civil War as an irrational, unnatural, accidental conflict brought about by a few religious extremists. The understandable reluctance of many to take an active part in the Civil War is assumed to come from a localist 'non-political' stance on the divisions between King and Parliament. Allegiance is seen as determined largely by contingent factors: the relative proximity of the king's army or of London; or the comparative strengths and energy of the small groups of local zealots.[5]

If the 'localist' model and the interpretation of the Civil War bases on it are unsatisfactory, what alternatives can be proposed? In the next sections of this essay I will make more positive suggestions about the nature of local politics and about the contributions local studies can make to our understanding of the Civil War.

Record-keeping arrangements in England make the county a very convenient generator of sources for many kinds of studies. But historians have thereby been seduced into an overestimation of the county's importance in the lives of the seventeenth-century gentry and others. There were no unitary local communities in seventeenth-century England whether these are sought in counties, parishes or villages. Rather, local communities were elaborate overlapping entities, 'an incredibly complex set of "planes" which may or may not overlap' in Macfarlane's phrase.[6] For some aspects of life the county clearly was a crucial 'community': it was the major legal and administrative unit and with the breakup of the regional power bases dominated by great territorial magnates, it was the most important arena for political debate and conflict after the kingdom as a whole. Even in these areas, however, some qualifications need to be made. Corporate towns and cities had a jealously guarded administrative independence from the rural counties they were sited in; relationships were often very tense as the frequent conflicts between Chester and Cheshire, Gloucester and Gloucestershire, Coventry and Warwickshire reveal. County administration itself often reflected geographical divisions within counties. Units of ecclesiastical administration, and so the focus for the many important aspects of life covered by the church courts, rarely coincided with county boundaries. Even as a political unit, the role of the county was not necessarily clear-cut: all but one of the knights of the shire for Warwickshire from 1604 until the Short Parliament came from the southern 'sheep-corn' areas of the county.[7]

Geographically, few counties were homogeneous while patterns of settlement or economic activity and marketing areas did not respect county boundaries. Great variations are found in Durham, Sussex, Norfolk and Wiltshire amongst many other counties; a distinction is usually made between 'wood-pasture' and 'sheep-corn' areas although agricultural historians are now insisting on subtler distinctions.

Loyalties based on social status or on co-residence of a particular county were cut across by differences in social environment, contrasts in relationships between the gentry and lower social groups. Loyalties were disrupted also by factional and ideological divisions.

I am not suggesting that England was simply divided into sub-units, communities smaller than the county. Rather, the fact that there were several, overlapping local communities on which people based their social, economic, religious or political affairs makes it harder to discern any coherent local entity that could be opposed to the nation state. More important are the possibilities for comparison and generalization created by an emphasis on the diversity *within* counties. A continuing problem with case studies in the humanities and social science is that of comparability. Many, however, would not accept this as a problem – the predominant conclusion drawn from county studies of the English Civil War is that each county is unique (as it must be if the crucial determinant of the behaviour of the gentry and of other ranks is mere co-residence of a particular county) and so no generalization is possible. This fragmentation of analysis of 1642 is often coupled, though, with a covert generalization, designating the overall provincial response to the cleavage between King and Parliament as localist and neutralist. This could be described in Clifford Geertz's phrase as the 'lowest common denominator' method of drawing conclusions from local studies and it ignores the complex and distinct patterns of allegiance within counties. A more fruitful approach is to see a local 'community', in this case a county, as a unique combination or configuration of various elements or components, the elements being present in all counties.[8] Each county may have experienced 1642 differently but its reactions were a product of a set of factors common to all counties, of which the most important were the geographical, economic and social divisions within them; the degree of cohesion amongst the social élite; and the nature of ideological, especially religious, divisions.

It is clear that, whatever the response in specific situations, no general distinction was drawn between the centre and the localities. At the funeral in 1640 of Sir Thomas Lucy, a leading Warwickshire gentlemen who had been knight of the shire for all parliaments from 1614 until the Short Parliament, the preacher declared:

A noble lady hath lost, not an husband (as she saith) but a father.
Many children have lost, not a father but a counsellor.
A houseful of servants have lost, not a master but a physician . . .
Towns full of tenants have lost a landlord that could both protect and direct them in their own way.
The whole neighbourhood have lost a light.
The county a leader:
The country a patriot, to whom he was not wanting, till he was wanting to himself in his former vigour and health.[9]

A prominent gentleman thus operated in overlapping and ever widening arenas from the family, through neighbourhood and county to the nation, with no sign of conflict or contradiction.

It is thus perhaps a misnomer to talk of the interrelationship of the centre and the localities because even this suggests too sharp a polarity; but as yet, no alternative presents itself. England was an integrated but not bureaucratized polity; consequently the Crown was dependent on the involvement and consent of some at least amongst local élites. Conversely, because local offices were appointed by the Crown and the English legal system was basically uniform, local élites needed central support. In pre-Civil War Warwickshire people sought the intervention of the Privy Council on a wide range of issues from the personal – Sir Thomas Lucy's attempt to get Privy Council intervention in his daughter's troubled marriage – to the generally significant: the complex and bitter dispute between Coventry and Warwickshire over the city's Ship Money assessment.[10]

Recent studies have indicated how King and Council could benefit from acting as the 'honest broker' in local struggles. The collection of the Forced Loan or of Ship Money could be facilitated as men exhibited an enthusiasm for the Crown's business in the hope of obtaining central backing in some local dispute.

Local conflicts also reveal a capacity for efficient and sophisticated lobbying, suggesting a political culture far removed from a 'sub-political' localism. Coventry aldermen addressed the Privy Council, mobilized London contacts and headed off influential men who might favour Warwickshire; similar examples are found in Bristol.

This skilled and knowledgeable lobbying derived from information about and experience acquired within a national legal–administrative–political system. A vast amount of news about local, national and international affairs circulated in a variety of media amongst a large literate and semi-literate public. A broad section of the male property-holders of England participated in administration and politics as electors or MPs, as jurors or litigants, constables or justices. They thus acquired a more or less sophisticated familiarity with legal rights, the role and functions of a parliament, factions or divisions in the Council and the Court. It was not just that those with most experience of 'central' politics – MPs for instance – took back a more sophisticated awareness to the gentry and freeholders of their counties; or that central emissaries, such as assize judges, were sent out to educate local governors on the finer points of the law or on central administrative priorities. Local experience and attitudes could have an influence on central policy and politics. The Elizabethan Poor Law was a summation of local initiatives while the supposedly 'centralizing' Book of Orders was based in part on practice in Northamptonshire.

A range of evidence suggests that their information and their experience led provincial people to view the political process as characterized by conflict and divisions rather than as the harmonious and consensual system depicted in recent studies. Particularly important to provincial opinion were the interlocking sets of attitudes and ideologies which were summed up as a 'Court and Country' polarity. The ambiguity of the term 'Country' in particular has caused much historiographical debate but it was precisely the ability of the concept to conjure up various shades of meaning that gave it its seventeenth-century resonance. Topographically, its meaning was imprecise: 'my country' could mean the most immediate neighbourhood, one's farming region or 'pays', occasionally the county (but by no means exclusively or even often), and finally, as in the quotation from Lucy's funeral sermon, it could mean the whole kingdom or realm and thus was very similar to the term 'commonwealth'. Like the 'commonwealth', the 'country' carried ideological connotations: ultimately 'Court' and 'Country' were not places at all, but sets of contrasting attitudes, ideal types which stood for vice and virtue, corruption and purity. Hence members of the Court like Archbishop Abbot or even Buckingham, when he resisted the Spanish match in 1624, could hold or adopt 'Country' attitudes and thus appeal to a broad constituency. This ideological polarity between Court and Country did not of course rule out practical links between the centre and the provinces which, as we have seen, were taken for granted. The 'Country' attitudes of a gentleman like Sir Richard Grosvenor of Cheshire included a commitment to the rule of law, and to regular parliaments with the active involvement of freeholders in elections which were seen as necessary precautions against the tendency towards corruption and popery at Court. A zealous commitment to Protestantism and to the struggle against popery were also involved. Finally, the Court-vs.-Country polarity shaded into rival conspiracy theories, alternative explanations of why the harmony and co-operation which all believed essential to the political system had broken down. The 'Country' view tended to a belief in a popish plot to undermine the laws and liberties of England, to attack Parliament and true religion, while Charles I and the Court became convinced of a popular Puritan plot, centred on Parliament, committed to depriving the monarch of his just powers.[11]

There was a wide awareness of such polarities in the localities. Local governors like Sir Thomas Lucy who dutifully collected subsidies and organized the levy and billeting of troops in the 1620s, were conspicuously absent from activity to collect the Forced Loan. Those who opposed the loan outright like Sir Francis Barrington of Essex or Sir Nathaniel Barnadiston of Suffolk, 'standing up for his country and the defence of the just rights and liberties thereof', were praised as patriots while the biographer of Lord Montague of Northamptonshire considered twenty years later that 'his paying the loan lost him the love of the country'.

The preceding account of the nature of local politics in the early seventeenth century makes a localist-neutralist response to the 1642 cleavage implausible. Indeed, much recent work, most notably Anthony Fletcher's thorough study of the outbreak, suggests a more complex picture. Fletcher concluded that very few were neutral in their opinions although many were understandably reluctant to engage in armed conflict. As significant is Fletcher's unpicking of localism and neutralism as *distinct* elements in provincial responses, whereas earlier studies too often conflated them. Neutrality moves were occasionally mere stratagems by one side to gain time, not truly pacific in their intention: pacts in Yorkshire, Lancashire and Cornwall are examples. More genuine peacekeeping initiatives such as that in Staffordshire were very complex affairs combining a general desire for peace with some inclination towards one side in the struggle and a particular set of local circumstances.[12] Petitions for accommodation such as those from Yorkshire in June 1642 usually blamed one side more than the other for the breakdown echoing the conspiracy theories discussed above.

There were, however, differences between 1642 and the 1620s or even between 1642 and 1640. The great expansion in Parliament's responsibilities between 1640 and 1642, the close involvement of MPs with Privy Councillors, and the mere fact of Parliament's sitting for so long gave MPs insights into Charles's attitudes and an understanding of political divisions which took some time to spread to the provinces. Inevitably, by the summer of 1642, there was something of a gulf in understanding between the provinces and central politicians although this was more a time-lag than a distinctive view of politics. Attempts to secure peace thus continued in the counties for some weeks or months after men in London had given up hope and were preparing for war. The seriousness of the crisis of 1642 meant that there was no necessary continuity between 'country' attitudes before 1640 and parliamentarianism in 1642. A fear of disorder, a simple loyalty, a bedrock devotion to a non-Laudian episcopal church, or alarm at the extension of Parliament's powers all brought many 'Country' gentlemen to the royalist side. For some the horrors of civil war prompted the 'construction' of a localist response, a separation of local loyalties from national allegiance.[13]

Nonetheless there were continuities and counties' responses in 1642 reflected the complexity of local communities discussed above. There were sharp ideological divisions in almost all counties: even in Puritan Essex, 'the first-born of parliament', a royalist element, with much Catholic support, promoted neutralist petitions while some actively fought for the king. These divisions were expressed most often in a religious form, or, following Underdown, as a cultural cleavage, rather than in the constitutional terms analysed by Sommerville. Brilliana Harley complained in June 1642 'at Ludlow they set up a maypole, and a thing like a head upon it, and so they did at Croft, and gathered a great many about it and shot at it in derision of roundheads'. The Herefordshire opponents of her parliamentarian husband called for the establishing of the 'uniformity of common prayer and the bringing of sectaries, separatists and all such recusants' to obedience to the king.[14] However, it is artificial to distinguish too sharply between religious and secular political attitudes. Parliamentarian adherents of godly reformation attacked the profane and the papists but amongst the crimes of the papists was a conspiracy to undermine the laws and liberties of England and to overthrow Parliament. Supporters of episcopacy and of a more settled, ritualized and ceremonial parochial worship attacked divisive, hypocritical Puritans. But they regarded such a church and such a worship as essential to order, hierarchy, authority and stability while seeing Puritans as subversives bent on the overthrow of monarchy. In most counties there were also patterns to allegiance which reflected their geographical diversity discussed above.

How are we then to draw general conclusions from these fragmented provincial responses in 1642 which incorporate the geographical patterns and emphasize the importance of ideological divisions? One valuable approach is to focus not on social categories – not on how many rising or declining peers, gentlemen or yeomen can be found on each side – but to examine instead the social relationships and alliances revealed in local patterns of allegiance. Crucial here are the variety of ways in which the landed élite and lower-born social groups reacted to, or coped with, the tensions arising from the economic and social changes of the previous century and the conflicts over authority and belief which derived ultimately from the Reformation. Divisions over religion and politics on the one hand, and the problems of social change on the other, came together in a mutually reinforcing way. Religious and political crisis intensified the fears which arose from social restructuring, while political and religious disputes can themselves be linked to social change: Court fears of 'popularity' against Country desires for wider political participation; godly attempts at moral reform versus communal solidarity expressed in ceremonial worship and parish festivities have obvious social contexts.

A variety of local evidence and local studies have helped to develop this basic framework. Directly relevant are the works of Brian Manning, William Hunt and David Underdown, which all emphasize the importance of social relationships to an understanding of the coming of civil war, and all use local evidence. Brian Manning has argued that the Civil War arose out of conflict within a feudal society between the 'people' and an aggressive landed and commercial élite. The 'people' usually include that ambiguous and, for Manning, unstable group, the 'middling sort', who are motivated by a Puritanism which provides them with an embryonic class-consciousness, a way of distinguishing themselves as the 'godly' from both rich and poor. Parliament acquired in 1640–42 a brief and precarious role as the focus of popular support against the king, the greatest and most aggressive of landlords. The royalist party of 1642 was a 'party of order' terrified by popular demonstrations in support of Parliament, particularly by the artisans and small merchants of London. Manning's characterization of the royalists as a party of order is convincing; it is less clear, however, why anyone from the élite should have supported Parliament and indeed Manning has an extremely attenuated explanation of élite parliamentarianism.[15]

In Hunt's account of Essex the opposite problem arises: here it is difficult to understand why anyone from the middle or upper ranks of society should be a royalist. In an account that echoes Wrightson's, Hunt locates the appeal of Calvinist Puritanism in its providing for the middling sort of parish élites and, to a lesser extent, the landed gentry and peers, a way to distinguish themselves from the 'rude' ungodly multitude and a means of subjecting the culture of the unruly poor to godly reformation, a 'culture of discipline'. Again, much of this is convincing but there remains the problem of explaining élite royalism.[16]

The value of David Underdown's account is that it does allow for divisions of culture and political principle amongst élites, and suggests that there was a variety of responses, at all social levels, to the problems of social change and ideological conflict. On the basis of research in Dorset, Somerset and Wiltshire,

Underdown presents the Civil War as a cultural conflict, connecting cultural divisions to the geographical and social diversity within his region. The war was fought between parliamentarians who were pressing for godly reformation of popery and profanity and royalists who supported the traditional social order, believed that parochial rituals and festivities were a guarantee of social harmony, and feared Puritan disruption more than any popish conspiracy. The 'wood-pasture' and clothing areas of north Wiltshire and north Somerset were identified with the parliamentarian stance: these areas contained large socially polarized parishes which had great numbers of unruly poor and had undergone rapid economic change. Like Hunt, Underdown emphasizes the appeal of Puritanism to the middling and upper ranks in these areas as a means to reform traditional culture and to discipline the poor; Underdown also sees a link here between Puritanism and market-orientated individualism. In the mixed farming downland areas, on the other hand, communal solidarity survived in deferential, hierarchical nucleated villages and was reflected in widespread support for parochial festivities; here economic change had been less rapid and royalism had most appeal.[17]

Underdown's work shows how local history can contribute more fruitfully to general interpretations of the Civil War. The social and ideological elements he has identified are surely crucial to allegiance in the localities; one may doubt, however, whether the elements should be slotted together as neatly as they are in Underdown's account. We can return to the suggestion made earlier that general conclusions are better derived from examining the many ways in which a constant set of factors can combine rather than searching for total similarities. It is clear from the recent work of agrarian historians that the wood-pasture/sheep-corn dichotomy adopted by Underdown (and most local historians) is itself too crude and that the social characteristics associated with such farming practices are more complex.[18]

Furthermore, the view of Puritanism as an ideology of 'social control' is open to question. Puritanism is also seen as divisive and disruptive, while it could also be a rousing, socially subversive, even liberating creed; as such its social appeal was wide.[19] A disruptive and liberating Puritanism is often associated with industrial or wood-pasture areas (in Derbyshire, Durham and

Warwickshire for example) but these are seen as relatively egalitarian rather than the polarized communities described by Underdown. On the other hand a disciplinary Puritanism has been found in East Anglian arable communities by Hunt and Wrightson but these are polarized, market-orientated and 'capitalist', not relatively homogeneous as in Underdown's West Country.

Finally it is not clear why all social groups within an area should react in a particular way. Among the possibilities not considered by Underdown there is space to mention only two. The first is that the support for Parliament and Puritanism apparent amongst middling and lower ranks in some industrial and wood-pasture regions encouraged the greater gentry of those areas into support for the king as the guarantor of social and political order. This process – a 'Manning model' – can be seen in north Warwickshire, in Derbyshire, and in the West Riding of Yorkshire, where royalist gentry outnumbered parliamentarians by more than two to one, a proportion greater than in the rest of the county.[20] On the other hand, it is possible that in some mixed farming, 'traditional', deferential areas the gentry's own sense of security made them more willing to risk opposing the king – again Warwickshire is an example. When looking at the ranks below the gentry in such areas it seems to be an open question as to whom deference was due when authority was divided: to lord of the manner, minister, bishop or king.

These points can be illustrated through an examination of Lord Brooke's leadership of the parliamentarian cause in Warwickshire. Parliament had secured Warwickshire by August 1642 despite the royalism or neutrality of most of the leading gentry. Indeed by background and belief, Brooke was ill-equipped to rally the county gentry. Robert Greville, second lord, was something of a parvenu; the adopted son of the first lord, he was himself from a minor gentry family, and his succession was resented by relatives who felt they had a better claim, including members of a senior Warwickshire family, the Verneys. More significant was the radical and uncompromising nature of Brooke's opposition to Charles I. In 1619 Brooke's adoptive father Fulke Grenville had lavishly entertained James I at Warwick Castle. In contrast, when Charles visited the town on 20 August 1636 Robert Greville was conspicuous by his absence.

In a departure from his normal practice of spending July and August in the country, Brooke returned to London on 15 August. In the Scots crisis which ended the personal rule,[a] Brooke's position was clear. Brooke and Saye were imprisoned at York in April 1639 for refusing the oath of loyalty required by Charles as he raised forces for the first Bishops' War. Brooke encouraged the spread of Scots propaganda in the provinces. In published work Brooke openly welcomed the Scots victory: 'blessed be God that hath delivered that Church and state from tyrannical prelates and will ere long deliver us also.'

While many English people showed little enthusiasm for Charles's war against the Scots, committed support for them was much rarer. Brooke's religious beliefs were equally distinctive. By 1640 there were many calls for reform of the national Church and much opposition to Laudian bishops. Brooke, however, praised the religious toleration practised in the United Provinces; presented the arguments of poor 'unordained' preachers as he had heard them delivered at ecclesiastical trials, refusing to condemn or condone lay preaching himself; and suggested that 'anabaptists', hated bogeymen in most seventeenth-century opinion, were less of a danger to religion than supporters of 'lordly prelacy'. As might be expected, Brooke gave practical support to a wide variety of ministers. His chaplains in the 1630s were Simeon Ashe, who had been ejected from a Staffordshire living for opposition to the Book of Sports and who was to become a leading presbyterian in the 1640s and 1650s; and the very different Peter Sterry, a Platonist like Brooke himself, who became an Independent after 1642 and was a chaplain to Oliver Cromwell during the Protectorate. Ministers harassed by the ecclesiastical authorities were welcome at Warwick Castle in the 1630s, as were local godly ministers and schoolmasters.[21] Brooke's contempt for the low birth of English bishops is well known and he clearly advocated a prominent political role for the peerage. But his political practice is marked also by support for broad participation and like Cromwell he chose his allies for their zeal to the cause, not for their social status.

Almost twice as many royalists as parliamentarians can be identified amongst the Warwickshire gentry, with an even greater royalist preponderance amongst senior families: 13 of the county's 21 resident JPs sided with the king; only 5, including Brooke himself, and 3 who were not of the quorum gave support to Parliament. Nonetheless it was the parliamentarians who won the struggle to control the county and Brooke's success can be attributed to three main factors. In the first place, the lack of a cohesive, county-wide gentry 'community' encouraged, or at least permitted, the emergence of an 'extreme' and determined parliamentarianism. Second, Brooke obtained more effective outside help than the royalists could muster: an army of some 6,000 men sent from London entered Warwickshire on 22 August, prompting the royalists to abandon their sieges of Warwick Castle and the city of Coventry. Most important of all, Brooke received the more significant 'popular' support, particularly in Coventry and amongst the lesser gentry, independent freeholders and metalworkers of the Arden region ('sectaries and schismatics' from Birmingham, as the historian Dugdale called them). In August 1642, as the king and his army approached Coventry, the city corporation prepared to receive him, arranging gifts and entertainment. But when the army arrived, the city gates were closed against it, and volunteers swore to resist the royal forces. Hence a vital breathing space was gained during which the relieving army could be dispatched from London. If Charles's forces had occupied the crucial stronghold of Coventry, the course of the Civil War in Warwickshire and the midlands as a whole might have been very different.[22]

Brooke was a skilled popular leader: volunteers were rallied with music and feasting; peals of church bells rang out when Brooke seized the county arms magazine at Coventry to take it to safety at Warwick Castle. The rank and file were involved in the struggle through the election of the officers for their troops and companies and through their assent to petitions to Parliament. Through anti-papist rhetoric Brooke linked personal concerns to a wider, indeed international, cause: papists and malignants had undermined true religion and the subject's liberties – their machinations were revealed in the Armada and the Gunpowder Plot but also, by 1643, in their plundering the towns and lands of local people. Above all, Brooke portrayed the war as God's war with Parliament's soldiers as the zealous agents of a godly cause, praying

that God almighty will arise and maintain his own cause,

scattering and confounding the devices of his enemies, not suffering the ungodly to prevail over his poor innocent flock. Lord we are but a handful in consideration of Thine and our enemies, therefore O Lord fight Thou our battles, go out as Thou didst in the time of King David before the hosts of the servants, and strengthen and give us hearts that we show ourselves men for the defence of Thy true religion and our own and the kingdom's safety.[23]

Ideological and social change had produced a situation where aristocratic leadership could not be based on landed power alone. Brooke's influence, like that of the Earl of Lincoln in Lincolnshire during the Forced Loan or the Earl of Warwick's position in Essex from the 1620s to the 1640s, reveals how effective an appeal based on ideology could be. These peers were patrons and leaders of the 'godly' and the 'Country', and supported as 'patriots' not just as landlords. In fact Brooke's appeal was best supported not near his own estates which were mostly in the more settled parts of south Warwickshire (where indeed there are hints of popular royalism – including in Warwick itself) but in the industrial and urban areas of north Warwickshire where men of middling wealth had a greater degree of independence and control over their own lives. Here Parliament's call to the defence of liberties, law and true religion seems to have had a particular attraction and early musters of Parliament's Warwickshire forces reveal much more successful recruiting in the north than the south. I do not want to suggest that this type of aristocratic leadership simply manipulated lower social groups. On the contrary, the existence of the broad, well-informed political nation, committed to Parliament and to Protestantism, had a vital influence on the kinds of aristocratic leadership that were possible in the first half of the seventeenth century.

A further significant aspect of Brooke's leadership is that it was not based on 'traditional' or paternalist attitudes to economic and social relationships. He was an efficient and improving landowner who had zealously defended his inheritance against legal suits by aggrieved relations and had attacked his adopted father's executors' handling of his property before he came of age. One function of Brooke's rousing Protestantism (though of course one cannot reduce it to this, or explain it only in these terms) was that it enabled him to combine apparently contradictory responses to the problems of social change. He could be an economically 'advanced' landowner while side-stepping possible problems in his role as a social leader by building a dynamic social alliance working for godly rule and the creation of a New Jerusalem.

Besides the popular support for Brooke, the other 'pattern' in civil war allegiance in Warwickshire is the committed royalism of most of the greater northern gentry. This suggests another possible combination of social and political attitudes. Most of these gentry were also improving landlords who had taken advantage of the insecure tenures on their mainly copyhold manors so as to profit from inflation; as discussed earlier, they lived in an area which had seen much economic change and were 'threatened' by a large landless population and independent middling groups who had given enthusiastic support to Parliament. Their royalism is surely, in part, a reaction to this insecurity, an aggressive adherence to a strict conception of hierarchy and order.

In a sense, the preceding discussion had focused on extreme though significant cases. Many other combinations existed: there were paternalist landowners who were Puritans and parliamentarians, usually moderate in their views; one example is Sir Thomas Lucy of Warwickshire. In other circumstances gentry who were 'traditional' in their economic attitudes were easygoing (rather than deliberate) promoters of parish festivities and episcopalian Protestantism, and royalists in 1642. There is great, not infinite variety, but this does not suggest that contingent or accidental explanations are appropriate. To return to the framework discussed earlier in the chapter, the way localities divided in 1642 was produced by a multitude of *different* combinations of *constant* factors. We do not yet have a sufficiently subtle explanation of how and why these factors are connected but a crucial element in explanations of the division of 1642 can be elucidated through analysis of the ways in which the landed élite and other social groups reacted economically, socially, politically and culturally to the tension in social relationships produced over the previous century.

I will conclude by clarifying the nature of the contribution local approaches can make. It is possible that the analysis sketched out above has more relevance to the cleavage of 1642 than to the 1639–40 crisis of Charles's personal rule. Charles's difficulties in mobilizing English strength against the Scots may be due in part to a simple localist reflex – a reluctance to provide enough men and money for the task. This sort of response was clearly more important in 1640 than in 1642, but also vital were the issues of what Charles wanted revenue and an army for and the unparliamentary and dubiously Protestant nature of his regime. A chronological distortion of a rather different kind has done more to produce misconceptions about 1640 and especially 1642: that is a reading back of attitudes which were a response to the war itself, to the time of its outbreak. By 1644–46 the massive demands for men and money, the plunder, billeting and troop movements, the attempts at militant Puritan reform and the general ecclesiastical disruption had indeed produced a conservative and localist response in many areas. This conservatism and localism was not natural, or pre-existing, but was created, called into being by the strains of war. Too often local historians forget that people develop new ideas, change their minds under the pressure of events, and argue for similar responses in 1642. Thus the conservatism and localism of provincial responses to the outbreak of war are greatly overestimated.

It is currently being argued that the most convincing explanations of the outbreak of the Civil War are to be found through studying central politics and particularly through looking at the policies of Charles himself. The approach I have adopted has an obvious relevance to explanations of how local people *reacted* to a conflict that was not entirely, or mainly, of their making. I want to suggest much more than this, however. In the first place studies of local politics show how difficult it would have been for Charles to establish permanently the sort of monarchy and church he wished for. Furthermore, much recent work stresses the importance of rival conspiracy theories in the division of 1642 (and in earlier conflicts): Parliament's popish plot versus the king's Puritan plot. Peter Lake has stressed particularly the explanatory power of the popish plot; the analysis here helps us understand Charles's fear of 'popularity' – of a Puritan-led subversive conspiracy focused on Parliament and aiming at the undermining or overthrow of monarchy. The roots of the king's fears lay in his understanding of local politics; indeed fear about the nature of local responses spurred Charles into devices like the Forced Loan in an attempt to avoid Parliament, and into the great reluctance to summon Parliament after 1629. Finally, an examination of the way local gentlemen like Sir Richard Grosvenor encouraged broad participation in politics, or of the broad social alliances of the godly, on which Brooke, Warwick or Lincoln based their local leadership, suggests that the king may have been justified in his fears of popularity.

EDITOR'S NOTES

Reprinted in abridged form with permission of the Longman Group UK Limited, from Richard Cust and Ann Hughes, eds, *Conflict in Early Stuart England* (London, 1989).

a Charles's eleven-year rule without parliment ended in 1640 when the king needed parlimentary supply for an army to repel the Scots invasion. The Scots had banded themselves in a 'National Covenant' and taken up arms against Charles's and Laud's attempt to force an English-style Prayer Book on their presbyterian and non-liturgical church.

NOTES

1 Conrad Russell, *Parliaments and English Politics, 1621–1629* (Oxford, 1979), p. 8.
2 J. T. Cliffe, *The Yorkshire Gentry From the Reformation to the Civil War* (London, 1969); B. G. Blackwood, *The Lancashire Gentry and the Great Rebellion 1640–1660* (Chetham Society, 3rd series, xxv, 1978). See the introduction, pp. 34–5.
3 The discussion of Everitt is based especially on Alan Everitt, *The Community of Kent and the Great Rebellion* (Leicester, 1966); see esp. pp. 14–15, 117–19.
4 Ronald Hutton, *The Royalist War Effort* (London, 1982), p. 201; John Morrill, *The Revolt of the Provinces* (London, 1976), esp. pp. 14–22, 34, 42–51.
5 See for example, Hutton, *The Royalist War Effort*; Morrill, *Revolt of the Provinces*; John Morrill, (ed.), *Reactions to the English Civil War* (London, 1982).
6 Alan Macfarlane, *Reconstructing Historical Communities* (London, 1977), pp. 12–13.
7 For Warwickshire in this and the following paragraphs see Ann L. Hughes, 'Warwickshire on the Eve of the Civil War: A County Community?', *Midland History*, 7 (1982), pp. 42–72.
8 This argument is based on Clifford Geertz, 'Form and Variation in Balinese Village Structure', *American Anthropologist*, 61 (1959), pp. 991–1012.
9 Robert Harris, *Abner's Funeral* (London, 1641), pp. 25–6.
10 Hughes, 'Warwickshire on the Eve of the Civil War', p. 56.

11 Peter Lake, 'Constitutional Consensus and Puritan Opposition in the 1620s: Thomas Scott and the Spanish Match', *HJ*, 25 (1982), pp. 805–25.

12 A. Fletcher, *The Outbreak of the English Civil War* (London, 1981), pp. 380–404.

13 Perez Zagorin, *The Court and the Country: The Beginning of the English Revolution* (New York, 1970), pp. 305–14; Fletcher, *Outbreak*, pp. 264–80 is more dubious about a central–provincial gulf in 1642.

14 C. Holmes, *The Eastern Association in the English Civil War* (Cambridge, 1974), pp. 40–7; David Underdown, *Revel, Riot and Rebellion: Popular Politics and Culture in England 1603–1660* (Oxford, 1985), which is discussed more fully below; *Letters of Lady Brilliana Harley* (Camden Society, 1854), p. 167; *Royal Commission on Historical Manuscripts, Report Portland MSS*, III, p. 85; J. Eales, *Puritans and Roundheads* (Cambridge, 1990).

15 Brian Manning, *The English People and the English Revolution* (London, 1976). Cf. Manning, 'The Aristocracy and the Downfall of Charles I', in Manning, ed., *Politics, Religion and the English Civil War* (London, 1973), an account that revisionists can largely agree with.

16 William Hunt, *The Puritan Moment: The Coming of Revolution in an English County* (Cambridge, Mass., 1983).

17 Underdown, *Revel, Riot and Rebellion*, esp. pp. 40, 73–105, 164–81.

18 Mark Overton, 'Depression or Revolution? English Agriculture 1640–1750', *JBS*, 25 (1986), pp. 344–52, and references there cited.

19 Among many challenges to the 'social control' view of Puritanism see M. Ingram, 'Religion, Communities and Moral Discipline in Late Sixteenth and Early Seventeenth-Century England: Case Studies', in K. von Greyerz, ed., *Religion and Society in Early Modern Europe 1500–1800* (London, 1984); Peter Lake, 'William Bradshaw, Anti-Christ and the Community of the Godly', *JEH*, 36 (1985), pp. 570–89; M. E. James, *Family, Lineage and Civil Society* (Oxford, 1974), pp. 195–6.

20 J. R. Dias, 'Politics and Administration in Nottinghamshire and Derbyshire 1590–1640' (University of Oxford D.Phil. thesis 1973), pp. 446–8; Cliffe, *The Yorkshire Gentry*, p. 338.

21 For Brooke and Warwickshire in general see Ann Hughes, *Politics, Society and Civil War in Warwickshire* (Cambridge, 1987), esp. ch. 4; Hughes, 'Thomas Dugard and his Circle in the 1630s: A Parliamentary–Puritan Connection?', *HJ*, 29 (1986), pp. 771–93; the quotations are from Brooke's *A Discourse Opening the Nature of that Episcopacy which is exercised in England* (London, 1641), repr. in William Haller, ed., *Tracts on Liberty in the Puritan Revolution 1638–1647* (New York, 1965), II.

22 Hughes, 'Warwickshire on the Eve of the Civil War', pp. 59–64.

23 *A Worthy Speech Made by the Right Honourable the Lord Brooke at the Election of his Captaines and Commanders at Warwick Castle* (26 Feb. 1643).

GLOSSARY

adiaphora literally 'things indifferent'; beliefs not essential to saving faith.

Admonition Controversy debate over church government initiated by the presbyterian Thomas Cartwright's publication of the *Second Admonition to the Parliament* (1572), reiterating the demands of John Field and Thomas Wilcox in a *First Admonition* some months earlier.

advowson right to present a clergyman to an ecclesiastical benefice.

antinomianism heretical belief that those elected to salvation have no obligation to obey the moral law.

Arminianism beliefs of the Dutch theologian, Jacobus Arminius (d. 1609), generally opposed to the Calvinist understanding of predestination. Arminians believed that the human will has a role to play in salvation, that election is based on foreseen faith, that proffered grace may be rejected, and that election may be lost.

assize twice-yearly court held in each county by royal justices.

attainder deprivation of rights upon conviction of treason or felony.

Bishops' Wars Charles's response to the 1639 Scots rebellion against the Prayer Book.

Book of Orders the Privy Council's instructions in 1630–31 for the enforcement of social legislation (especially Poor Laws) in every county.

Book of Sports royal declaration of 1618, renewed by Charles I in 1633, permitting Sunday recreations.

canon ecclesiastical law.

chantry endowment to maintain clergy to say masses for the souls of the dead; chapels were often erected for this purpose before the Reformation.

coat and conduct money levy by the king to pay for maintenance of an army.

convocation general assembly of the clergy in an upper and lower house, held at the same time as Parliament.

Council the monarch's advisers at Court, formally constituted as the Privy Council.

Covenanters Scots rebels opposing imposition of the English liturgy on the presbyterian kirk (church) in Scotland.

enclosure construction of a hedge or wall around previously common land in order to graze sheep and profit from the wool trade.

episcopacy government of the church by bishops.

Erastianism doctrine that the church is properly governed by the secular magistrate.

Forced Loan Charles's attempt after his failure with the 1626 Parliament, to finance war with France and Spain by compelling taxpayers to 'lend' him money. It was a loan in name only, vigorously pressed by members of the Privy Council, and resented although not resisted by most. Defaulters were gaoled without charge and deprived of offices.

gentry a slippery term even for contemporaries. Gentlemen were substantially landed and recognized as having the right to a coat of arms.

guild association of craftsmen or tradesmen for religious and social purposes.

Hampton Court Conference 1604 meeting of moderate Puritans with the new King James I to discuss further reform of the Church of England. The only reform that James decreed in consequence was a new translation of the Bible, completed in 1611.

impositions revenue in addition to that granted to a monarch at the beginning of the reign, imposed under the prerogative right of the Crown to regulate trade.

Inns of Court schools of common law in London.

Jesuit member of the Society of Jesus, a militant Catholic religious order founded by Ignatius Loyola in 1540.

Justice of the Peace (JP) gentleman commissioned by the Crown to preside over quarter sessions and perform administrative functions in the county.

Lambeth Articles strictly Calvinist expression of the theology of election, adopted in 1595 to quell theological controversy in Cambridge University. The articles were never incorporated by royal or parliamentary authority into the official (Thirty-nine) Articles of Religion, despite the desire of many Calvinists.

liturgy formal text of a religious service; in England, the Book of Common Prayer.

Lollards late medieval heretical movement similar in some points to Protestantism; followers of John Wyclif.

lord lieutenant nobleman charged with military administration in a county.

ordinary clergyman who exercised jurisdiction in ecclesiastical cases, generally a bishop or his deputy.

Pelagianism doctrine named after the fifth-century British heretic who believed that salvation could be acquired apart from divine grace by means of voluntary effort. Pelagius was the target of Augustine's works on predestination.

Personal Rule period between 1629 and 1640 when Charles I ruled without summoning a parliament.

prerogative powers traditionally held by the Crown apart from Parliament (e.g., regulation of trade and foreign policy, exercise of pardon). Prerogative courts like Star Chamber and High Commission rendered judgement on grounds of prerogative rather than common law.

presbyterians those who believed in a national church governed by assemblies of lay and clerical 'elders' rather than by bishops.

proclamation royal decree having the force of law but issued without consultation of Parliament.

purveyance enforced purchase of food at prices fixed by the Crown to feed the army or the royal household.

quarter sessions regular meetings of Justices of the Peace in the shires to deal with legal and administrative matters designated by parliamentary statute or by the Council or monarch.

recusant one who declined to attend the state church; generally refers to Catholics after 1559.

sheriff local agent of the Crown, performing financial and administrative duties such as the calling of elections and serving of writs.

Ship Money rate levied on coastal communities by virtue of the monarch's emergency powers, to provide protection of the narrow seas from threatened naval invasion. Some, like John Hampden, refused to pay this traditional levy when Charles I extended it to inland towns and imposed it annually, on the grounds that it amounted to taxation without parliamentary approval; his case, heard in 1637, helped to mobilize the opposition.

statute law enacted by Parliament and approved by the monarch.

subsidy tax granted by Parliament to the Crown, levied according to the value of a taxpayer's land or goods.

Synod of Dort clerical conference in the Netherlands, 1618–19, summoned to settle quarrels between Remonstrants (Arminians) and Contra-Remostrants (Calvinists); James I sent five British delegates, all Calvinists.

Thirty-nine Articles Church of England's confession of faith, approved by Convocation in 1563 and confirmed by statute in 1571.

trained bands portions of a county's citizen militia given special military training.

visitation investigation of a diocese or parish by a bishop or his representative, for judicial and administrative purposes; *metropolitical* visitation was carried out by an archbishop.

SUGGESTIONS FOR FURTHER READING

Students who wish to pursue the themes represented in this volume should begin with the works noted in the Introduction and the prefatory notes to each essay, as well as the full volumes of the authors excerpted here. For easy reference, the most important of these are listed below by author:

Thomas Cogswell, 'The Politics of Propaganda: Charles I and the People in the 1620s', *JBS* (1990).

Patrick Collinson, *The Religion of Protestants* (Oxford, 1983).

——*The Birthpangs of Protestant England* (New York, 1988).

Richard Cust, *The Forced Loan and English Politics, 1626–1628* (Oxford, 1987).

Richard Cust and Ann Hughes, eds, *Conflict in Early Stuart England* (London, 1989).

Julian Davies, *The Caroline Captivity of the Church* (Oxford, (1993).

A. G. Dickens, *The English Reformation* (revised edn, London, 1989).

Eamon Duffy, *The Stripping of the Altars* (New Haven, 1992).

Jacqueline Eales, *Puritans and Roundheads* (Cambridge, 1990).

Geoffrey Elton, *The Parliament of England, 1559–1581* (Cambridge, 1986).

Kenneth Fincham, ed., *The Early Stuart Church 1603–1640* (London, 1993).

Anthony Fletcher, *The Outbreak of the English Civil War* (London, 1981).

Christopher Haigh, ed., *The Reign of Elizabeth I* (Athens, Georgia, 1985).

——ed., *The English Reformation Revised* (Cambridge, 1987).

——*English Reformations* (Oxford, 1993).

Derek Hirst, *The Representative of the People?* (Cambridge, 1975).

Ann Hughes, *Politics, Society and Civil War in Warwickshire, 1620–1660* (Cambridge, 1987).

Mark Kishlansky, *Parliamentary Selection* (Cambridge, 1986).

Peter Lake, *Moderate Puritans and the Elizabethan Church* (Cambridge, 1982).

——*Anglicans and Puritans?* (London, 1988).

J. S. Morrill, *The Revolt of the Provinces* (London, 1976).

——'The Religious Context of the English Civil War', *TRHS* (1984).

——'The Causes of the British Civil Wars', *JEH* (1992).

——*The Nature of the English Revolution* (London, 1993).

Conrad Russell, *Parliaments and English Politics 1621–1629* (Oxford, 1979).

——*The Causes of the English Civil War* (Oxford, 1990).

——*Unrevolutionary England, 1603–1642* (Oxford, 1990).

——*The Fall of the British Monarchies, 1637–1642* (Oxford, 1991).

J. J. Scarisbrick, *The Reformation and the English People* (Oxford, 1984).

Kevin Sharpe, *The Personal Rule of Charles I* (New Haven, 1993).

David Starkey, *The English Court* (London, 1987).

David Underdown, *Revel, Riot and Rebellion* (Oxford, 1987).

——*Fire from Heaven* (New Haven, 1992).

Peter White, *Predestination, Policy and Polemic* (Cambridge, 1992).

Robert Whiting, *The Blind Devotion of the People: Popular Religion and the English Reformation* (Cambridge, 1989).

In addition, the problem of the Reformation is illumined in a local study by Susan Brigden, *London and the Reformation* (Oxford, 1989) and by Margaret Aston's *England's Iconoclasts* (Oxford, 1989) and *Faith and Fire: Popular and Unpopular Religion 1350–1600* (London, 1993). On the slow evolution of a protestant culture, Tessa Watt's compendium, *Cheap Print and Popular Deity 1550–1640* (Cambridge, 1991) is a useful way to pursue some of the points made by Collinson in chapter 2 of this volume, and Susan Doran and Christopher Durston, *Princes, Pastors and People: The Church and Religion in England 1529–1689* (London, 1991) offers a useful introductory overview of the 'long Reformation' and a substantial bibliography. Dewey Wallace, *Puritans and Pre-destination* (Chapel Hill, N.C., 1982) is an extensive and fairly accessible treatment of Calvinist theology in England from 1525 to the end of the seventeenth century. Kenneth Fincham's *Prelate as Pastor* (Oxford, 1990) is an excellent treatment of the early Stuart episcopate, and the essays in his collection, *The Early Stuart Church* (1993), are extremely important. Kevin Sharpe's article on Laud and the University of Oxford is reprinted in a collection of his essays, *Politics and Ideas in Early Stuart England* (London, 1989). On Laud, see also J. Sears McGee, 'Archbishop Laud and the Outward Face of Religion', in Richard DeMolen, ed., *Leaders of the Reformation* (1984). Anthony Milton's *Catholic and Reformed: The Roman and Protestant Churches in English Protestant Thought, 1600–1640* (forthcoming from Cambridge University Press) treats a hitherto underexplored aspect of early Stuart religion and may well help to reshape the debate. The persistence of Prayer Book Anglicanism during the Civil War is treated in an interesting essay by John Morrill, 'The Church in England 1642–9' in his collection, *Reactions to the English Civil War 1642–49* (London, 1982); read it alongside Derek Hirst's 'Failure of Godly Rule in the English Republic', *Past and Present* no. 132 (1991).

Important revisions of Elizabethan parliamentary history besides Elton's include Norman Jones's *Faith by Statute* (Oxford, 1982) and essays in Jones and D. M. Dean, eds, *The Parliaments of Elizabethan England* (Oxford, 1990). Jennifer Loach's *Parliament under the Tudors* (Oxford, 1991) is a useful introductory survey reflecting newer interpretations. For the early Stuart period, see Esther Cope, *Politics without Parliaments* (London, 1987). Kevin Sharpe, ed., *Faction and Parliament* (Oxford, 1978), includes revisionist and counter-revisionist essays and might be usefully read along with the critique of revisionist scholarship by T. K. Rabb and Derek Hirst, 'Revisionism Revised', and Christopher Hill, 'Parliament and People' in *Past and Present* no. 92 (1981). Hirst's *Authority and Conflict 1603–1658* (Cambridge, Mass. 1986) combines narrative history and analysis in a readable survey text. A detailed study of domestic and parliamentary politics after the failure of the Spanish match is Thomas Cogswell, *The Blessed Revolution* (Cambridge, 1989); a broader view of early Stuart foreign policy is Simon Adams, 'Spain or the Netherlands? The Dilemmas of Early Stuart Foreign Policy', in H. Tomlinson, ed., *Before the English Civil War* (1983). On the 'British problem', see Brian Levack, *Formation of the British State* (Oxford, 1987).

Ann Hughes's *The Causes of the English Civil War* (1991) is a concise historiographical summary of currently raging debates on the subject; R. C. Richardson, *The Debate on the English Revolution Revisited* (London, 1989), offers a comprehensive summary of the historiography on the issue as it stood just before Conrad Russell's newest contributions. A brief and readable discussion of divergent socio-cultural interpretations of the Civil War is John Morrill, Brian Manning and David Underdown, 'What Was the English Revolution?' in *History Today* (March 1984). Gerald Aylmer, *Rebellion or Revolution* (Oxford, 1987) and J. C. D. Clark, *Revolution and Rebellion* (Cambridge, 1986) offer divergent views of the nature of the conflict.

The problem of popular political consciousness and Protestant culture is explored by David Cressy, *Bonfires and Bells* (London, 1989); K. Wrightson and D. Levine, *Poverty and Piety in an English Village* (New York, 1979); Margaret Spufford, *Contrasting Communities* (Cambridge, 1974); essays in Anthony Fletcher and John Stevenson, eds., *Order and Disorder in Early Modern England* (Cambridge, 1975); Peter Clark, *English Provincial Society from the Reformation to the Revolution* (Sussex, 1977); William Hunt, *The Puritan Moment* (Cambridge, Mass., 1983); and many other local studies. John Morrill, *Cheshire 1630–1660* (Oxford, 1974) and Anthony Fletcher, *A County Community in Peace and War: Sussex 1600–1660* (London, 1975) remain the best county studies for this period; see also Fletcher's *Reform in the Provinces* (New Haven, 1986) on local government.